STU MASCHWITZ

THE
DV REBEL'S
GUIDE

An ALL-DIGITAL Approach to Making
KILLER ACTION MOVIES
on the CHEAP

The DV Rebel's Guide
An All-Digital Approach to Making Killer Action Movies on the Cheap
Stu Maschwitz

Peachpit Press
1249 Eighth Street
Berkeley, CA 94710
510/524-2178
800/283-9444
510/524-2221 (fax)

Find us on the World Wide Web at: www.peachpit.com
To report errors, please send a note to errata@peachpit.com

Peachpit Press is a division of Pearson Education

Editor: Karyn Johnson
Production Editor: Hilal Sala
Interior designer: Maureen Forys, Happenstance Type-O-Rama
Compositor: Maureen Forys, Happenstance Type-O-Rama
Copyeditor: Doug Adrianson and Hope Frazier
Indexer: Jack Lewis, j & j indexing
Cover design: Mimi Heft

ISBN 0-321-41364-4

9 8 7 6 5 4 3

Printed and bound in the United States of America

For Xixi.

Acknowledgments

I do a lot of public speaking, so I've become comfortable in front of crowds. But in 2006 I was asked to give the graduation speech at a San Francisco Bay Area media school, and on the day of the event I felt myself becoming uncharacteristically nervous. The reason? I wanted to do a good job. I felt like I had something to say, and I wanted to say it well—it was important to me not to let those graduates down. This book has been like that. What I thought was going to be painless blatherings about stuff I do every day has become a passion project, and the self-imposed pressure to deliver the good stuff has had me dangling from buildings, watching the sun come up, and imposing no small amount on the good graces of my friends, family, and colleagues.

There is acknowledging, there is thanking, and then there is recognizing deep indebtedness. Somewhere beyond that is what I must attempt to convey about my beloved and luminous wife Michelle. Her support of my efforts on this book requires no enumerating, as it quite simply composes every ounce of what you now hold in your hands. She even let me take pictures of her holding big guns—what more could a guy ask for?

My deepest thanks to the cast and crew of *The Last Birthday Card, Skate Warrior,* the 2005 teaser trailer, and *The Green Project.* I may be a Rebel but thankfully I have never been without my crew.

Thanks to Mark Christiansen for early advice and for occasionally reminding me of just how much work this might turn out to be. Thanks to Eric Escobar, filmmaker and friend, for sage council over eggs benedict. Thanks to Sammy Rodriguez of The Orphanage's editorial department for authoring the video portion of the DVD. And thanks to my partners at The Orphanage—Scott, Jonathan, Carsten, and Daniel—for relinquishing a percentage of my brain to this project.

And on the subject of family, I remain in awe of my brother Eric's contribution to this book. From careening through Chinatown with a madman on his heels (a madman with a DV camera, that is) to creating the Ghettocam, my bro is always the first one I turn to when I come to the shocking realization that computers can't do everything.

Mad props to the filmmakers who contributed images from their work. Macgregor, co-director of *Similo*, Sharlto Copley and Simon Hansen, co-directors of *Spoon*, and Gregg Bishop, director of *The Other Side*.

A big shout out to the Adobe After Effects development team, for their years of patient absorption of my feedback, and for creating the single greatest filmmaking tool that doesn't have a lens. Thanks especially to Jeff Almasol for the amazing scripts he wrote to turn my onlining toys into a real toolkit.

And lastly, a very special thanks is due to the original Rebel, Robert Rodriguez. When I first saw *El Mariachi* in a dingy theater in Minneapolis, I had the same sensation that I had when I saw *Star Wars* at age five—I was looking down the barrel of my career as a filmmaker. I could not have imagined that years later I'd be helping him put his cinematic visions on the screen. In no small part this book is an effort to expand on the teachings of his book, DVD commentary tracks, and 10-Minute Film Schools. His stamp of approval on this book is the best sign I could have that I got some of that good stuff into these pages.

Contents

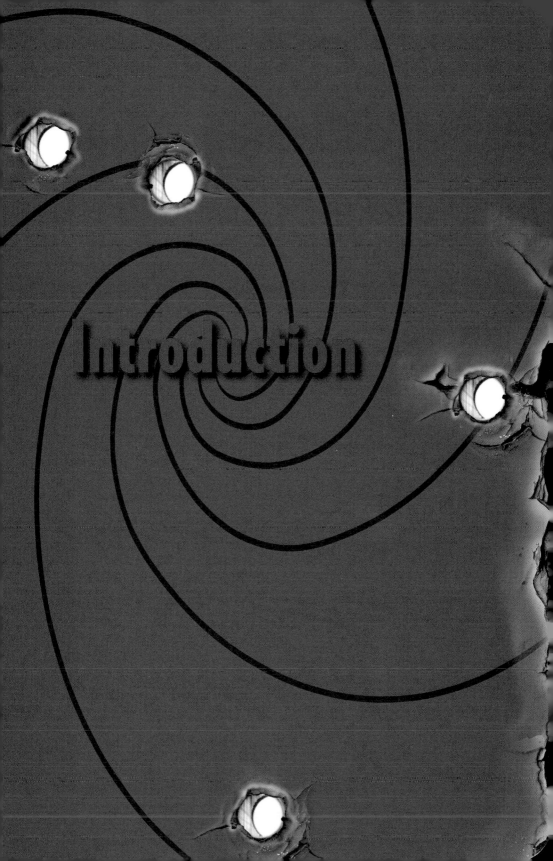

Introduction

Why should you make a low-budget action movie? Simple. The people making the big-budget ones have lost their touch. It's time for the baton to be passed, and this book will prepare you to receive it.

Action movies—the very term invokes visions of brainless adrenaline injections set to techno music. But things weren't always this way. It's easy to forget that *Die Hard* has a full 30 minutes of engaging story before the first gun is fired, or that *Lethal Weapon* features an attempted suicide so gripping that director Franco Zeffirelli cast Mel Gibson as Hamlet based on that scene alone. It's easy to forget that director John Woo (*Face/Off, Mission Impossible II*) is best not just when his guns are blazing, but when he wears his heart on his sleeve. Who remembers that *Predator* is an intricate suspense film for its entire second act, or that *The Goonies* and *E.T., The Extra Terrestrial* both feature kids who actually talk like real kids? Or that one of the most captivating scenes in *Raiders of the Lost Ark* is one of pure exposition? Or that *The Terminator* has a love scene in which you actually believe that the couple, who had first met the previous day, is in love?

There was a golden era of action films that spanned almost exactly the decade of the 1980s. No doubt owing much to the successes of *Jaws* and *Star Wars,* the '80s warmed up to the concept of the "blockbuster" movie before it was an established genre in and of itself. There was still an idea, held over from the '60s and '70s, that a film should be a cinematically authored work—and the spirit of summer spectacular one-upmanship was a healthy cherry atop a sundae of substance. Even as commercial directors made the move into film, they created movies, not two-hour American Express ads.

You begin to see the end of this great era in the sequels to some of its best examples. The slickness of these follow-ups became a veneer so thick it didn't matter much what was underneath. The sequels to *Die Hard, Predator,* and others, fun as they are, seem to be set in some fake movie reality—whereas the originals, fanciful as they may have been, took place in the real world.

Studios have always spent a lot of money on action films. And once they got the idea that polish, body count, star factor, "trailer moments," and other easily quantifiable assets could reliably provide a return on that investment—even without a compelling story to back them up—they went for it whole hog. Thus we've entered a time when action movies generally deserve the bad rap they've always endured.

Why did Hollywood freak out when Robert Rodriguez's $7,000 *El Mariachi* hit the screens? Sure, it was novel that he had made the film so inexpensively, but what the industry really reacted to was its freshness. It was unlike other movies in theaters at that time. It was a new voice—an action movie *and* a personal story.

A fresh new voice, by definition, must come in under Hollywood's radar—radar that responds to only one signal: Cash. *The Terminator* was made for $6 million. *Aliens* cost $18 million. *La Femme Nikita* $5 million, and *Point Break* $24 million. Spielberg's directorial debut, *Duel,* was shot for less than half a million dollars. As I write this, there are no films in the box office top 10 made for anywhere near those low numbers, even adjusted for inflation—and tentpole films typically cost upwards of $250 million.

The future of the action film genre rests firmly in the hands of the adept, digital-savvy independent filmmaker with more brains than bucks. But you probably already knew that. Why else would you buy this book?

Jargon Watch

Throughout the book, you'll find these *Jargon Watch* sidebars to help define esoteric film terms.

A *tentpole* film is one the studio is betting it all on—a big-budget monster like *Titanic* or *Spider-Man* that the studio expects to be its highest-grossing film that year.

The Big Idea

There are plenty of books about filmmaking. Some promise that you can make a movie for spare change; others expect you not only to spend some money, but to actually keep track of it. Most admonish you to aim low, keep your whole film to one location, shoot it in a week, and avoid anything in the script that you might be tempted to type in all caps. You know, stuff like A THUNDERSTORM HITS or THE T-REX ESCAPES THE PADDOCK or EXT. MOSCOW.

Screw that. You may have already discovered the dirty little secret of this book, which is that it's not just for aspiring action filmmakers. It's for anyone whose cinematic ambitions extend beyond the self-imposed restrictions of standard indie fare. If the story about which you are passionate involves exotic locations, visual spectacle, weather, Kung Fu, or any other stuff that makes movies better than plays, then welcome to the book that won't try to talk you off the ledge. Nope, it'll jump with you, just like Mel Gibson in *Lethal Weapon*.

Pop Quiz hotshot: What's this?

Image courtesy of Panasonic.

It's a video camera that costs less than a cheap used car and makes images that can be shown on a movie theater screen without anyone unconsciously cleaning their glasses.

Now, what's this?

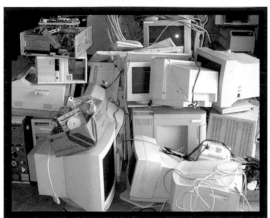

Image courtesy of Washington University.

That's a few computers with specs that were state of the art a couple of years ago, that are now being recycled for parts. They're no different from computers that high-end visual-effects facilities are still using to create shots for blockbuster feature films.

Put these two together and you've got everything you need to make a movie. What's Hollywood got that you don't?

Oh yeah: millions of dollars, movie stars, and hundreds of trained crew members.

You know what? That's OK. Because you have a couple of things that Hollywood will never have. The first is a great script. I know, if that was so easy you'd be a paid screenwriter reading this book atop a giant stack of cash. Or maybe not. Hollywood buys scripts for tons of money, sure—but look what they're buying. Your script has the luxury of not needing to be sellable. Take advantage of that! Pander to no one—tell *your* story. If you can do that, you will have a great script.

The other thing you have that Hollywood doesn't is time. Who the hell cares when you finish your film? There's a festival deadline? Guess what, it will roll around again next year.

If you're willing to tell a personal story and take your time executing it, you can leverage inexpensive, off-the-shelf technology to make a kinetic, exciting film with tons of production value. The key is to exploit the strengths of your tools and your life, work around your limitations, and think outside the box of Hollywood filmmaking.

About the Lunatic

In 1996 I was a visual effects artist at Industrial Light & Magic, George Lucas's premiere visual effects facility. I had been teaching myself Avid during my off hours, editing some old footage I shot in film school (California Institute of the Arts in Valencia). That footage was meant to be an action-packed mini-feature called *Skate Warrior*. After completing my edit, I realized that at no point did my "film" ever need to touch tape again. I had begun to assemble the 45-minute epic in Adobe After Effects 3.0, and immediately fell in love with the idea of mastering an entire movie using such a fluid and capable tool. The only thing that was missing was a shooting format that was as digital as the rest of my workflow.

During a chance trip to a consumer electronics store a few weeks later I saw the answer to my prayers. There was the Sony DCR-VX1000, a 3-chip camcorder that recorded to a digital tape format called "MiniDV." It had the strangest little connector on the back—IEEE 1394, or, as I was already loving calling it, *FireWire*. Someday soon, I knew, I'd have a similar port in my very own computer.

I bought the camera that day, took it home, and in one weekend wrote the script for *The Last Birthday Card*—a 20-minute short that would become the last project I ever worked on at ILM.

Birthday Card took more than a year to complete, but by then I knew I'd discovered the method of filmmaking that I would pursue into my professional career. I left ILM, joined Scott Stewart and Jonathan Rothbart in a tiny office in downtown San Francisco, and attended the 2000 Sundance Film Festival accompanied by a front page *Hollywood Reporter* story announcing our new production company, The Orphanage.

Since then I've directed numerous commercials, with budgets large and small, and tried wherever possible to experience and learn from the big, expensive ways of putting images on the screen—and continue to subvert them whenever possible with my DV Rebel bag of tricks.

The Orphanage

In 1999, three employees of George Lucas's premiere visual effects company, Industrial Light & Magic, struck out on their own with a simple vision: to change the way movies are made.

The company name immediately became synonymous with the "DV Revolution." The Orphanage produced a series of shorts utilizing existing digital camera technology, and preparing them for film using their proprietary Magic Bullet technology. They offered this service to the independent filmmakers who were already embracing digital acquisition, and continued to push other technology companies to support this new way of making movies. When Sony and Panavision announced their 24p CineAlta camera to the world, The Orphanage was the first company to complete a film with it—and finished it (*bigLove*, 2001) on home computers. Later they would be consulted on the design of Panasonic's revolutionary 24p DV camera, the DVX100.

Magic Bullet went from a service to a product that any DV filmmaker could use, and The Orphanage went from a tiny production company to a top visual effects facility with over 100 employees. While the folks at The Orphanage were working on complex computer graphics for films like *Charlie's Angles 2: Full Throttle*, *Sin City*, and *Hellboy*, they were also quietly developing their own feature film projects out of their Los Angeles office. In 2005, they went into production on their first movie, *Griffin and Phoenix*.

The three founders continue to push the company forward on all fronts. Scott Stewart writes and develops stories for the feature films division. Jonathan Rothbart is a visual effects supervisor on such films as *Harry Potter and the Goblet of Fire* and *Superman Returns.* The author directs several commercials a year while continuing to pioneer new filmmaking technologies. In everything they do, at every budget level, the DV Rebel spirit thrives.

What This Book Will Not Do

This book will not train you to be a producer. It doesn't contain sample budgets, schedules, advice on how to cheat a camera rental for an extra day, or tricks for avoiding paying people until the last possible moment.

This book will not offer more than the tiniest bit of advice about writing your script. Books about screenwriting abound, and reading any one of them is an excellent alternative to actually sitting down and writing. What if I told you your 10th script would be great? Would you still be interested in writing the first nine? Well, your 10th script will be great, now get to work.

This book will not beat around the bush. There are lots of ways to get things done—you came here because you want to hear mine. Any time I say "you could do it this way or that way," it will be blatantly obvious which way I think is right. You are free to disagree, of course, but you'll never feel like this book is copping out.

And of course, this book will not offer legal guidance. In fact, quite the opposite—you may find some decidedly unconventional advice. I'll suggest some omelet recipes that most assuredly require breaking a few eggs. The safety of your cast and crew and anyone who gets in their way is *your* responsibility—an important one that no person or book can take off your hands.

What Are You Prepared to Do?

The way I make low-budget films is not for everyone. I use an approach that is postproduction heavy. I integrate my visual effects knowledge into every aspect of my filmmaking, and am always looking at my film from 50,000 feet, strategizing the best way to get my story on the screen using whatever techniques seem best.

Ultimately, you are the author of your film. *Your* sensibilities will inform your choices, and the film you make will be one that no one else could have. Some of the things you read in these pages will sound absolutely crazy to you, but some will cause you to throw down the book immediately and go try them out.

I hope there's a lot of the latter. I promise you I'll give you the best of my cool ideas about moviemaking, if you promise you'll give them a shot!

The Homework

Throughout the book, I make specific references to several movies. It will be handy for you to have the DVDs of these films available to study the techniques and shots I reference. To help you prepare, each chapter includes a list of the films mentioned. Have a good DVD player with easy-to-use pause and slow motion controls (a jog/shuttle control is best), and if you suspect there might be some DVDs you're missing, skip ahead to the lists so you can rent them before you get to that chapter!

Computers Are the Devil

And you will make a pact with them.

This book will suggest a number of solutions for achieving high production value on a shoestring budget. Some of them—in fact, many of them—involve some form of postproduction computer intimacy.

Some filmmaking books assume that you'll be able to make heads or tails of the mock budgets they helpfully supply. Some assume you're the kind of person who can spend $15 at Home Depot and an hour later have a Steadicam-like device. And yet somehow there's been a taboo about assuming that people are willing to teach themselves a little about doing computer effects. Well, I have bad news: I don't know any other way to make movies other than involving computer-heavy techniques from day one.

There are some computer-graphics how-tos in this book. I'll try not to assume too much, but I wouldn't use this book as a first step in learning about digital compositing and effects. Still, this stuff isn't that complicated. All I ask is a willingness to try.

Don't Make Your Short in Hollywood

I apologize if you are in Hollywood, although I'm sure you realize that it's possible to leave, even for a short time. If you're not in Hollywood, or the Los Angeles area, rejoice.

Why not shoot a film in Hollywood? Hollywood is where films are made! That's exactly why. I've seen a lot of short films, some made in L.A. and some not, and I have come to be able to recognize the ones made in L.A. Quite simply, they have high production value and terrible direction.

People in L.A. know how movies are made, so they think they know what it takes to make a movie. To them, all filmmaking requires the accoutrements they see on the set of every big-budget effort they've ever crewed on or performed in. So they work their favors and get a full 35mm package for free, and a big grip truck and crew for free, and they weasel their way onto someone else's set the day before it's slated to be struck.

These shorts turn out terrible. The truth is the mechanisms of professional Hollywood filmmaking are cumbersome. They conspire to create mediocrity. It's quite difficult to work through them and create a compelling film. You finagle a fancy Fisher dolly, and suddenly all your shots are between two and six feet off the ground. You hook up with a great DP (Director of Photography) looking to build his reel, and suddenly, since you're not paying him, you have no leg to stand on when he takes three hours lighting an insert of a hand on a phone. Your short winds up undercovered and overproduced. And that set? It *looks* like a set.

If you learn your nunchuck skills with those lightweight plastic ones, the worst thing you can do is look silly. If you decide to learn using the heavy wooden ones, you may wind up with a concussion. Beginning filmmakers would do well to avail themselves of the most agile means of production available. Why do you think Robert Rodriguez infamously released half his crew the first day of filming *Desperado?*

Another strike against L.A. is that everyone in or near "the zone" (a 30-mile radius centered on the Beverly Center mall) is *over* film production. It's a business to them, not a magical window into glitz and glamour.[1] In my hometown of Minneapolis, if you walk into a coffee shop and tell the owner you'd like to film a scene there, she may be flattered and fascinated. In Los Angeles' trendy Silverlake neighborhood, they'll simply hand you their standard form and fee structure—the same one they gave Bruckheimer last week.

We are not interested in *emulating the process* of Hollywood filmmaking—we are interested in *simulating the finished product,* by any means necessary. Contrary to popular belief, there are more ways to get great images and performances on screen than with a lifetime supply of lighting equipment waiting in a truck down the street.

What Is a "Low" Budget?

Filmmaking costs money, almost without exception. Many how-to books define their intentions based on a specific budget range.

I'm not going to do that. Everyone will have a different idea of how much money is too much to spend on a film, and how much is not enough. For one director, setting a film in a large, suburban home will be the least expensive choice (because he lives in one), whereas another may live in a tiny apartment but be able to exploit her uncle's exotic car collection for her climactic car chase scene.

What every DV Rebel will face is the constant opportunity to spend money and the constant struggle to avoid doing so. Often this struggle is

---

1 They're right, of course — but people who've yet to learn this sad fact are our stock in trade.

born out in the age-old relationship between money and time. If you have the time and patience to assemble your *online* by eye in After Effects, you can save $500 on Automatic Duck (see "Owning the Means of Production" below). If you're short on time, the $500 will suddenly seem like the best deal in town.

Jargon Watch

Online is both a noun and a verb that refers to the process of creating the final, high quality version of your film. You online your film, you work on your online, or you are stuck in traffic and late for your online. The term *mastering* is sometimes used interchangeably with onlining. Chapter 6 is entirely devoted to the onlining process.

Most important, the money-saving, production value-enhancing tricks described in this book are ones that I routinely use in both zero-budget video projects and million-dollar TV commercials. Every technique is equally relevant to projects of any budget level.

In 2004, I directed a commercial that needed a big look on a small budget. It opens on a wide shot of a suburban neighborhood in a thunderstorm. The power goes out, and after a pause, the lights come on in one house.

The rest of the spot plays out inside the house. To afford a 12-hour nighttime shoot in an actual home in Los Angeles, we saved money wherever we could. We shot with the Panasonic Varicam instead of film, and mastered the entire spot in Adobe After Effects using the exact techniques described in Chapter 6. But I still had a problem—my opening shot. I knew it was to be a visual effects shot, but the problem was how to shoot the plate. Not only was there no good place to do it near my interior location, there was also no time.

Jargon Watch

A *plate* is a shot that is to become the basis for a visual effect. There are numerous variations on the term, such as *background plate* and *clean plate*. Where a plate provides the foundation for an effects shot, an *element* might be something small that is added to it. So an average shot in a dinosaur movie might have an *action plate* consisting of a hallway with a pile of boxes that get knocked over. The computer-generated dinosaur will be synched up with the boxes so it looks like he knocked them down. Visible in the shot might be cables or rigging used to pull the boxes over, so you'd also have a clean plate to allow you to more easily remove the cables. Finally, a separate *dust element* might be shot and laid over the moment of impact.

After losing some sleep over this, I finally proposed to my producer a solution to get the shot in the can for $8. Oddly enough, he agreed. I spent the next few nights scouting locations on my own and eventually found the perfect spot: a hillside overlooking a row of houses from which a simple tripod—rather than the crane we had originally envisioned—would be able to capture the sweeping vista. I set up my digital SLR and snapped a few exposures at dusk. This element would be color-corrected day-for-night and used for the lights-out portion of the shot. I then sat and guarded my camera for about two hours while the sun went down and the streetlights came on. During this time I ate my take-out burrito which, along with a tasty beverage, had cost me about $7, putting me $1 under budget. When the sky went dark and the neighborhood lights came on, I snapped a few more exposures and left. In postproduction, not only did we add the rain and wind effects that we would have had to create digitally under even the best of circumstances, we also added a camera move that gave our opener the look of an expensive crane shot.

Under our "shoot it for real" plan, the platform would have been a static cherry-picker, incapable of such a move.

The exciting behind-the-scenes action of a $7 visual effects plate shoot.

I don't think many people realize how often "stolen" shots like this wind up in big-budget productions. Many famous commercial directors have their own small 35mm camera packages for augmenting their million-dollar shoots. In my days at Industrial Light & Magic, I worked on a Pepsi commercial where shots nabbed without permits out of the back of a van were intercut with state-of-the-art visual effects. Years later I would use this same trick on a music video for Cher. These days, anything from an HVX200 to a Panasonic LX1 point-and-shoot still camera (that happens to shoot 16:9, 30p movies at greater than NTSC resolution) can be used to pluck a freebie out of the air when fate smiles on you. For more on "stealing" shots, see the section on locations in Chapter 2.

Conversely, sometimes spending the same bucks that the big guys do is just what the DV Rebel needs. For *The Last Birthday Card,* one of my most expensive single purchases was an order of breakaway glass props from a Hollywood special effects company. Google around and you'll find several sites happy to instruct you in the ways of making your own "sugar glass." I just couldn't see myself perfecting this technique and molding my own beer bottles the night before a long day's shoot. Instead, I spent around $350 on the real deal. I was able to create a very violent scene, in which my hero escapes a hail of gunfire, by shattering these bottles (made of a brittle resin material, not sugar) with well-aimed BBs (see Chapter 4). The broken pieces would then be collected and lovingly thrown at my actor in other shots. I milked every last bit of production value out of those props and was overjoyed with the results. Best $350 I spent out of the whole budget.

Breakaway pint glass plus BB gun equals DV Rebel happiness.

Jargon Watch

What's the difference between *special effects* and *visual effects?* Special effects are the devices and events that are rigged on the set or location, as a part of principal photography. Breakaway props, explosions, a fire hydrant that's rigged to break open and pour water on cue—these are all special effects, or, as they are sometimes known, *practical* effects. *Visual effects* are added in postproduction or filmed by a unit separate from the main unit. A full-scale explosion filmed on a rooftop is a *special effect*. Shooting the miniature helicopter exploding and compositing it into the full-size building explosion is a *visual effect*.

If *Birthday Card* had been just that scene, the breakaways would easily have represented the majority of the budget—and still been well worth it. In the case of my commercial, the money I saved by giving up a few evenings and risking the ire of a Valencia homeowner was more than the entire budget of *Last Birthday Card,* and bought me extra time to make sure the live-action shoot wrapped on schedule. In both cases the methods I chose also happened to be the ones that yielded the best possible on-screen results.

I am always perplexed that some people plan their moviegoing around the migration of films from the large theaters to the bargain matinee houses. A film they may be unsure about they'll wait to see for a few bucks, whereas for a much-anticipated flick they'll drop the full ticket price. I don't see things this way. I figure I'll see a bunch of movies this year, some good, some bad, some for free or cheap, and some at exorbitant cost. It all comes out in the wash. I encourage you to take a similar view of the cost of various items in your budget. You may spend a ton of money on a prop used in only one scene (Scott's sniper rifle in *Birthday Card:* $300), or you may score a killer deal on something that would ordinarily cost you a bundle (total location fees for the building-lobby assassination scene in *Birthday Card*: only $250 instead of the $4000 we were quoted elsewhere). In the end, it all comes out in the wash, and only you know how much is too much.

One thing's for sure—you will spend some money. But by following the guidance in this book, you'll be confident that you spent as little as possible and never sacrificed production value.

Are You a Mouser or a Machinist?

My brother is a gifted sculptor and fabricator. He has always had a Rain-man-like skill for making things with his hands, as you will see in Chapter 3. My sculpting talents consist of making that shape of the inside of your hand that you get when you squeeze a lump of clay really hard. But I've always been able to make moving pictures with computers.

Occasionally throughout the following pages I'll discuss techniques that can be approached using a crafty, corporeal approach or a computer-aided one. Beyond your own skills and proclivities, there are a couple of things to bear in mind when considering whether to build it or binary it.

Real Is Always Better Than Computer Generated

Almost without exception, real stuff looks better than Computer Graphics (CG). If you can get the shot "in camera" (requiring no post-effects at all), you will have a huge advantage over someone who commits to synthesizing the same shot out of whole cloth in post.

In-camera effects capture a lot of stuff for free that even advanced CG struggles with, like complex lighting interactions and atmospheric effects. Best of all, in-camera effects allow for happy accidents—little touches of reality that are hard to plan for. Chapter 4 includes some fun examples of in-camera effects and as you'll see, they can be very rewarding compared to postproduction intensive shots, because after you shoot them they require no further work!

Practical Effects Cost Money

When you're shooting your effects you're spending shooting time, which often means that you're spending money and/or using up favors. When you're tinkering around with your shots in post, you're just spending your own time. This is another opportunity to ask yourself which you have more of, money or time. The answer for the DV Rebel is usually time. Time is your greatest advantage over the Hollywood big boys. If they want it to rain, they rent rain towers at hundreds of dollars per day and make it rain on the day they need it to. A week later it rains for real and they lose a day or move to a cover set. You just wait for the rain and shoot on that day—and your free rain looks way better than their million-dollar rain! The DV Rebel melts down time and re-forms it into production value.

The same thing applies in postproduction. For *The Last Birthday Card,* I shot the helicopter attack scene first. The rest of the film took me a whole year to get in the can (way, way more time than money!), and the whole time I was crafting the handful of effects shots in that sequence. If I ever got frustrated that I couldn't shoot another scene on a particular weekend, I'd work on my helicopter animation instead.

Scenes from the helicopter attack sequence in *The Last Birthday Card*.

The best approach for an effect is the one that suits your schedule and resources, not necessarily the one that looks the best on paper.

Jargon Watch

In the can refers to a film canister, of course. When a shot or scene is in the can, it's been shot in its entirety. We'll be saying "in the can" long after the last film canister is melted down to create spaceships helping transport the human race off this dying world.

Are You P.T. Barnum or Jackie Chan?

My colleague Corey Rosen has an amazing skill. Sure, he's a talented visual effects artist and a gifted comedian, but his most impressive skill lies in getting his friends to help him out with stuff. He's a born producer, and he occasionally turns this talent on the world of the short film. His most ambitious effort to date is a short called *Keep Clear*. It's a fun film, and a masterpiece of calling in favors from friends. Corey knows that people are attracted to ambition and positive energy—two commodities that he has in spades. I have coined a term for this magnetic force—the Cor-tex. As in, "Corey asked me to rotoscope these ninjas for *Keep Clear* and for some reason I said yes—I've been sucked into the Cor-tex!"

The author both perfomed as and rotoscoped these ninjas.

I don't have this skill. I roto my own ninjas. In fact, I'm usually the guy in the ninja suit as well.

Jargon Watch

Roto is short for *rotoscope,* which was the name for a modified animation camera that could both project and shoot film. By projecting images onto animation paper, the camera allowed an artist to trace a matte for a live-action element. This painstaking process would be done by hand for every single frame of a shot. The projector was then reconfigured as a camera and the animated matte would be photographed. Today, of course, we trace mattes by hand using digital tools, but we still call the process *rotoscoping.*

Everyone is good at something. Make sure you bring your special skills to bear in making your film. Corey's film was designed more to launch his career on-camera than behind it, so he delegated wisely to allow himself the ability to focus on his performance as the star of *Keep Clear*. As the sole creative force behind the film he could design the production around his unique abilities, and you should do the same. There's a reason Jackie Chan wrote, produced, and directed many of his Hong Kong action films—no one else could conceive of those insane stunts, or in good conscience ask someone to perform them!

Don't think your abilities translate to the film you want to make? A skilled cook should have no trouble getting friends to work on her magnum opus if she tempts them with the best craft service table this side of the Naked Chef. Use what you got.

Owning the Means of Production

You should own your own camera, computer, and software. That probably sounds expensive, but it doesn't end there—I also insist that you own your own car (New Yorkers excepted), clothing, and have regular access to a bed. If those last items sound painfully obvious, you get my point—a camera and a computer are as essential to the filmmaker's lifestyle as shoes, protein, and lattés.

What makes DV Rebel filmmaking possible is the accessibility of consumer tools that can, if wielded properly, produce professional-looking results. Those tools are principally cameras and computers, and the key word is accessibility. Your leg up on your big-budget brethren is your ability to grab your camera and run out the door every time you hear sirens, or yank the camera out of the trunk when the perfect sunset materializes on the drive home from dinner.

You could rent a camera for your shoot, but that gets you into a situation that I just hate—it enforces a *schedule*. Just ask any producer I've ever worked with: I hate schedules.

A couple of lucky shots nabbed for *The Last Birthday Card,* as they appear in the final film.

When shooting the *Last Birthday Card* scenes in Scott's apartment, our schedule was thrown off by an unexpected situation. Scott's place was right next door to a fire station, and every Sunday the firefighters would exercise their trucks, pulling them out into the street. This caused a lot of noise that kept us from shooting. But as I stared out the window at the gleaming red ladder truck in front of Scott's building, I realized I had been given a gift. I ran outside and shot a couple of field-reporter-style shots of the trucks surrounding Scott's place. Later I would composite smoke pouring out of the apartment and play these shots back on the TV in Baxter's studio, creating the faux news story about Scott's alleged demise—something I thought I'd have to suggest with audio alone. Owning the camera and other gear allowed me the flexibility to roll with the punches and take advantage of dumb luck.

An even more extreme example occurred back in my film school days. I was helping a friend with his stop-motion short in his studio late one night when one of my filmmaking cohorts burst in, exclaiming that there was a huge brushfire just down the I-5 freeway from CalArts. I grabbed the Hi8 camera and we were off, actors donning costumes as we drove. We managed to shoot the entire climactic "ninja battle in hell" finale of our martial arts epic on a frontage road backed by a spectacular vista of the blaze. We got all our shots in the can before we were politely escorted the hell out of there by some gentlemen in uniform who very much wanted to take our wooden swords away.

The "ninja battle in hell" scene from *Symphony of Slaughter*.

I once shot an entire *spec spot* based around a piece of construction equipment that was parked in the middle of the street near The Orphanage. I drove home, grabbed my DVX100a, came back, and shot for three hours. The next day the construction equipment had been moved, but my spot was already edited.

Jargon Watch

A *spec spot* is a commercial that is shot *on spec,* or without paid commission. To lend authenticity to a spec spot, its director often bases it on a real-world product or brand. There's never any real hope that the brand owner will buy it or its underlying concept— creating a spec spot is strictly a reel-building endeavor. It's commonplace but potentially risky to create a spec spot for a well-known brand without permission. In the days of hand-carried ³⁄₄-inch tape reels, there wasn't much cause to sue a kid making her own Nike spot, but with the advent of the Internet, companies have begun cracking down on unlicensed use of their brands.

The director, cameraman, star, and stunt driver are all featured in this shot from an Isuzu spec spot.

OK, I didn't just grab my camera. I grabbed my mobile DV Rebel kit. This includes the camera and some accessories.

An example DV Rebel camera kit, including a DVX100a 24p DV camera, Apple PowerBook with Final Cut Pro HD, a roll of gaffer's tape (not pictured), ND gradient filter, wide-angle lens adaptor (not pictured), extra tape, and battery—and a padded, water-resistant bag that holds it all, complete with straps to hold a lightweight tripod.

As the CEO of The Orphanage often says, "Success is where luck meets preparedness." You'll find little talk of scheduling in this book, despite the fact that, much like getting up in the morning, it is occasionally a necessary evil. Your biggest production value scenes probably won't be schedulable—they'll be dumb luck for which you were prepared. Owning a few pieces of production gear that you'll use on every film you make will save you money in the long run, but most importantly, it gives you the agility to turn twists of fate into production value you could never afford.

Besides a camera, the other big piece of gear you'll want to own is a computer. These days, it's hard to buy one that doesn't have enough horsepower to edit video, so insisting you have one seems reasonable enough. But before you go crossing that one off your list, I have some bad news—you also need software. That part of the cost equation can add up fast, but a computer without software isn't much use. Here's what I think you should have on your machine besides Minesweeper and iTunes:

A Non-Linear Editor (NLE)

Editing is an important part of the filmmaking process—in some ways, the most important part—so I recommend jumping up a step from the software that comes free with your computer or video card. On the Mac, there are really only two choices, Apple's own Final Cut Pro HD and Avid's Xpress Pro. These are both excellent, and so similar in feature set that your choice should be based on personal preference. These applications are in the $1000 range, which could well exceed the value of the computer you run them on. Alternatives include the entry-level versions of each, Final Cut Express HD and Avid Xpress DV, which are only a couple hundred bucks. They have some limitations that make the workflow described in this book difficult, so this is one of many places where you get to decide what you have more of: time or money.

On Windows, your choices are more varied. There's Avid again, Pinnacle Studio, Sony Vegas, and many others.

For those whose operating systems support it, I recommend Adobe Premiere Pro (2.0 or greater), because of its tremendous interoperability[2] with Adobe After Effects, the lynchpin app in our workflow. Again, your choice may boil down to personal preference—just make sure there's a way to get your edit from your NLE of choice into After Effects (see the section, *Automatic Duck* below).

Adobe® After Effects® Professional 7.0 or Later

The vast majority of the techniques described in this book revolve around After Effects Professional 7.0. It's not that there aren't any other compositing applications out there—most of the visual effects tasks described in this book could be performed in Shake, Fusion, or Combustion. But After Effects provides the magical combination of a highly stable, timeline-oriented application with good interoperability with major NLEs, and yet

---

2 Some of which is only available as a part of the Adobe Production Studio bundle.

it is also able to tackle complex compositing tasks, including 3D. There's a vast quantity of high quality training available, and a generous online user community. But most importantly, *I* know After Effects well enough to set up sample projects for you that should handily automate many of your common postproduction tasks.

You're going to be using After Effects for everything from previsualization to mastering your final film. I highly recommend that you become comfortable with the fundamentals of this great piece of software. One excellent resource is *Adobe After Effects 7.0 Studio Techniques* by Mark Christiansen (Adobe Press, 2006). It's one of the few After Effects books focused specifically on visual effects for film and video.

Adobe® Photoshop®

Perhaps you've heard of it?

Automatic Duck

If you are not editing in Premiere Pro, you will want some sort of "bridge" between your NLE software and After Effects. Automatic Duck is a company that specializes in exactly this. They sell a wide variety of tools for sharing EDLs (Edit Decision Lists) between NLEs and compositing applications. For instance, if you edit with Final Cut Pro HD, you'd use Automatic Duck's Pro Import AE product.

At roughly $500, Pro Import AE might seem like a luxury. It's important to remember that what you get with a product like this is more than just software—it's support, online tutorials, and more time to spend on the creative aspects of your postproduction.

That said, conforming your edit in After Effects is something you can do by hand. Depending on how long your film is and how many cuts it has, this may be something you'd like to consider. Or make your life easy and use Premiere Pro, which provides direct interoperability with After

Effects. As always, the balance that only you can know is how much money you're willing to spend weighed against how much time you're able to invest.

On the DVD

Included with this book is a DVD that contains both a video and a data partition. In your DVD player, this disc contains my short film *The Last Birthday Card,* including a commentary track and a visual effects breakdown. It also includes a segment called *The Green Project,* which is a tiny snipped of a very DV Rebellious project that you will work with yourself in a tutorial in Chapter 6.

In your computer's drive, the disc not only contains the tutorial files to follow along with *The Green Project* example and several others, but also includes some useful bullet hit elements that you can use in your films, as well as some After Effects Professional 7.0 template projects for creating common effects such as gunfire, night vision, and even a hand-cranked film look. You'll also find some amazing scripts that will transform After Effects into a full-featured mastering studio for color correcting your final film.

Now, with your DVD player warmed up, your software installed, and your camera batteries charged, let's get to work!

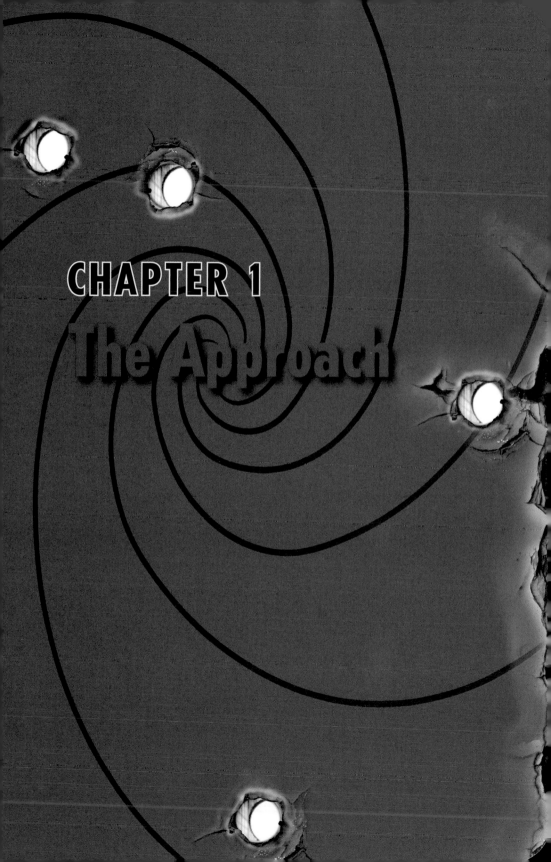

CHAPTER 1

The Approach

There are many ways to approach making a film, and there are even many ways to approach making a film on a modest budget. But the DV Rebel approach is special. It centers entirely on *production value,* that nebulous quality that makes a film feel big—or not. Production value doesn't have to cost money—think of an episode of "Project Runway" where each of the designers gets $50 to buy fabric, but only one of their creations "looks expensive" to the judges. You can fake production value. You do it by knowing how the barest minimum of resources can look like a million bucks, and by planning your film out in detail to ensure your every effort finds its way onto the screen.

Work Backward, Not Forward

Hollywood action movies are made using an effective but somewhat luxurious process. The key to achieving a high production value on a tight budget is turning this process on its ear.

Consider an action scene in any big movie. The process of creating it sounds like pretty much the only way to make a movie.

- First it is scripted, and possibly planned out using storyboards or even animatics (see Chapter 2).

- Then it is budgeted and scheduled.

- On the shoot, the action is *covered* per the plan. Multiple cameras might be used to maximize the coverage on an expensive stunt or pyro event. Retakes are done after resetting scenes, which can include redressing squibbed walls or rolling another brand-new Mercedes off the truck to be crashed. In order to ensure good coverage, much more material is shot than is strictly required to match the boards.

- In the cutting room, the editor uses the coverage to create the scene. She sculpts the story using the shots, creating that all important *mis en scene,* the illusion that all these separately filmed events are actually one reality seamlessly unfolding before us.

- Sound, music, and digital effects are added to complete the scene.

Jargon Watch

Cover is a term used to describe the process of portraying an event with a shot. When you shoot the same action from different camera positions, that's called *covering the action.* What every editor is looking for when screening dailies is *good coverage*—in other words, enough variety of shots that she can string together a scene that will flow past the audience effortlessly. Every first-time director is nervous about getting good coverage, especially if he runs out of time and has to drop setups from his schedule.

Sounds great! What's wrong with that? Nothing, if you can afford it. I encourage you to examine the supplemental materials on disc 2 of the *Bad Boys 2* DVD. There are some excellent mini-documentaries there that give an instructive picture of how large-scale action scenes are executed.

After watching these, your response will be, quite rightly, that you can't afford any of this stuff. The *Bad Boys 2* production probably spent your film's entire budget each day on donuts alone. But pay particularly close attention to the segments that show how much time and effort goes into shots that are ultimately cut from the movie, or featured only fleetingly. Much of the effort involved in creating a big-budget film never actually makes it to the screen.

While many action scenes in multimillion-dollar movies will, of course, be outside the reach of the low-budget action filmmaker, you might be surprised by what you can achieve. You just can't afford to waste one drop of effort in the process.

Mis en Scene, Dans la Cuisine

Luc Besson's groundbreaking *La Femme Nikita* is a perfect film for us to study, because it was made without a tremendous budget. Instead of offering audiences explosion after costly explosion, Besson gave us memorable characters and a few signature action scenes that are not only exciting, but are drenched in the emotion of the title character. In fact, it is our emotional connection to Nikita's situation that makes the scenes so gripping. If you already have the special edition DVD of *La Femme Nikita,* great. If not, I highly recommend you get your hands on it for this chapter. I've included several images from the film in case your Netflix queue is a little backed up.

The scene we'll examine in depth is Chapter 14 on the film's DVD, where Nikita goes out to dinner with Bob—her first journey outside the confines of her training facility. What she thinks is a lovely "graduation dinner" turns out to be her first assignment. Bob abandons her with a pistol, two clips, and an escape plan that turns out to be bogus. After she successfully performs her hit, a gunfight ensues in the confines of the restaurant's kitchen.

Watch that scene now. It's a solid scene, very well directed with a flair that would later become Besson's trademark.

You could never shoot this scene.

But now watch it again, and try this: Don't watch the *scene,* watch the individual *shots.* Pause the DVD on each one, and ask yourself this question: Could I create this shot? This less-than-two-second little snippet in time? Could I figure out a way to shoot that with my little DV camera?

The answer is yes (or it will be after you finish this book) for all but maybe a few of the most pyrotechnic-intensive shots. No single shot in the scene is so elaborate that you couldn't dream up a way to create it. And if you can create the shots, you can create the scene.

So emerges the DV Rebel approach: Plan the shoot, shoot the plan. Pre-edit your movie on paper, shoot only what you absolutely need, and lean on the universal fact that half of the reality of a movie is what the audience creates in their minds *in between the shots.*

By starting with a firm idea of what you want the end product to look like, and reverse-engineering the least expensive way to get there, you are putting a lot of pressure on your ability to plan and previsualize. In fact, the low-budget filmmaker must be a better action director than the average Hollywood blockbuster helmer. Just about anyone can stage some action and cover it with a dozen cameras for take after take until he produces enough footage that a talented editor can craft a scene. I'm sure you've seen examples of this technique. You don't have the luxury of "discovering" your scene through coverage and cutting, however. You need to plan it out in rigorous detail and execute your plan using the tricks found in the following pages.

Jargon Watch

Helmer is a silly industry term for director, the person "at the helm" of the film.

Break It Down

You're probably still thinking I'm crazy for telling you that you could create the kitchen scene in *La Femme Nikita*. That's OK, you should be thinking that at this point. In this section we'll break the scene down to its individual components and tackle them one at a time.

First of all, the scene takes place in the kitchen of a restaurant. I'm going to assume that you could somehow get yourself access to such a location for a couple of nights' shooting. I'll also assume that your friend's friend who owns the restaurant is not interested in your destroying his kitchen, or even setting off the fire alarm. There's a whole section about locations in the next chapter, although unfortunately it does not contain names and phone numbers of gullible restaurateurs.

To understand what I mean by breaking down a scene, let's look at an example from a truly no-budget enterprise, my student film entitled

Skate Warrior. After a chase scene, the antagonist vents his frustration by unloading his 9mm on the skateboard left behind by the kid he was trying to run over. We only had toy guns for this film, but we had an assortment of them. One had a decent-looking blowback effect[1]; the other was a cap gun that looked almost the same but fired paper caps, creating a nice smoke effect but no blowback.

I knew from my detailed storyboards that the edited sequence would go like this:

1. Alex (the antagonist) watches as our heroes escape, and then turns and begins to fire at the skateboard.

2. The skateboard gets shot up.

3. Alex stops firing when he runs out of ammo, puts his gun down, and turns to leave.

In a regular movie, shots one and three would be the same setup, probably the same take. The actor would fire, glower, and exit, and the editor would later insert shot two into the middle. But I wanted some smoke lingering in the air after all this gunfire, and the toy gun with the realistic firing action wasn't going to give me this. So, knowing that I'd have an

Although shots one and three appear to be the same setup, each required a different gun prop to complete the illusion of running out of ammo.

---

1 *Blowback* is the name for the physical motion that you see on the slide of a firing automatic pistol. For a detailed discussion of this effect and how to achieve it safely and inexpensively, see the "Guns Guns Guns!" section in Chapter 4.

edit between one and three, I jumped in mid-take and swapped out the gun. For shot three, the actor simply fired a bunch of paper caps and then lowered the gun out of frame. It took a few tries to get the timing right, but on take three we got it. The shot would never work as one continuous chunk, but that's OK—my plan told me I'd never need to use it that way.

The audience sees the two shots and creates the seamless reality between them. They see a gun fired until empty and spewing smoke. My two plastic guns become one real one inside the audience's head.

This is the definition of the fancy French term *mis en scene*. It's the reality that a film creates inside the viewer's mind. The audience is an active participant in this, willingly suspending their disbelief. Although they know what they're seeing is manufactured, they allow themselves to be swept up in it. *Mis en scene* is the triumph of our emotional response to cinema over our intellectual skepticism.

If you think only low-budget filmmakers need to "cheat" like this, relying on the audience's willing participation to create the illusion of reality, think again. In *The Abyss*, director James Cameron found a cost-effective way to stage the final scene on the surface of the alien craft. He used a hanging foreground miniature (see Chapter 4) to show Bud (Ed Harris) walking through an enormous arch-like feature in the craft's design (*The Abyss* Special Edition DVD Chapter 52). He cut away to a few shots of the crew's reaction, and then cut back to the approaching Harris, now much closer. For the second shot, Harris is actually standing right in front of the large miniature, although it looks very far away. The part of the scene that could never have been filmed, the transition between his distant and nearby walk, is effortlessly imagined by the unsuspecting audience.

As long as you obey the rules of film grammar, you will be surprised how generous your audience will be in believing what you show them. See the section "Lines of Action" in Chapter 2 for more on this.

The very first video footage I ever shot and edited was of my high school friends and me skateboarding. We would often use editing tricks to make it look like we pulled off a trick that was beyond our ability. To me, this technique will always be known by the name we called it in our school's video editing room—the *Ollie to Edit*.[2]

Check out chapter 15 of the *Back to the Future 2* DVD. Michael J. Fox's hasty vault into the stairwell to avoid Mr. Strickland's (James Tolkan) gaze? Classic Ollie to Edit.

Build It Up

Got your *La Femme Nikita* DVD all cued up? We're going to dissect a few tricky shots from the kitchen scene and examine how, at the individual shot level, it's a doable scene for the DV Rebel.

By the end of this book you'll be staging exciting action scenes like this one in *La Femme Nikita*. You must provide your own French-speaking ballerina assassins.

Images from "Nikita," a film by Luc Besson, Production Gaumont (1990)

---

2 The Ollie is the first step of most freestyle skateboard tricks—the getting-airborne maneuver in which the skateboard stays somehow magically attached to the skater's feet.

From the very first shots, the sequence oozes production value. But upon closer examination, this is more due to the style of filmmaking than to anything ultra-expensive going on. The lighting is broad and flat, probably not that different from what you'd get for free in a real kitchen. But the camera is moving smoothly and smartly on dolly tracks. Chapter 3 covers several options for low-budget dollies. One of those options is grabbing anything you can find with wheels and setting your camera on it. It's not hard to imagine some wheeled carts lying around a kitchen. Some locations provide their own dollies!

It's fairly easy to imagine your actor with your realistic prop gun skulking through your borrowed kitchen set followed by your make-shift dolly. And then, if you're following along with your DVD, you'll notice that people start shooting at each other. Your first clue will be the stack of plates violently exploding behind Nikita.

This effect was created with a small pyrotechnic charge called a *squib*, handled by a practical effects technician. On each take he would explode those dishes on cue, and between takes he would have to

A pile of plates explodes behind Nikita, a gag that the DV Rebel can easily find a way to stage without any pyrotechnics.

Even the pros sometimes resort to ghetto pyro, the fine art of chucking handfuls of junk at your actors.

take time to reset the dishes and the charge. The safety concerns surrounding an effect like this are numerous, and the time it takes to reset could have a major impact on your schedule. The DV Rebel prizes safety, speed, and flexibility, so you would not use a pyrotechnic event for this effect. Chapter 4 details several ways to create bullet hits on set and in post, none of which involve gunpowder. In this case, assuming you can afford some thrift-store plates, the technique I would recommend would be smashing them with a baseball bat! "Paint out" the bat handle in Adobe After Effects and you've got a safe but spectacular pyro event that costs only a few bucks.

This is a perfect example of reverse engineering. If you go into the scene with predefined notions of how movies are made, you would see "plates explode" on the shot-list and immediately think squibs, which would then make you think of a hundred legitimate reasons why you can't do the scene, from location issues to safety concerns to expense. But if you examine the effect in slow motion on your DVD player, you can see that there's little difference between an expertly squibbed stack of plates and one at which a crowbar has been swung or that's been hit with a slingshot. You haven't shot your scene yet, so you don't have it to slow-motion through—instead you must use your storyboards to plan the most effective DV Rebel bullet hit you can. Maybe the way to do this is to destroy something less sturdy and dangerous than a pile of plates. It's possible that an exploding bag of flour could look just as impressive.

In fact, while there is certainly a lot of real pyrotechnic action in this scene, there's also plenty of what I call "ghetto pyro." Ghetto pyro is where you take a handful of whatever kind of debris you could imagine flying through the air and throw it at your star. Rinse and repeat. I imagine that's exactly what's going on in this tense moment in *Nikita:*

In Chapter 4 I describe some of my ghetto pyro moments from *The Last Birthday Card*. It involves combining the on-set debris with some spark elements created in post.

I predict that you're going to want lots of bullets ricocheting in your movie. Never mind that bullets don't really spark when they hit things— they do in movies, and it's a movie that we're making here. Following my nonpyro rule, you'll be making these sparks digitally. On the DVD at the back of this book, there's a small collection of squib elements, and there's a tutorial for compositing them in Chapter 4.

"OK," you say, "but what about all the gunfire in this scene?" Glad you asked.

When the actors in *Nikita* are firing their guns, a few things are happening on the set. A highly trained, well-paid specialist is supervising this gun action. The guns are rented

When the time comes to composite a digital muzzle flash into your movie, your entire DVD collection becomes reference material.

In *La Femme Nikita*, a stylish bullet point-of-view (POV) shot helps show the power of Nikita's turning point in the kitchen scene.

props, actual firearms that have been custom-modified to fire blanks that cost over a dollar each. The guns undoubtedly jam a couple times during filming. This may be why the guys with the submachine guns are firing them in semi-automatic mode rather than full auto. The actors and any crew in the room would be wearing hearing protection, because blanks are very loud. An insurance policy covers the entire production in the event of an accident. While accidents involving guns on movie sets are rare, when they do happen they can be lethal.

For all these reasons and more, most people will advise the budget-conscious filmmaker to avoid not only guns but also the entire genre of action. Not me. Chapter 4 features a section devoted to safe, cost-effective techniques for including guns in your movie. By the time you finish reading it, gunfire won't be intimidating at all.

Luc Besson has become known as a master of stylized action. He hinted at this predilection with one fancy shot in the kitchen scene, a bullet's POV as it flies through the room.

No computer graphics were used for this shot, as *Nikita* was made before computers were allowed anywhere near movies. This shot looks like it was accomplished completely in-camera. There's nothing all that difficult about it, but what's worth noting is that Besson thought to do it at all. Nikita's one asset in this scene, besides her training and high heels, is her gigantic hand-cannon of a pistol. When she finally concentrates and brings her training to bear, the massive power of her .50-caliber Desert Eagle is neatly conveyed by this in-your-face shot, as is an important character moment—Nikita is going to fight back.

Jargon Watch

POV stands for Point of View, and a *POV* shot is one that literally represents exactly what someone is seeing. Or some*thing*—there have been great *POV* shots for everything from bullets to sharks to bombs to alien predators.

The bullet POV is not the only inexpensive but effective stylistic flourish in this scene. In fact, the very first shot features one. Go back and watch it now—you may note that the shot of Nikita entering the kitchen begins with a flash of white. While this is nothing you couldn't do in your NLE software, you may not have the idea to use such a "dirty trick." The flash is accompanied by an audio cue that has a jarring, gunshot quality. It clues you in right away that this will be the setting for the showdown that determines Nikita's fate.

If you don't want to get shot in an action movie, then don't wear a white shirt.

When bullets aren't flying into piles of plates or stainless steel shelving, they're hitting people. This sad fact is *de rigueur* in action films, so we may as well figure out how we're going to pull it off on a budget. Chapter 4 details some ways to both practically and digitally squib your actors.

We've been breaking this scene down a shot at a time and so far haven't come up against any deal breakers. Each action beat has a DV Rebel equivalent. Each dangerous pyrotechnic has a safe and inexpensive replacement. By now you're starting to see how, after reading the referenced chapters, you could put together a sequence like this. You could even imagine how you could tune the scene to take advantage of assets to which you have special access. Maybe your dad runs an auto body shop and he'll let you film there at night. Maybe your aunt is remodeling her kitchen and would be OK with you blowing a few holes in the wall she's about to tear out. Part of the focus of this book is to train your mind to always be on the lookout for production-value enhancing elements you could somehow incorporate into your film.

Outrunning the explosion, an action movie staple. If you do digitally what Besson staged on set, you'll be in the company of such mainstays as John McTiernan, Peter Hyams, Renny Harlan, and Andrew Davis.

What Is Production Value?

The DV Rebel approach is all about creating a high production value on a modest budget. But what exactly constitutes production value? As I mentioned, there's no difference between real production value and the illusion of production value. In other words, production value is one of those "perception is reality" things—if the movie *feels* big to the audience, then it *is* big. The qualities that make a movie feel big can be broken down into several small things—and a couple of popular myths.

Image Quality

DV cameras are capable of capturing some very high quality images, but they are just as capable of capturing images that look terrible. The two images below were both shot with the same camera, my Panasonic DVX100a. The first image looks like it could be a shot in a movie, and the second looks like Uncle Bob's Hi8 home movies. Getting your hands on a nice 24p DV or HD camera is a first step to creating great-looking images, but it's hardly the last. DV can look amazing, but only if you treat it with respect.

These two images were both shot with the same camera on the same street in Seoul, about ten minutes apart. The reason one looks like a shot from a movie and the other looks like camcorder footage has nothing to do with camera settings or CCD resolution.

MEGAPIXELS

There's a common feeling that high resolution means high quality. In fact, the movie you make with your DV camera will be shown on the same DVD player and the same TV as a major Hollywood production. As you'll see in this book, even in the days of inexpensive HDV cameras, it still can make a lot of sense to shoot on standard-definition DV. The key is to treat those few pixels your camera makes with respect. Chapter 6 goes into meticulous detail on how to avoid unnecessary image degradation throughout your postproduction pipeline. The low-resolution nature of your gear should in no way limit your ability to create production value.

DYNAMIC RANGE

More than resolution, the single characteristic of film that sets it apart from digital is its dynamic range. *Dynamic range,* sometimes referred to as *latitude,* is a term for the range of light values that can be faithfully reproduced by a given medium. If you've ever tried to videotape someone who was heavily backlit, you know the limitations of video's dynamic range.

Generally speaking, in a case where video blows out to pure white, film would do a much better job of holding detail in the highlights. And while it's not always necessary to avoid overexposed areas in your shots, uncontrolled clipped whites in an image are usually a giveaway that you're seeing video, not film.

The same scene shot on 35mm film (left) and DV (right). The blown-out sky in the video image is a dead giveaway.

That's why I say you must treat DV with respect. Even film productions, with the broad dynamic range of their color negative stocks, go to great lengths to control the light before it enters the camera. They may line the windows of a room with neutral density (ND) filters, or "tech down" a white T-shirt, or hit a shiny chrome bumper with dulling spray to tone down its reflections. Because DV is even more sensitive to these overexposure situations, it's generally understood in the cinematography community that lighting for DV (or HD) is more difficult than lighting for film. That's right—the belief that DV's light sensitivity allows for smaller, less expensive lighting packages turns out to be a myth.

Jargon Watch

The need to control the range of light on a set is so well understood that even the wardrobe department gets involved. Rather than leave a white garment pure white, they'll often make it a *tech white* by darkening it with dyes (often as simple as a bucket of water with a few teabags). A tech white T-shirt looks gray to the eye but appears white on the screen, where an actual clean white T-shirt might have been overexposed. The process of darkening a too-white object or garment is known as *teching down*.

Of course, we're DV Rebels, and we won't be carrying around enormous lighting kits. But we will be keeping our cameras' zebra modes on and watching for ways to avoid overexposure wherever possible. There's much more detail on this in "The Camera" chapter that's on the DVD.

DEPTH OF FIELD

Turn to the next page and compare the two images shown. Which appears more "cinematic?"

Chances are you picked the second one. The only difference between the two images is the depth of field, but this simple characteristic is enough to subconsciously trigger an association with big-budget film. Focus is yet another way for cinematographers to isolate the part of the image that's telling the story. This is one of many cases where *less is more*—de-emphasizing a distracting background allows the viewer to focus on the important action in the frame.

There are two mechanical features on any camera that determine the depth of field. The first is the aperture, or "iris." This is the bladed opening inside the lens that acts as an adjustable valve for the light coming in. When it is open wide, it lets in more light—but this light comes through a less precise gate and can spill across more of the frame. Thus you get a

Cinemek G35 lens adaptor before and after images courtesy of Macgregor.

shallow depth of field. "Stopping down," or making this opening smaller, lets less light in and creates sharper focus at all depths, increasing the depth of field.

But no matter how far you open your iris, you can never achieve as shallow a DOF with a DV camera as you could with a film camera. This is because of the second determining factor in DOF: the size of the imaging plane. The larger the area onto which light is focused, the harder it is to keep that light focused. If you frame up the same shot with equivalent lenses on both a Super 8 camera and an IMAX camera, it will be much, much harder to maintain deep focus with the IMAX camera. At the same *f-stop,* or aperture setting, the Super 8 image will have greater depth of field, because its imaging plane is so much smaller.

Our DV cameras have tiny little CCD chips that act as the image plane. These chips are much smaller than a 35mm film frame, making it difficult to match film's lovely shallow focus look. In "The Camera" chapter on the DVD, you'll learn how to "shoot wide-open" and use focal length choices to control your depth of field—but there is only so far that these techniques can go. I'll run you through some tools for eking out the shallowest depth of field your DV rig can muster, as well as some techniques for faking shallow focus in post.

Sound Quality

Without a doubt, the single most important factor in conveying production value to your audience is audio quality, particularly in dialog recording. This may be surprising, coming from an author with such a visual background. But the truth is, we live in a time where out-of-focus shots or grainy footage could be considered a valid artistic choice, but this will never be the case for difficult-to-hear, reverberant dialog. Audio quality is usually the first giveaway that the short you're watching was produced on a low budget, and that impression informs the entire viewing experience.

Having said that, you bought a book by a former visual effects artist, so you'd probably expect most of the material within to be about the visual end of filmmaking, and you'd be correct. I have too much respect for people who know audio to pretend to be an expert. But I will throw out the following bits of advice:

- The built-in mic on your camcorder is for decoration only. Use an external mic piped into your camera's audio inputs.

- Watch your mic input levels. Get the hottest signal you can without risking overmodulation. Do not use Auto Gain Control.

- Sound recording equipment is not limited to mics and boom poles. Strategically placed moving blankets, A.K.A. furniture pads, can drastically cut down on unwanted echo.

- If you get stuck with bad production audio, loop it in post. *Looping*, or ADR, is the process of re-recording dialog in a studio to replace the sync sound.

- If you can't get your mic near enough to your actors in a wide shot, make sure to record "wild lines," which means on-set audio with no corresponding picture. Better to spend time syncing audio in post than to have distant-sounding dialog. All of *El Mariachi* and much of *Primer* were done this way.

- Don't be literal-minded about sound design. You know that music is a purely emotional experience, but sound effects are too. Choosing not to add sound effects (see the film *The Thin Red Line)* is as valid a choice as adding sound to silent events (a metal grate makes a dramatic sound as it passes though a beam of light in *Die Hard).*

- Recognize that audio post may require more of your time than editing and color correcting your entire film. A good audio mix takes work, and is well worth it.

- Pick up *Sound for Digital Video* by Tomlinson Holman (Focal Press). Holman's book is an excellent primer on audio for those of us still recovering from the discovery that the picture isn't the most important part of the movie.

Locations

Action films have what are called "set pieces." These are the scenes that your friends use to show off their new surround-sound setup—the major action moments. Set pieces are often a tool to show just how big and world-changing the events of the film are, such as the flying Golden Gate

Bridge in *X-Men: The Last Stand* or the destruction of Grand Central Station in *Armageddon*. In other words, staging dangerous events at well-known locations is a hallmark of action movies.

And guess what: In both of those examples, the locations in question were never actually filmed! The *X3* scenes were shot on a set in Vancouver, and *Armageddon*'s Grand Central Station was a miniature.

The DV Rebel can apply this same approach to locations. If you want a scene to take place in Times Square, maybe the best approach would be to pose as a tourist and shoot some background plates, and then comp your actors in later.

In his quest to avoid shooting his entire film in his own apartment, the DV Rebel will resort to one of three choices: Borrow it, fake it, or steal it. I discuss these options, especially the last one, in the next chapter.

Lighting

I have a deep respect and awe for the craft of cinematography. While visual-effects supervising on the set of a major movie, I used my DVX100a to record some reference material. I aimed my lowly DV camera at the same scene that had been professionally lit by a truly gifted director of photography (DP), and was shocked by how great the image looked in my viewfinder. It drove home how much production value comes from good lighting. Did my DV images look as good as those made by the priceless Panavision camera next to me? No way. But they did look like a movie.

Great lighting can make DV look unquestionably cinematic, and is a mysterious art that, at least in this case, required a few tons of expensive equipment. So how does the DV Rebel with some worklights and a bounce card achieve anything close to this?

The answer is simple: Just do your best. There are no rules of good lighting. Throw out your books with the three-point lighting diagrams. Re-stage your shot if you don't have the resources to light it well with the framing you originally had in mind. Give yourself the freedom to see that halfway down the block the sun is doing something amazing with the shadows from the barbed-wire fence. You will achieve good lighting by simply being conscious of lighting whenever you shoot. And, of course, read the section on lighting in Chapter 3.

Effects

Yeah, there's a whole chapter on effects, but there are some on-set, or *practical,* effects that you can use to lend your film a more polished look. Smoking the set is a good one (see Chapter 4), and so is making it rain. These shots from a short project by Orphanage director Aaron Rhodes were made with an $8 hardware store light fixture and a garden hose.

If you're shooting a dialog scene in a parked car, you'd almost be stupid not to spray a hose on the windows while you're at it. For whatever inex-

Rain is instant production value, and it comes out the end of a standard garden hose with little provocation.

plicable reason, rain adds production value. As does the indication of rain—have you noticed how often you see shiny wet streets and sidewalks in movies? Even those that take place in bone-dry Southern California? In 2004 I shot a low-budget commercial in San Francisco, and while we couldn't afford a water truck to do a "wetdown," we did have a very persuasive location manager. While we set up our shot atop the steepest hill in the city, he knocked on a few doors and asked the locals if they would lend us a hose. Three doorbells later we had a wet street on a sunny day, and great production value pouring into the lens of our DVX100.

Stars

There is one kind of production value that sits apart from the rest, and that is star power. Having a name actor in your film instantly elevates the stock ticker of your movie.

The only way I think it makes sense for the DV Rebel to attempt to play this card is if (a) you are actually crafting a business plan around your film, one that involves seeking distribution or (b) you are best friends with Tom Cruise and he sees your new HVX200 and says, "Dude, we should totally make a movie with that thing!"

If (a) is the case for you, you can make a financial assessment of how much of your budget you want to spend on attracting name talent. But once you do that, you probably won't be able to take advantage of many of the DV Rebel tricks, such as creative permitting, catch-as-catch-can scheduling, and nonexistent craft services.

WORKING ~~YOUR~~ *WITH* ACTORS

There is a style of acting that audiences have come to associate with short films, and that style is called "bad." Bad acting is the hallmark of shorts, and I can't say I've disproved that with *The Last Birthday Card*.

One may think that the root cause of bad acting in shorts is the dearth of good actors in Denver, but sadly we DV Rebels must own up to a little-known filmmaking fact: Bad acting is always the director's fault. The corollary to this is that good acting equals that most sought-after commodity for the DV Rebel: production value. So what do we do?

The first thing to do is read a book, and not this one. Judith Weston's seminal book entitled simply *Directing Actors* is a must-have. I discovered it halfway through shooting *Birthday Card*, and as I pored through it the performances from my actors and nonactors noticeably improved. Note that it was I who needed to change tactics in order for this to happen, not my performers.

The biggest mistake that inexperienced directors make is thinking that their actors are there to *act*. They are actually there to *be*. Your job as the director is to provide the correct environment for them so that all they have to do is *be* for you to get the results you want on the screen. It's easy to imagine that what makes a great actor great is that she can emote sadness, for example, on cue. But in fact the actor's craft is not to emote, or pretend, but to actually *feel* sad. On cue. Each actor's process will be different, but it's safe to say that generating a legitimate sense of sadness will take some time, and be difficult to do in the hectic environs of a low-budget shoot. A director who takes the time to quiet the set, who designs the sequence so that actors have time to prepare, protects the actors from a hundred crew members accosting them between takes, keeps clear eyelines,[3] and provides a safe and unhurried bubble in which the actor can work is going to put a better "sad" on screen than the guy who bellows, "Cut! Do it again, but sadder!"

In fact, words like "happy" and "sad" have no place in the director's vocabulary. Using those terms constitutes giving *result direction*, and that's the biggest no-no. It's an easy no-no to commit because it's such a logical thing for directors to do—describe what they want to see. But to do so guarantees that you will not see it in the performance.

Here's an example of how result direction backfires, borrowed from an acting class I took at CalArts. The teacher asked for a volunteer to stand in front of the class at one end of the blackboard. "Now walk to the other end of the blackboard, and I want you to walk *sneakily*." The guy proceeded to do his best Hamburglar impersonation, projecting overt sneakiness broadly and clearly with his tiptoed steps and suspicious glances. "OK," the teacher continued, "now walk that same path again, but this time we will all be very quiet, and your goal is to cross the room without making a sound." We all hushed up and the aspiring actor set about silently crossing the room's creaky wooden floor. The result was, of course, nothing like the "sneaky" walk. He tested each step before putting

---

3 Although Chapter 2 discusses the concept of on-screen eyelines, in this case the term means something different. On the set, an actor's *eyeline* is the space directly in front of her while she's working. It's good to be conscious of keeping clear eyelines for your talent, i.e., keeping distracting people or stuff out of their field of view.

weight on it, focusing intently on his task. It looked real because it was real. When directed to a specific result, the actor naturally began to act, to perform. But when given a clear task, he was allowed to simply be.

Had we videotaped both room-crossings and shown one version each to two separate classes, we could bet that the class shown the first walk would identify it as "bad acting." But we know that the only thing that changed between takes was the directing. Bad acting is bad directing. Once you take that fact to heart, you will become the kind of director who prioritizes above all else creating a supportive working environment for your actors.

But Seriously, What Is Production Value?

In 1977, there were no computer graphics in movies, no digital compositing, no paint-that-out. And yet a film was released that blew people's minds with its visual effects: *Close Encounters of the Third Kind*. If you watch that film now, you'll see that those effects still hold up today, which is quite an accomplishment. There's a good reason why those shots still look good: The filmmakers chose to only create the type of effects that they could execute well using the bleeding edge technology of the day.

In Roger Ebert's review of the $7,000 mind-bender *Primer,* he said that the budget never interferes with the film, because "every shot is exactly as it should be." Taking our cue from *Primer's* masterful bang-for-the-buck factor, I've coined a little mantra for the DV Rebel:

DO WHAT ONLY YOU CAN DO WELL, DO ONLY WHAT YOU CAN DO WELL.

The first part is simple, and we've already discussed it —you should make the movie that you alone can make. Tell us *your* story and use the resources that only you have.

The second part is tricky, though. It means exercising some self-control, just like Spielberg did in 1977. It means acknowledging that on your budget you won't be making *Terminator 2*—but if you stretch and strain and get really creative, maybe you can make *The Terminator*.

DV Rebels aim high, but we have to make sure we don't make a film so beyond our modest resources that every prop, costume, and location betrays our budgetary constraints.

Don't Make Shots, Make a Movie

The last trick to achieving a high production value is perhaps both the most important and the most elusive. It's all about where you place your camera. Given any room with a couple of people in it, there are a hundred places to put a camera, but not all will create *cinema* when cut together. In Chapter 3, I do my best to describe the difference between pointing a camera at something and making a movie in the section called "Making Memorable Shots."

There are many ways to make a movie, and in Hollywood one common way is by surrounding yourself with a great crew. But as DV Rebels, the pressure is all on us. Our movie will shine or stink based purely on our abilities. If it was easy, everyone would be doing it. Are you ready? Then dive in!

Movies Referenced in This Chapter

The Abyss, Special Edition

Armageddon

Back to the Future 2

Bad Boys 2

Close Encounters of the Third Kind

Die Hard

La Femme Nikita, Special Edition

Primer

The Terminator

Terminator 2

The Thin Red Line

X-Men: The Last Stand

CHAPTER 2

Planning

It pains me to say that most films must be planned. Many creative people, myself included, derive no great pleasure from planning, scheduling, or amassing the resources required to make a film. However, planning your film can be a very rewarding creative experience. The directing process begins the instant you sketch your first rough storyboard. Alfred Hitchcock said that storyboarding his scenes was the only part of the filmmaking process that was truly creative—every stage after that was simply a compromise of this original vision. The best news is that the filmmaking process rewards planning with tangible results. Your camera is a machine for capturing not just what lies before it, but all the decisions that led up to the moment it was switched on. Your audience will feel the effort that went into what they're watching.

Looking for a Producer?

No matter how much you know about traditional film production, you probably know that a producer is a very important person on a film crew. Producers come in different flavors (executive, line, associate), but in general a producer's role is simple—to make sure the film gets made.

Line producers in particular are a director's best ally. They oversee the day-to-day scheduling and logistics of the shoot, and they make sure that stuff, people, and you are on time, prepared, and hopped up on caffeine on the shoot days.

Sounds great, huh?

I Have Bad News for You

You are the producer.

No one cares about your film as much as you do, and no one but you is going to make sure this thing gets made. You can hire or cajole someone to help, but the very fact that it's *you* doing these things indicates that, ultimately, you're in charge.

You absolutely should find help in this area. Do call in that favor, do delegate. But it will serve you well to remember that your film will get made only by the force of *your* own will.

Resources

With his blessing, it's now time to steal some wisdom from the godfather of the microbudget, Robert Rodriguez. When concocting *El Mariachi*, his $7,000, 16mm action movie, Rodriguez started by creating a list of available resources: cars, props, locations, people—anything he knew he could borrow for long enough to put in front of his camera. He then wrote his script to exploit these resources.

The importance of this document, which I'm calling "The Rodriguez List," cannot be overstated. You don't have unlimited resources, but you do have access to stuff that other filmmakers don't. Milk it! When you actually write down all the cool cars, apartments, horses, and samurai swords your friends collectively possess, you will not only be surprised at the length of the list, you may also begin to see a story emerge.

This is how *The Last Birthday Card* came about. My Rodriguez List included my friend Scott, whom I wanted to star in the short. He came with an apartment. David Nakabayashi came with a cool nickname ("Nak"), a great vehicle, and a willingness to try his hand at acting. Other items on my list included my own two dingy vehicles, my roommate's car, the art gallery where a college friend worked, and a friend's bayside house with a fabulous view. From this list, the story of two rival hitmen somehow emerged. The creative limitations imposed by The Rodriguez List are the best kind of inspiration.

Make your Rodriguez List and use it as your muse. Don't miss an opportunity to put production value on the screen.

A Uniquely Rebel Plan

How the DV Rebel plans her shoot is yet another major difference from, and advantage over, the traditional Hollywood approach. Planning a regular film shoot is hard because in order to be cost-effective, a traditional low-budget film must be shot all at once. This is the permeating wisdom of many "make a movie for cheap" books—that you should shoot your film on as compact a schedule as possible, in one location. While that will indeed save money, it may also make it quite evident to the audience that you saved money.

By owning a few key pieces of equipment, enough to stage a DV Rebel shoot anywhere, anytime, you completely eliminate this constraint, and enable a new kind of planning—the kind where you can take advantage of many more opportunities than may occur in the one week you chose to shoot.

The Last Birthday Card features an unholy number of locations packed into its 20-minute runtime. This was an intentional plan to keep it moving and exciting and to differentiate it from other shorts, but it was also an effective way for me to get the film made. It meant that I could break down my shoots into bite-sized chunks, each of which could be staged on one weekend. This was important, because I also had a day job at the time. I could plan and execute each short scene as its own little project and take a week or two to recover afterward. This resulted in a shooting schedule that spanned more than a year. That might not sound too appealing to you, but to me, it was an ideal way to get a film made while holding down a demanding job.

The DV Rebel doesn't blow up a building. The DV Rebel plans his shoot to coincide with the demolition of a local high-rise. The DV Rebel doesn't rent rain towers—he watches the forecast for rain. The DV Rebel doesn't shout "cue the fire engines" into a megaphone, she patiently waits across the street from the fire station with her finger poised over the record button.

Your Script

Here's where I join the chorus of every other "filmmaking is easy, just buy this book" book and sing: The script is the most important thing.

Blah blah blah no good film was ever made from a bad script blah blah the script is your blueprint blah blah if it's not on the page, it's not on the screen blah blah blah use two brads, not three blah blah.

OK, now that I got that out of my system, let's talk about your script. The real reason that your script is so important is that it is where you will do the two things that afford you a huge advantage over the Hollywood big-boys:

Make Waves

Your script should be controversial. Challenging even. This doesn't necessarily mean violent and gory; it means thought-provoking. *Primer, Reservoir Dogs, A Clockwork Orange,* and *Oldboy* are great examples of movies that take informed, controversial stances on relevant issues.

Think about it—*Reservoir Dogs* is a story about a brutal criminal (Harvey Keitel as Mr. White), but the film tells us that the only true mistake he makes is tragically trusting his fellow bank robber. *A Clockwork Orange* concludes that it is better for society to have violent criminals running free than to attempt to control the thoughts of the populace. The mind-blowing Chan-wook Park film *Oldboy* goes even further, but I won't spoil it for you as long as you promise to go see it immediately. The point is, these bold thematic stances cost the filmmakers nothing but keystrokes and propelled their films to the front page of the trades.

Even a moderately budgeted Hollywood film has a number of masters to serve, from its initial studio backing to its eventual distributors. The more money that is spent on a film, the less likely it can contain controversial ideas. This is probably the biggest strike against Hollywood movies today, so it's our ace in the hole. The tough-guy lines and leading actor charm that work well in a summer blockbuster have no place in our world. Make damn sure your film is about something worth arguing about. Create a stir, put your characters through hell, and challenge your audience.

Authenticity

The other thing you get to do as a low-budget filmmaker is to lend your script the kind of authenticity that Hollywood tends to eschew. This isn't a case of something Hollywood can't afford, or something that can't survive the decision-by-committee process. This is just Hollywood being lazy; another Achilles heel for you to take aim at.

Authenticity is free. Tom Clancy has the same word-processing software as any other writer, but his research and attention to detail lend his military thrillers a sense of production value that his competition can't touch. Whatever the subject matter of your film, read up on it, Google the living hell out of it, ask around, and do it justice.

Heat was widely praised for its brutal accuracy in depicting a highly trained gang of robbers in a bank job gone bad (Chapters 32–33 on the *Heat* DVD). While you probably won't be staging any shootouts in the middle of downtown L.A. on your DV Rebel budget, if you take the time to educate yourself a little you can give your gunmen the same credibility that Val Kilmer and Tom Sizemore exuded. Chapter 4 explains further why some movie characters look like they know what they're doing with a gun in their hand, and some don't.

You know how to use a computer. Your mother knows how to use a computer. So why do characters in films and television always use bogus terms and silly, outdated computing concepts? Does a list of 20 or 30 names of international spies need to be transported on a high-density optical disc? The text-only file would compress down to about 2 kilobytes and could be stored as a text message on a cell phone, emailed from a Blackberry, or encrypted into the barcode on a box of cereal. Does an analyst in a high-tech counterterrorist organization need to put a file on a Zip disk and scoot her chair across the room to hand it to a colleague? And why is every computer in every movie running some non-Mac, non-Windows, non-Linux operating system with a giant font and a text window for entering plain-English commands like "find the informant" or "shut down the reactor"? Most 10-year-olds know enough about Photoshop to realize you can't enhance a blurry photograph to the point where the nostril hairs of the bad guy leap into crisp focus.

But you know what? Google "enhance blurry photograph" and I bet you'll find some Stanford computer science grad student's SIGGRAPH paper about a cool new way to do just that.[1] The results won't be miraculous, but they'll be cool-looking with all their funky digital artifacts, and if you can duplicate the look, your audience will buy it big time. The freeware image enhancement software you download and compile yourself will produce results far more authentic than the slick, overproduced graphics of a Hollywood thriller.

Technology authenticity is a win-win because it's actually cheaper to do it right. It's far more likely that a master thief would disable the alarm codes at the Louvre with a spray-painted black PocketPC running Linux than some milled-aluminum production designer's wet dream. The sci-fi thriller *Primer* is the ultimate example of this—it's the hacked-together, Radio Shack feel of the characters' garage efforts that make their miraculous invention believable.

Give your audience a window into your area of interest or expertise. Michael Mann did copious research with real-life cab drivers to develop Jamie Foxx's character for *Collateral*—but imagine the film an actual cab driver could make. He won't get Tom Cruise, but he'll get a level of believability Mann could never buy.

Edginess and authenticity are the slings with which the low-budget filmmaker can slay the mighty Goliath of Hollywood.

---

1 In fact, the term you really want to Google is "deconvolution," but you'd probably discover that after a few searches.

I Am But a Shadowy Reflection of You

I will mention one thing about your script that has nothing to do with budget, but it's so important to the success of an action film that, purely as a fan, I have to touch on it.

An action movie is never any better than its bad guy. Every great action film has a memorable antagonist who—and this is the key—has a deep, personal connection with the hero.

In *Die Hard,* Hans Gruber (Alan Rickman) may be holding Holly, John McClane's wife (Bonnie Bedelia), hostage, but more importantly he *represents* everything in life that has taken her away from John. He wears the same suit as her boss at the Nakatomi Corporation, and the hapless Ellis (Hart Bochner) even points out to Hans, "Business is business—you use a gun, I use a fountain pen." Hans is the turned-up-to-11 version of Nakatomi itself. As another example, *Predator* pits the most elite, badass hunters from this planet against the otherworldly incarnation of themselves. The brute strength and armament that the heroes wield so cavalierly is precisely what nominates them to become prey. In *Raiders of the Lost Ark,* Belloq's (Paul Freeman) speech about how he and Dr. Jones are "not so different" has become classic. Indy and Belloq are both after the same thing and both willing to bend the rules to get it.

No one takes this philosophy further than the undisputed action master, John Woo. In many of his films, the protagonist/antagonist relationship spans two close friends, or even brothers. In *Face/Off,* the hero actually takes on the identity of the bad guy and vice versa, a compelling enough idea even without the poetic beauty that comes when they actually fix what's broken in each other's personal lives while occupying their bitter enemy's skin.

The more you think in these terms, the more you'll appreciate this rule. Is it an accident that Jack Walsh (Robert De Niro) playfully adopts Agent Mosely's (Yaphet Kotto) persona in *Midnight Run?* Or that Johnny Utah (Keanu Reeves) must learn to surf to track down the Ex-Presidents (and his own identity) in *Point Break?*

It's worthwhile to approach the structure of your script as if it was the antagonist's story. He or she creates the situations and pushes the film forward by seeking goals, and the hero reacts. The hero's *story* springs out of his or her efforts to resolve the *plot* created by the bad guy—but this inevitably involves resolving issues along the way that existed before the movie began.

Your Storyboards

Storyboarding is the process of drawing rough sketches of your shots in order to plan a sequence. It's a great way to approach any film project, but in the case of action movies, it's almost a must. For the DV Rebel, it's mandatory.

Mark Andrews, a director at Pixar and one of the greatest storyboard artists alive, shows exactly the kind of board that the DV Rebel probably doesn't need.

As I discussed at the very beginning of the book when I dissected the kitchen scene in *La Femme Nikita,* one of the ways you'll work DV Rebel miracles is by doing the hard work up front. You'll create a plan so detailed that shooting and editing may well feel like paint-by-numbers exercises. Your storyboards are not just where you begin to make important

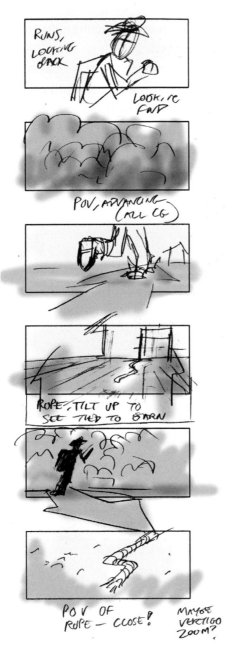

RUNS,
LOOKING
BACK

LOOKING
FWD

POV, ADVANCING
(ALL CG)

ROPE, TILT UP TO
SEE TIED TO BARN

POV OF
ROPE — CLOSE!   MAYBE
VERTIGO
ZOOM?

One page of boards from one of the
author's projects.

artistic decisions about how a sequence will flow, they're also where you'll break down exactly how you're going to accomplish the scene, what resources you'll need, what you'll do in-camera versus what you'll do in post, and where you may be exceeding your modest means.

Learn to Draw Badly

When I sit down to draw storyboards, I focus on getting the flow of a scene sketched out as quickly as possible. I am sure to mention this prioritization of speed to anyone who may view these "thumbnail" boards, usually right after they say something like, "What's that supposed to be" or "Oh, is that a guy?"

That's right, despite four years of expensive art school, I don't draw very well—at least not when I'm in a hurry. But it's OK. Storyboards don't need to be artistic masterpieces; they only need to communicate a few basic ideas about a shot.

The figure to the left shows an average example of the author's storyboarding style. Note that the actor is represented by nothing more than a stick figure. Simple construction lines suggest a face.

Not much to look at, but look again. You can see where the character is looking and what he's doing. In fact, there are only three key things that you and those on your crew need to be able to discern from your storyboard panels:

1. What's happening in the shot, including which characters are featured.

2. The predominant lines of action of the shot (more on this later)

3. A rough idea of the camera angle, including the type of lens (wide or telephoto), the composition of the frame, and any camera motion.

If you draw well you can communicate such lovely nuances as emotions, lighting, and hairstyles. But these things can also be noted textually alongside the panel, and that's exactly what I usually do. The board is a visual tool for setting up a shot, not a replacement for a script.

Observe how these two panels are almost identical, but give the impression of a slightly different camera angle:

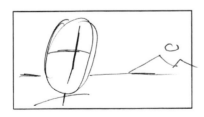
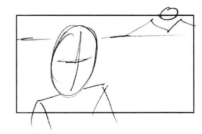

The placement of the horizon line clues in the viewer to the height of the camera.

The only difference between the two drawings is the height of the "horizon." There's a handy rule-of-thumb here: If you (or a camera) face a person of equal height, the horizon will appear to line up vertically with their eyes. So, to suggest a low angle, draw the horizon below the eye-height of your characters. To suggest a high angle, place the horizon above their eyes.

Eyelines

So far so good—you've established that with an oblong circle and three lines you can show the framing and camera height of a shot, as well as the eyeline of the talent.

This second bit is one of the really handy aspects of storyboards—eyelines. Entire books have been written on the subject of matching and maintaining eyelines, and covering complex, multicamera scenes in such a way that audiences can easily follow the action. As I mentioned in Chapter 1, the basic idea is that an audience can get confused if the camera crosses an imaginary line stretched between the faces of the people in a scene. This means that a filmed conversation between two people will feature one of them facing left, the other right.

 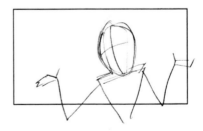

These two people appear to be having a conversation because the camera remains to one side of an imaginary line stretched between their faces. This most basic type of coverage is called *matching reverses*.

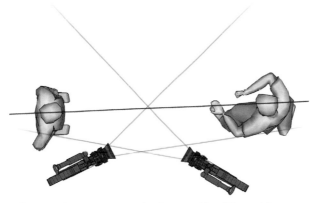

As long as the camera remains to one side of the red line, your audience won't get confused.

If you cross this line, the same action becomes confusing—the characters seem to be facing the same direction. This is called "crossing the line," or "breaking the 180° rule."

These two people appear to be looking in the same direction.

One major exception to this rule is that you can freely cross the line if you do it by moving the camera during a shot. If you do this for one side of a conversation made up of matching reverses, then you will need to do the same for the other side, otherwise when you cut away you'll be breaking the rule.

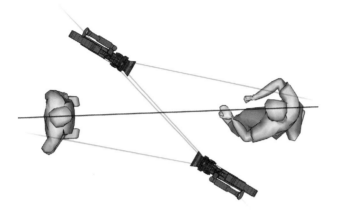

Even though the actors are facing one another, cameras on opposite sides of the red line create the illusion that they are facing the same direction.

A well-choreographed crossing of the line can be a great storytelling tool. In Nora Ephron's *You've Got Mail*, the initial meeting between Tom Hanks and Meg Ryan contains an overt crossing of the line at a pivotal moment in the conversation (*You've Got Mail* DVD Chapter 20). In *The Lord of the Rings: The Return of the King*, director Peter Jackson staged an ingenious play on the 180° rule for the scene in which Gollum (Andy Serkis) battles his own schizophrenia. First the camera dollies across an imaginary line to establish matching reverse angles on Gollum for each of his personalities. In one angle Gollum faces screen left, the other screen right, even though he never moves. Once these angles are established, Jackson cuts back and forth between them, and Gollum appears to be having a conversation with his darker personality.

For the action filmmaker, the idea of eyelines expands into a larger concept of "lines of action," and I'll go into more detail on that later.

Drawing Through a Lens

Back to the topic of minimal but effective storyboard. You've seen how to show what direction a person is facing and how high the camera is, but how can you give the impression of a particular type of lens?

Suggest a wide lens with radiating perspective lines.

Wide-angle lenses emphasize perspective. If you draw some radiating perspective lines, you're suggesting perspective and therefore a wider lens.

Long lenses often exhibit shallow depth of field. If you draw a character isolated against a vague background, you suggest a long lens.

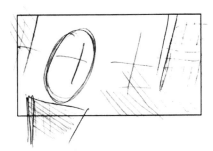

Suggest a telephoto lens with a flat, vague background.

Better still, you can suggest your lens choice by drawing the desired visual characteristics of that lens. In the following board, the gun on the left is drawn very large in comparison to the person's face. This instantly suggests a wide lens. The gun on the right is closer to the correct size in relationship to the character's head. It feels like we're father away and on a longer lens.

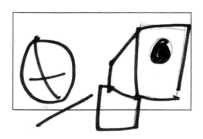

Two different ways to (badly) draw a guy with a gun. One clearly indicates a wide lens (left), the other a long lens (right).

Shoot it, Nerd it, Steal it

There are other ways of creating storyboards, ways that don't involve any drawing. One great way to create boards is to simply shoot photographs of willing subjects in the correct poses. All the better if you can work this into your location scout, because then you can get a real sense of how shots might work in, or be limited by, your location. When I do this for a TV commercial that I'm shooting on film or with a rented HD rig, I have to go through a process of converting my point-and-shoot camera's focal lengths to the equivalent 35mm lens sizes, but when I'm shooting DV Rebel-style, I simply use my DVX100a as the still camera on the scout. If I feel like being super organized, I'll even verbally slate any relevant information onto the tape, such as "I'm zoomed all the way out, the camera is about three feet off the ground, and this is where the sun will be at four in the afternoon" or "Hey, why don't we just shoot this stupid shot now?"

These four photo-boards are from a Toshiba commercial I shot in 2005. Two willing production staff members, Athena Portillo and Jonathan Vohr, helped mock up a scene in which a woman dangles from a helicopter. The frame of their clasped hands was shot sideways. Before we shot one frame of this commercial, we had a full animatic comprised of these parking-lot shots, stock footage, and clips stolen from well-known movies. More info on this commercial is in Chapter 6, and the finished spot can be seen in HD at theorphanage.com/ocp.

Another option is to use a 3D graphics program to create storyboards digitally. This has the disadvantage of being slightly slow compared to sketching or photographing, but it can make up for this in flexibility. You may, for example, have trouble shooting digital stills of a minivan being chased by a velociraptor (piloting an F18)—but this would be a relatively easy image to create in 3D.

The trick is to avoid getting bogged down by the complexities of 3D software. There are actually a few commercial applications out there designed specifically to help you storyboard your film. They come with a library of common cinematic props such as Handsome Men and Desks. Instead of these applications, I tend to turn to an amazing but little-known piece of architectural software called SketchUp. SketchUp has a really cool interface for building simple 3D shapes, and a decent library of people, props, and even some film industry-specific stuff like cameras and cranes. What I really dig about SketchUp is that its renderings look, well,

like sketches. They have loose lines and a "concept art" look about them, which makes them much easier on the eyes than the bad-videogame look of many 3D storyboards. Best of all, there's a free version of SketchUp available from Google.

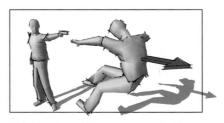

This storyboard frame was created in minutes using SketchUp Pro.

There's one more way to create a storyboard, and that's by stealing. A Google image search, a scan through the offerings of a stock photo house, or a quick DVD rip may be the fastest path to a storyboard panel that eludes your pen or your mouse. This can even become the beginnings of a moving storyboard, or *animatic*. You'd be in good company using this technique—George Lucas famously pre-edited the space battles of *Star Wars* using World War II air combat footage. For more on this, see "Animatics" later in this chapter.

Google SketchUp and Sketchup Pro

SketchUp Pro is a 3D design program that is aimed primarily at architects, but it provides a great interface for quickly designing anything in 3D. I've used it to design sets, plan shoots, and create great looking storyboards. SketchUp is now a Google product, and a free version (called Google Sketchup) can be downloaded at sketchup.google.com. The pro version, which adds some film-related functionality, sells for $495.

Lines of Action (Big Red Arrows)

The special relationship between action films and the storyboarding process is best summed up by one image—the Big Red Arrow.

I first remember becoming aware of the Big Red Arrow in Joe Johnston's amazing storyboards for *Indiana Jones and the Temple of Doom*. Johnston's arrows, drawn in perfect perspective and shaded a vivid red, were so tangible and commanding that the storyboard really did spring to life on the page.[2]

What Spielberg and Johnston knew then, and I have come to learn after years of bad filmmaking, is that action scenes are cut together well when adjacent shots have consistent motions across the cut, and when entire sequences have visual flows that are connected in this way. When

The Big Red Arrow.

I storyboard a scene, I'm staging action and planning coverage, but more importantly, I'm choreographing the visual flow of the scene. When I want actions to seem connected across shots, I make sure they follow the same on-screen direction. When I want to jar the audience, I create a sequence of shots with jumbled lines of action.

---

2 We can't reprint them here, but at the time of this writing there was a tremendous collection of *Temple of Doom* storyboards on this site: indianajones.de/indy2/texte/pictures_storyboards.php

The importance of lines of action can be illustrated by a fun little homework project. Grab your camera and a friend and quickly shoot the two shots shown below. The only prop you'll need is a stir stick.

The first shot of this example features Captain Sideburns (A.K.A. Dav Rauch) launching a common stir stick left-to-right.

It will take a few tries, but the key to the second shot is syncing up the timing of the left-to-right whip-pan with the motion of the actor's head jerking back.

In the first frame, you shoot your friend throwing the stick out of frame, left-to-right. In the second, you use that same friend and the same stick. Have him carefully hold the stick up to his head by pinching it in his hand as shown. Don't even bother having him move his hand at all, simply have him hold it against his forehead. When you call action, he should jerk his head back and look dazed.

On this second shot, you should do a left-to-right whip-pan that ends on the indicated frame. The faster the whip-pan, the greater the impact. It will take a few tries before your pan and the actor's motions sync up just right.

Bring these two shots into your editing software and cut them together. Play with the timings a bit and you'll quickly find a surprisingly convincing cut that makes it look very much like your friend has just assassinated his clone with a stir stick.

We know that your friend can't be in two places at once. We know that a stir stick cannot easily penetrate a human skull (yes, we do know that). And yet somehow this cut "works." In fact, the only reason it works is that you shot the stick going left-to-right in both shots, and you found a cutting point where the motion from the throwing shot carried through perfectly to the motion in the impact shot. To see how important this motion continuity is, use your editing software to "flop," or mirror the second shot, left to right. Play back this new sequence—it doesn't work at all, does it? The next time you see an action movie with a knife being thrown at someone (*The Matrix, Battle Royale, Scream 2, Big Trouble in Little China*, and many more), slow-mo through the shots. Even with all the modern technology available to filmmakers, the stir stick trick is still as popular as ever.

Motion continuity is to the action scene what the 180° rule is to conversations. In fact, they are the same rule. But whereas you obey the rule in conversation scenes to avoid confusing the viewer, you embrace the rule in action scenes because of all the dirty tricks it affords you! I mean, check it out—you just turned your friend into a Ninja assassin using only a stir stick and an understanding of lines of action.

Below is a three-shot sequence from *Skate Warrior*. The action consists of Steve being thrown out the back of the moving Jeep and landing on the hood of the car alongside it. Of these three shots, only one is really a stunt—the last one. For this shot Steve really jumped from the Jeep to the ugly green car. He did so not from the back seat, but from the outside edge of the Jeep. The cars weren't going very fast and the stunt, while dangerous, was not the stupidest thing we did with Steve and those two cars. We really maximized the impact of this unwise stunt by cutting to it from the previous shot, which has Steve airborne for a good long time and clearly shows him being propelled from the far side of the back seat.

For this middle shot, of course, the Jeep is not even moving. It's parked on the side of the road and being jiggled by off-screen hands as Steve jumps over the camera onto nice, soft grass. That streetlight blurring past in the background is CG, and probably not necessary for the shot to work.

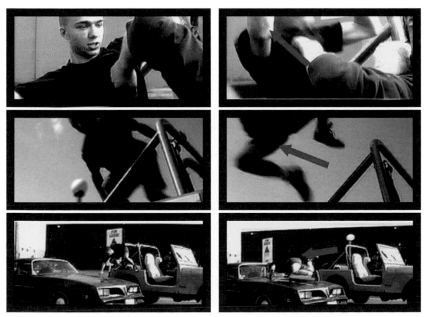

A three-shot sequence from *Skate Warrior* showing Steve being thrown out the back of a Jeep. The second shot was staged with a stationary Jeep.

By cutting from the shot of Alex's hand moving right-to-left, to Steve leaping convincingly right-to-left, to him landing on the hood and completing that right-to-left motion, we create one continuous action in the audience's mind. Had we broken screen direction for any of these shots, the illusion would not be so seamless.

To help plan out these little bits of motion trickery, I recommend bedecking your storyboards with Big Red Arrows. The primary motion of a shot should be clear at a glance, both to help you assess the continuity issues while creating your boards and to make sure that in the flurry of the shoot day you stay true to your plan and get a shot that will cut brilliantly with its neighbors.

Animatics

An animatic is simply a moving storyboard. I say "simply," and yet animatics can wind up being very elaborate. They can be as basic as a rough edit of scanned storyboard panels (this is often called a *story reel),* or as complex as an animated 3D film complete with lighting and effects.

While boards are a great tool to help plan your vision, animatics are more conducive to helping sell your vision to someone else. In other words, most directors don't feel that they require a fully realized animatic, edited, and set to temp music and sound effects, in order to plan a shoot. They tend to prepare such luxurious presentations more for the benefit of people who need to be sold on the effectiveness of the sequence— potential investors or studio execs, for example.

There are exceptions, of course. If you have a scene that has critical timing elements, such as the robbery set to music in *Hudson Hawke,* you may find that loading your storyboard panels into your NLE and roughing in some timings will help you proceed with confidence.

Creating an effective animatic does not have to involve hours of tedious labor. The animatic I made for the Cher video I directed in 2001 consisted of simple text cards in After Effects set to music. Rather than draw each frame, I simply typed little descriptions to help figure out the master timings of where Cher would be and when. For a commercial I directed for the funky San Francisco footrace called "Bay to Breakers," which featured costumed actors singing "I Left My Heart in San Francisco," I edited together still photos that were shot during our location scout into a solid 30-second plan that told me exactly how long I had for each line of the song.

These days I never scout a location without a point-and-shoot camera that has a video function. My favorite as I write this is the Panasonic LX1. This little monster features a 16:9 chip and a nice, wide Leica lens, and it shoots widescreen 30p movies. These movies can easily be cut together in an NLE to create a rough animatic.

If you decide to create an animatic for a key sequence, just remember that its only purpose is to aid in planning your shoot. You should resist the temptation to spend time finessing it, and remind yourself that on the shoot day you'll probably have a few new ideas that you'll want to try as well.

Being too locked in to an animatic or a storyboard can cause you to miss creative opportunities that arise during the shoot. My worst offense was during *Skate Warrior.* I storyboarded a scene in a skateboard shop that I'd secured as a location. My boards were careful not to cross the 180° line, with the shop owner on the left and the antagonist entering screen right. When I arrived at the location, I set up my shots this way, not even thinking about the fact that I was aiming my camera at a vast expanse of painted white brick, while behind me was an entire wall full of colorful skateboard decks hanging row after row. I'm still kicking myself about that one, and since then I've made a conscious effort to not let a plan keep me from seeing what's cinematic about a location or set.

The rule of thumb is that the animatic or board should be a good worst-case scenario. Say to yourself, "If this is all I shoot, I know I'll have the sequence covered." Then leave room in your day for the happy accidents and on-the-spot inspirations.

Turning a Storyboard into a Schedule

My opinion of scheduling is that it's the producer's job to schedule the shoot as a whole, but it's the director's job to schedule the individual shooting days.

On a "real" shoot, the first assistant director (First AD) usually plans out the shoot day based on the director's shotlist or boards. These mission-critical people are really good at what they do and are often given only the vaguest idea of what the director wants to accomplish that day. The result is usually that, despite the AD's best attempts, these directors don't get all the shots they'd like and have to make up the coverage elsewhere or lose shots.

I always give my AD the most detailed plan I can. Sometimes it's agonizingly detailed, and sometimes it's just a simple shotlist. Either way, I feel that only I can be held responsible for whether or not we get all the shots that I envisioned, so I work closely with the AD to make sure we're both comfortable with the plan.

The DV Rebel is usually her own producer (see below) and assistant director. This means you're on your own in creating a plan to shoot a day's worth of shots. If you make a smart plan, you'll get all your shots and feel great about the day's work. If you make a bad one, you'll lose shots, slip behind schedule, and, worst of all, lose the trust of the people donating their time to help you. Just wait until you tell your volunteer crew that you need them to drag that grand piano back into the ballroom for just one more shot—ten minutes after you proclaimed that the piano was "wrapped."

On one of my early guerrilla shoots I wrongly estimated that one night of shooting would be all we'd need to cover several scenes in one large (and ill-gotten) location. Instead what happened was that we spent the whole night shooting a short fistfight in a bathroom, using only two of the five actors who showed up that night. As the sun was coming up, the three guys who had been sitting around all night in costume were understandably upset with me. I vividly remember this as the moment I became tangibly aware of the importance of scheduling "the day."

Jargon Watch

The day is short for "the shoot day," and is often used in conversation to emphasize the special nature of that square on the calendar. "Who knows if the dog will actually remember his tricks on the day?" When we say we can figure something out "on the day" we're saying that it falls outside the scope of what can or should be planned in advance. The term has even been expanded to simply mean "when we actually shoot it," regardless of what the calendar says—in other words, you can say, "We'll rehearse at half-speed, but on the day we'll really go for it."

We wound up spending four full nights at that location getting all of our coverage. Aside from a more realistic appraisal of the time involved, there was another big difference in the first shoot and the subsequent three. After our dismal first night, I went home and carefully sorted through my storyboards for the rest of the scenes at that location. I used colored markers to code shots based on which actors were in the scene, what part of the building we were in, and what, if any, special equipment or props we needed. I then cut up my storyboards and resorted them based on the color coding.

I thought I was pretty clever, but little did I know I was doing something very common. I was taking my boards out of *sequence order* and putting them in *shooting order*. With these newly reordered boards I could easily see how many shots I had with which actors or special needs, and develop a much better plan for breaking down the shoots into bite-size chunks of long, lonely nights in a university building for which we had no shooting permit.

Another benefit of this process was that I could place similar shots one after the other and discover some efficiencies that would help me get through my shots faster. For example, I noticed that not only did I have several shots in a row looking down a long hallway, I actually had a couple that were the exact same angle. I scheduled the first to be the last shot we did with one actor. With the camera still set up, he then went home and the next actor arrived right on schedule. We already had the camera perfectly set up for his first shot.

When that actor showed up promptly at two in the morning and we were exactly on schedule and ready for him to work, I realized that while we may be rebellious about many things (we had, after all, broken into the building in which we were shooting a gunfight scene using realistic-looking plastic guns!), the schedule of the shoot day is not one of them. You owe your cast and crew the respect of their time, and you'll make a much better movie if you get all your shots in the can before then sun comes up.

Planning your shoot day is a bit like solving a puzzle, and it's a different puzzle every time, with many possible solutions. I can only hope to give you general advice about organizing your shoot days, and then, like me, you'll just have to learn from your mistakes.

Cut 'em and Code 'em

After you've completed your storyboards, photocopy them and cut them apart so that each shot is on a separate slice of paper (or do this same process virtually in Photoshop). Your task is now to plan the most logical and productive shooting sequence for these shots. The factors you weigh in doing this will be different every time, but here are some things to bear in mind:

YOUR LOCATIONS

Obviously this is a big one. If you're shooting in two locations on one day, it's easy enough to see that this is the first and simplest way to divide up your sliced-up boards.

THE TALENT

Your actors are your most vital resource, and you should give them first consideration when scheduling. Unless you can't. Actors do wait, which is why on "real" movies they get such nice trailers. Keeping them waiting is not a sin, but abusing their time is. Try to group together shots that use the same actors.

LIGHTING AND SETS

Setting up a new shot is always time consuming, but the worst kind of resetting is "reversing," or moving the camera to shoot in the opposite direction that you just shot in. You not only have to relight, you usually have to clean up all the crap that has a way of sprouting up behind the camera when you're not looking. What you desperately want to avoid is reversing more than you absolutely have to. For a conversation between two people, you should schedule your shots so you reverse only once. Re-reversing is a sure sign of a poorly planned shoot, and you'd be surprised how often it happens.

WIDE SHOTS FIRST, CLOSE-UPS LAST

Your director of photography (who may well be you) will want to shoot the master first to establish the lighting, and then move in to cover the close-ups. This also helps with the blocking of the scene.

CLOSE-UPS FIRST, WIDE SHOTS LAST

Some actors give their best performances on their earlier takes. Know this about them so that you don't waste all their best work on your wide master. You can also utilize this knowledge when deciding which half of a conversation to cover first. You may be lucky enough to have one actor who's best fresh and another who takes a while to warm up—the ideal shooting sequence will be obvious.

CAMERA RIGGING

If you're busting out some cool tricks like a jib arm, Steadicam-like device (see Chapter 3), or dolly, you may want to try to group shots that use these special mounts close together.

WHERE'S THE SUN?

Often when shooting outdoors, the position of the sun in the sky is a governing factor in planning a shoot. By shooting one side of a conversation before lunch and the other after, both of your actors will be nicely backlit by the sun, even though they're facing each other! See the section on lighting in Chapter 1 for some hints on how to plan for the most cost-effective of all light sources.

THE _____

Every shoot has something special around which everything else must revolve. When I needed both a bright yellow VW GTI and Land Rover

Defender 90 together in one shot for *The Last Birthday Card*, I dropped everything when the GTI showed up. We ran out and shot the establishing shot with the two cars, and sent my generous friend on his way in hopes that he might feel like loaning it to us again for another day's shoot. There's also one "magic hour" shot in *Birthday Card*—another occasion for dropping everything and grabbing a shot when the gettin' is good.

Jargon Watch

Magic hour is the time at either the very beginning or end of a day when the sun is low in the sky, casting a pleasing, warm light and creating long, dramatic shadows. You're lucky if it lasts a full hour, and you're risking a lot when you stage a scene during this enticing but fragile window of time.

These special-case scheduling anomalies will be easy to spot and worth the juggling they create. We DV Rebels often get our best bits of production value by being willing to jump on brief, juicy opportunities, and by meaning what we say when we only need the cops to turn on their flashers for "just one second."

OR JUST SHOOT IT IN SEQUENCE

All the above suggestions have you shooting potentially way out of sequence, which is standard enough and a part of the magic of moviemaking. But sometimes it makes the most sense to shoot in cutting sequence. You may be staging a fight scene in which the character's clothing, or the set, or the planet, is gradually being destroyed. Or you may have a scene in which complex plans are being drawn on a chalkboard. Or maybe your DV Rebel lighting is simple enough that reversing isn't such a hassle. You can save big continuity headaches by shooting in-sequence, even if it breaks some of the above rules.

Binder the Universe Together

Once I have my shots in shooting order, I either clip them into a binder or pin them up on a big board. I write detailed notes to myself alongside the boards, so that in the hectic atmosphere of the shoot I can actually remember what the hell the purpose of the shot is, and how it fits in the cut.

This can be more important than it sounds. It's surprising how easily a shot can lose its meaning when pulled out of its cutting sequence. You'll stand there, looking at your bad drawing, and think you've got the shot in the can when in fact you've shot the drawing but missed the point of the shot. Your notes are a glimpse back into the purity of spirit with which you crafted those original boards, back before the crew was shouting a hundred questions at you and the neighbors were threatening to call the cops. Keep the original, sequence-ordered boards around and consult them often. Remind yourself how each shot needs to fit into your master plan. Pull out a stopwatch and make sure your action is happening at the speed you liked in your animatic.

And then, when you've got at least one great take and one backup in the can, cross off that board with a big, red pen. There's no better feeling, and it feels better and better as the day goes on.

Jargon Watch

The last shot of the day is called the *Martini.* This is a great name for it because after you shoot it, you'll want one. Everyone on a shoot loves to hear "We're moving on to the Martini!"—it's a great way to get everyone's energy up at the end of a long day. The shot just before the Martini has a name too—it's called the *Abby,* after a First AD named Abby Singer who habitually announced the Martini one shot too early.

Putting the "Guer" in Guerrilla

All the planning in the world won't change one simple fact: You're a DV Rebel, also known as a guerrilla filmmaker. You shoot first and ask permission later.

Or do you? The truth is, there are numerous pros and cons to "going legit" and asking permission, but you may wind up doing it more often than you expect.

On Asking Permission

The romantic view of DV Rebel filmmaking is that it's a "grab your camera and go" affair. *The Green Project,* the sample film in Chapter 6, was done this way, and it can be fun. But I find that as soon as I start including more than just my friends, spouse, and dog in my plan, I get more and more nervous about staging a shoot in a location for which I have not secured permission.

It's a classic case of weighing the pros and cons. On one hand, if you ask permission to use a location, you could be surprised and get the green light. Or you could be told no, in which case you're really playing with fire if you attempt to shoot there. If you show up to an unsecured location with you and your camera and one actor, it's not a big deal if you get escorted off the scene by a security guard. But if ten friends converge on that one day to do you the ultimate favor of crewing on or appearing in your movie, then you'll really regret being forced to leave. And if your scene involves props or activities that might arouse the interest of local law enforcement, the cons can be quite serious indeed—but so can the exhilaration of successfully pulling off a "stolen" shot.

Let's consider the concept of "stealing" a shot. Like stealing second base, stealing a shot is harmless activity, yet one to which you will encounter many obstacles. However, you will be in good company! Big Hollywood movies steal shots all the time. Listen to the commentary track on the DVD of *The Bourne Identity* to hear director Doug Liman talk about trying to steal shots of Matt Damon in a European train station. His biggest obstacles were concealing his 35mm camera under his coat and cracking off a useable shot before the crowd recognized his megastar. These are two problems for which the DV Rebel has excellent solutions.

There's some great supplemental material on the DVD of *Lost in Translation* where the feat of stealing a shot of the famously busy Shibuya Crossing in Tokyo is discussed. Similarly, the commentary track of *Zero Effect* features director Jake Kasdan confessing to almost spitefully stealing a shot of the one building in Portland the film commission won't allow to be filmed. A few scenes later he relates the struggle he experienced with an uncooperative shop owner on a street location for which he did have a permit.

Stealing shots is a part of filmmaking at any scale. The big guys do it, the indies do it, and DV Rebels do it better than any of them. Our cameras are smaller, our stars aren't famous, and if push comes to shove we can pull our shorts up over our belly buttons and pose as camcorder-toting tourists while our actors stroll across the Golden Gate bridge wearing rented wireless lavaliere mics.

The Pickup Truck Loophole

I'm not a lawyer, and I don't play one on TV, but I do remember one bit of legal advice that I've put to use a few times. Most cities, including Los Angeles, have a definition of what kind of shooting requires a permit. If you want to shoot on public streets or sidewalks, you will need a permit if you "put down sticks," which is to say, set up a tripod. As soon as you plop a piece of gear on city property, they want you to go legit with the paperwork.

One popular workaround for this is to eschew the sticks and shoot handheld. Reasonable, but not always conducive to the production value we're trying to exude. A much cooler solution is to set up your tripod in the back of a pickup truck. This is an amazing trick because it gives you both a tripod and a dolly. You can actually drive down the street and get a real classy tracking shot following your talent, all without asking permission.

Be a Rebel, Not a Jerk

Like I said in the introduction, I'm not seeking to offer you legal advice. The DV Rebel style is definitely built on creative and opportunistic use of locations. But also remember that when you're shooting in public, you're an ambassador for the DV Rebel nation. I look at it this way: On the way in to work this morning you might have broken the speed limit. But you're a good person, and you didn't drive so fast that you were endangering anyone, and you didn't cut anyone off. Like most drivers, you believe that breaking the law just a little is OK, and maybe inconveniencing other drivers is OK, but never both at the same time. That's the way I feel about making movies. If you're going to be impacting people's lives by blocking traffic or lighting assorted things on fire, get permission. But if you aren't hurting anyone, then make your movie by any means necessary.

Movies Referenced in This Chapter

Battle Royale

Big Trouble in Little China

The Bourne Identity

A Clockwork Orange

Collateral

Die Hard

El Mariachi

Face/Off

Heat

Hudson Hawke

Indiana Jones and the
Temple of Doom

The Lord of the Rings:
The Return of the King

Lost in Translation

The Matrix

Midnight Run

Oldboy

Point Break

Predator

Primer

Raiders of the Lost Ark

Reservoir Dogs

Scream 2

Star Wars

You've Got Mail

Zero Effect

CHAPTER 3
Shooting

Wait! Don't start reading this chapter until you've read "The Camera," a supplemental chapter on the DVD. As one lazy filmmaker to another, trust me, it's worth it. In that chapter you learn the *how* of camera work, and in this chapter you'll learn the what. I describe some techniques for getting great shots that tell your story and boost your production value, and then offer some tools and techniques for moving the camera smoothly, achieving motion effects such as the all-important slo-mo, and lighting your movie on a budget. You'll find several After Effects tutorials as well as some DIY camera mount projects, so get your mouse in one hand and your Makita in the other!

Making Memorable Shots

When I discussed production value in Chapter 1, I mentioned that the simple choice of where to place the camera can greatly influence the apparent budget of your film. The truth is, many low-budget shot-on-video efforts betray their modest means by their boring, badly framed shots. Heck, most B movies shot on 35mm suffer the same problem. We DV Rebels get so obsessed with mimicking all the technical aspects of film—24p, widescreen, a plug-in that reproduces this or that film stock—but the truth is, what makes a movie a *movie* is much more style than substance. *Blade Runner* is *Blade Runner* not because it was shot on film or because it was expensive, but because Ridley Scott's directing is so damn stylish. That film is science fiction even when there's nothing fanciful on the screen at all.

The Usual Suspects, Reservoir Dogs, Primer, and El Mariachi all teach us that bold, cinematic camera work can elevate the production value of a low-budget endeavor. As director Shane Carruth says on the cast and crew commentary on the *Primer* DVD, "Composition is real cheap." So how do you go from being a person with a camera to a master of cinematic art? Obviously no book can close that gap for you.

But this one will try. If you think you can use some improvement in this area, here's a checklist that you can follow every time you set up a new shot. Even if you're perfectly happy with your cinematic sensibility, running through this list in your head as you set up a shot is a great exercise for stimulating creativity.

Slow Down

This may sound obvious, but in the hectic environment of a shoot we could all use a little reminder to slow down and think about the shot. What part of the story is it telling? What shots might it cut with? Are your lines of action correct? Are you crossing the 180-degree line? Are you intercutting this with a shot that's too similar? Too different? Are you cross-dissolving to or from another shot, one that you could match somehow? Is this the first shot in a scene? Or the last? Is there some cool transition you could do?

Take a moment to try viewing the shot as if you're seeing it in dailies, or cut into the final film. This is where having a separate monitor is handy—just viewing your shot somewhere other than through the viewfinder can provide that much-needed bit of objectivity. Make a conscious effort to cut through the din of the shoot and really *see* your shot.

Think in Thirds

The rule of thirds is a handy guide for framing a shot. It's as simple as drawing a perfect tic-tac-toe board on top of your image:

The rule of thirds framing guide is a tic-tac-toe grid overlaying your image.

Generally speaking, pleasing compositions tend to place one or more key elements on the intersections of these lines. Another way of looking at this is, if you want to draw attention to something, place it on one of those four corners, which I call "sweet spots." Even compositions that don't target the sweet spots reference them indirectly, just as they do the edges of frame. The rule of thirds is always alive in your shot whether you know it or not—so know it!

Some still cameras, including my Panasonic point-and-shoot, offer an option to superimpose this framing guide in your viewfinder to aid in composition. Even without this feature, you can easily eyeball your way to success with the rule of thirds. Getting close to those sweet spots is usually just as good as nailing them precisely, and of course it's always most important that your shot *feels* right.

The rule of thirds scales to match the aspect ratio of your final film, so if you're shooting Standard Def and letterboxing later, make sure to bear that in mind as you compose your shot:

This image looks unbalanced at 4:3...

...but a rule-of-thirds overlay hints that we may have a nice frame at 1:2.40.

Sure enough, not a bad shot at its final aspect ratio.

Like all rules, the rule of thirds was made to be broken—but knowingly. Sometimes you can transmit important information to the audience by not following this framing guide. More on that in bit.

Make Triangles

Another purely aesthetic consideration when framing a shot is something you learn in a basic art class: the power of triangles. There's a reason those big tombs in Egypt aren't square: Triangles are powerful. When elements in your shot create triangles in the frame, you are communicating something to your audience. Once again, since they more than make up for their lack of brilliance with their availability, I'll use some shots from *The Last Birthday Card* as examples.

The triangle that Scott creates is solid, balanced, and nearly lines up with the bottom corners of the frame. This type of triangle tells the audience that Scott is in control and a force to be respected.

An off-balance triangle, one that does not use the bottom edge of the frame as its base, creates a dynamic or active impression. The helicopter lines up with the buildings to create a massive, heavy triangle that focuses on Scott's window. Compositionally, this triangle backs up the idea that mighty force is being directed at a puny target.

Triangles can also help provide visual clarity in a busy shot. There's a lot to look at in this frame, but wherever your eye wanders, lines always lead you back to Baxter's (Billy Brooks) face.

Triangles help associate elements in an image. In the shots that are intercut with Baxter's above, Scott is framed alongside his bucket of paintbrushes.

Moments later, Scott resigns himself to going forward with his next contract killing, and we have another shot that combines both static and dynamic triangles. While Scott creates an imposing, static triangle, the lines of the room create an unsteady tipping point right at its base. Scott may be a powerful hit man, but he's in an unstable place in his career, and things are about to change for him in a big way.

Free Your Mind and Your Camera Will Follow

Your tripod allows your camera to be anywhere between two and six feet off the ground. When you handhold the camera, it's at about your shoulder height. These are the most convenient locations for the camera, so do yourself a favor and assume that they are most likely wrong for your shot.

All new parents with digital cameras are barraged with the same advice for shooting their kid's birthday parties: Get down to their level. In other words, if you're telling a story about three-foot-tall dudes, don't shoot it from six feet in the air. Unless, of course, you're trying to emphasize the fact that they're small. In other words, there'd better be a reason that your camera is at the height it is, a storytelling-driven reason.

Stand on a chair and look at your scene. Is this a better angle? Lie on the floor and see if maybe a worm's-eye view isn't what this scene is asking for.

Don't use these funky angles "just because." Use them for a reason. That low angle will make your SWAT team bursting through the door seem imposing and powerful. The angle from up on the chair will instantly make the audience suspect that someone has a surprise in store for those SWAT guys.

The importance of driving every camera choice off the story also holds true for lenses. The same medium shot will look completely different if you use the wide end of your zoom from a near perspective versus the telephoto end from far away. Do you want to feel distanced from your characters and lend them an isolated, portrait-like prominence? Or do you want to feel in-the-mix with them, and lend them a vibrant immediacy? A long lens will provide the former, a wide lens the latter.

The rule of thirds helps you create nice-looking framings, but nice-looking is vastly less important than storytelling. Towards the end of *The Birds (The Birds* DVD Chapter 17), there's an amazing shot of Tippi Hedren on the sofa, recoiling in terror as the birds attack the exterior of the house. As she pushes herself deeper and deeper into the corner of the couch, she also pushes herself into the corner of the static frame. The vast, empty left side of frame overwhelms the viewer with the haunting notion that she's cowering from nothing—from an empty room. In *Heat,* after Waingro (Kevin Gage) loses his cool during a holdup and implicates the rest of the team in a homicide, his ostracism from the group is demonstrated by framings that pin his face uncomfortably against the edge of the screen (Chapter 7 on the *Heat* DVD).

Tell the Story

This may sound obvious, but aim the camera at the things that are helping to tell your story. I've seen many student films where two people talk on a couch in front of a white wall. Since it's a "two shot," a shot with two characters in it, and the aspect ratio is 4:3, there's a ton of unused space at the top of the frame. Usually there's some horrible artwork or cuckoo clock hanging there, and I wind up staring blankly at it, distracted, confused, and hoping the scene, if not the film, will soon end.

Contrast this with a shot in *The Shining* of Dick Hallorann (Scatman Crothers) answering his phone. *The Shining* is shot in a 4:3 aspect ratio, and Kubrick uses that tall frame to include some outstanding wall art in the frame with Dick. Far from extraneous, this inclusion provides an instant summary of the chef's personality.

Tim Burton acknowledges that the training he received in hand-drawn animation has contributed to his signature visual style. When you have to hand-draw every single thing that appears in your film, you quickly learn not to bother unless that thing is helping you tell your story. But in live action that is a subtractive, not an additive, process.

In other words:

SHOW LESS

Once you've got the things that tell your story framed in a pleasing and appropriate manner, look at the image again and notice all the things in your shot that have nothing to do with your story. Is there a busy freeway in the background that's distracting from the foreground action? Is there a potted plant that, upon close inspection, appears to be sprouting out of your lead actor's head?

Reduce your depth of field, change your framing, turn off some lights, or insert a foreground element into your shot—do whatever it takes to make sure your storytelling elements don't get upstaged.

BE EFFICIENT

The script calls for a young man to enter a hotel room, where he discovers an older woman awaiting him in a seductive pose. One way to cover this action would be to start the shot on the door, allow the man to enter, and then pan over to the woman. But we know that's boring, so maybe we'd try something more clever—like open on the door, and then dolly straight back, revealing the woman as she enters the frame from the side.

But if you took a moment to think about how to capture this shot with the least amount of camera movement, if you asked your actors to hold their position as you walked around the room with your camera looking for the shot that told the story as cleanly and efficiently as possible, then maybe you'd stumble upon an angle on the young man through the triangle formed by the woman's seductively bent leg. No camera movement, no complex setup time, and boom: instant, powerful conveyance of the story. Even though your audience is all the way across the room from him, they'll instantly know how much trouble Benjamin Braddock (Dustin Hoffman) is in (Chapter 6 on *The Graduate* DVD).

How you cover a scene is one way you build trust with your audience, the trust that allows them to lower their defenses and suspend their disbelief. One sure way to lose their trust is to be inarticulate with the camera. In the same way that grammarians advise us to take a sentence like:

"I feel that I'm finally ready to engage in the process of realizing my plans for my future as a filmmaker."

...and turn it into:

"I'm ready to make my film."

...we owe our audiences conciseness in our coverage of a scene. When you find the shot that tells the story with as little effort as possible, you will have found an elegant and seamless presentation of the storytelling beat of the shot, and your audience will be swept up in the story without even thinking about your camerawork.

Study Simplicity

Some examples of simple, elegant shots that told their part of the story effortlessly:

Close Encounters of the Third Kind, DVD Chapter 2. A minute or so into the Sonora Desert scene, Spielberg masterfully reveals the WWII fighter planes one by one in a simple pan that follows the investigative team. Then François Truffaut and Bob Balaban enter from the left and the shot becomes a medium on Balaban, framed beautifully by one of the aircraft, as he calls out Lacombe's instructions to the team. Watch carefully how the camera both dollies and pans left, then tracks back along its path to the right as the shot ends. Spielberg takes a simple dolly move and makes it sing, and he achieves both a wide master and a medium shot in one setup by simply having his actor walk towards the camera.

The Professional, DVD Chapter 5. The very first shot in this chapter is the reveal of Gary Oldman's character. It's a slow dolly in as his henchmen scope out the empty hallway and take their positions. As each tough guy enters, pulls his gun, and looks around, the sense of dread and impending violence builds and builds until Oldman finally fills the center of frame that's been carefully left empty for him the entire time. You know the shot is building towards something, and when that something turns out to be a psychotically calm, drug-addicted cop, the danger for Natalie Portman's character is ratcheted up several notches.

Se7en, DVD Chapter 29. Director David Fincher is a master of understated simplicity of coverage. Here a left-to-right dolly follows Morgan Freeman and Brad Pitt as they approach the 14th Precinct building. The camera comes to a stop, a taxi enters the frame, and an unassuming man gets out and follows them in. As with the example from *The Professional,* the shot builds anticipation and then pays it off, all without breaking a sweat.

Designing efficient shots is not just good filmmaking, it's also inexpensive filmmaking. Each of the examples on the previous page could have easily been two or more setups if the filmmakers hadn't been committed to finding an elegant solution. The *Close Encounters* and *Se7en* examples are shots for which one might think a large crane would be the tool of choice, but the filmmakers chose a simple dolly instead. Can't even swing a dolly, but want a dramatic push-in? Steal Spielberg's trick and give your actor some motivation to walk up into the frame, creating her own close-up in the process.

Moving the Camera

After buying fancy cameras and microphones, it gets a little daunting to start shopping for camera stabilizers and mini-cranes, and yet those are the tools to help you move your camera in cinematic ways. Even if you can easily afford all these toys, they could become yet further encumbrances to your DV Rebel agility. And if you're like me, your rebellious spirit is repulsed by the "click to buy" button on the Hot New Camera Toy Web site.

I am mildly obsessed with small, lightweight, and, above all, inexpensive ways to move my DV camera smoothly and cinematically. Even as I sit in my director's chair on a big commercial, designing a shot with a 30-foot techno crane, I can't help but ponder how one might build such a thing out of PVC pipe and zip ties.

Sticks

By far the most important piece of camera support equipment is the simple tripod. Some of our DV brethren seem to feel that a tripod is an obsolete holdover from the days when cameras were too heavy to lift. No. Using a tripod is to filmmaking what wearing pants is to walking around in public—it's something you do because you have at least a tiny shred of respect for yourself.

The tripod, or *sticks,* is your default camera mount. When in doubt, use sticks. Even when not in doubt, use sticks. As long as a stiff breeze isn't blowing, the audience won't be able to tell the difference between a static shot made from a $30 tripod and one made from a professional film rig costing ten times as much. Put simply, a tripod is the cheapest and easiest boost to production value you can find.

Dollies

Dollies rule. They just do. You can shoot a whole movie from a dolly. They're everything that's good about a tripod, plus they have wheels.

The really good ones have wheels for days. They can go forward and backward, they can "crab" sideways, and they can go in a circle. Plus many dollies have some kind of boom arm for smooth vertical travel.

Yeah. Anyway, you probably don't have one of those dollies. The light est one JL Fisher makes is 300 pounds, and I can't even tell you what they cost, because you can't buy them—they are rental items only.

I knew I wanted several dolly shots in *The Last Birthday Card,* in several of my locations. One solution I came up with was a *wheeled spreader.* A "spreader" is a tool for receiving and stabilizing the legs of a tripod. Older, film-style tripods rely on the spreader entirely to prevent the tripod legs from splaying in all directions. Most video tripods have their own built-in spreaders, so few DV shooters would ever consider buying a separate one. But Bogen makes a nifty one that has a caster wheel on each of its three legs. This, I thought, could be my ultimate portable dolly. It packs up small and can be operated by one person.

The downside is that it must be operated by one person. It's quite dif-ficult to drive both the wheels and the pan/tilt head, and every time I tried to do a complex move with this rig I wound up doing several takes just to get the move right. There's a decided advantage to the camera operator riding along on the dolly, concentrating only on framing and focusing.

And so we come to another DV Rebel Axiom: If you can ride it, it's a dolly!

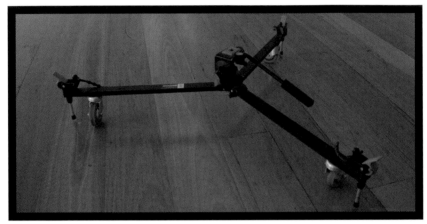

A wheeled spreader is a decent low-cost alternative to a dolly.

Grip Alfred Wentzel pushes camera operator Sunel Haasbroek, wielding a Silicon Imaging camera, for the film *Spoon*. Photo provided by the film's directors, Sharlto Copley and Simon Hansen.

THE $60 DOLLY

With that in mind, I made a trip to my local home improvement store and came home with a cool little collapsible cart from Rubbermaid that looked like a perfect ultra-portable DV Rebel dolly. While I was tempted by some of the larger garden wagons with flat decks and pneumatic tires, I decided that compactness was more important to me this time. Those wagons do make excellent dollies, though, and you can buy them from Amazon for between $100 and $200. My Rubbermaid cart was on sale for about $60.

This little cart was just a bit too small to hold me and my compact tripod, so my brother Eric came to my rescue with a lightning-fast DIY project. He crafted some plywood outriggers that unfold to give the tripod a wider base. When folded in, these "wings" allow the handle to fold flat as designed.

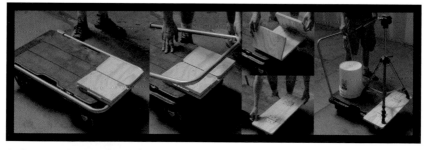

An inexpensive cart from a home improvement store can become a dolly with the addition of a little extra surface area.

Riding the Rubbermaid dolly feels a little silly if you're over six feet tall, but on a smooth surface this inexpensive tool can make some nice moves, and it can also help you load and unload gear from a location!

Jargon Watch

There are specific terms for the many ways that you can move a camera, and they are often misused.

Pan means rotating the camera head side-to-side. You pan left, but you *tilt* up. You never pan up.

When you *boom* up that means you travel straight up, or as straight as the mechanics of your camera support will allow. Boom up and down. Sometimes on a crane or jib you can say "boom left," so as to distinguish between dollying left (which would mean moving the base of the crane).

When you dolly in towards your scene that's a *push*, a *truck*, or a *dolly in*. You can pull out, or truck out, or dolly out as well.

When you dolly to the side that's a *dolly*, a *track*, or sometimes a *crab*, as in "push in and then crab left," "truck out and then dolly right," or "track with them as they walk along the beach."

When you dolly one way and pan the other to keep someone in frame, that's called *back panning*.

Any dolly-like move that is slow and subtle can be called a *drift*. Any slower and it becomes a *creep*.

Dutching is when you roll the camera so that the image appears to spin. This requires a Dutch head, or just your hands. When you Dutch your camera you create a *Dutch angle*. I guess Holland has lots of hills.

On a crane that has a linear extension, like a Techno Crane, there are many colorful terms for the practice of lengthening and shortening the arm, but the closest I've heard to a standard is *telescope in* and *out,* often shortened to *'scope in* or *'scope out.*

Regardless of which hardware-store dolly you decide to hack for your DV Rebel needs, here are some tips for getting the best moves:

- Tape off your desired path on the floor so your *dolly grip* can match the same motion on each take.

- If you pick a cart with casters (like mine), get one with swiveling casters at only one end. This will help you execute curving moves in a repeatable fashion, as the casters will steer the cart like a car rather than crab off your taped path.

- If you choose a wagon or cart with pneumatic tires, deflate them slightly for a smoother ride.

- If your location features rough terrain, bring along sheets of plywood for a smooth dolly surface.

Slider

The only thing cooler than a dolly is a "slider." No, not a tiny hamburger that comes in a six-pack, a slider is a short set of rails that mounts on a standard "plate" instead of a pan/tilt head. You then mount the head to the plate on the rails. Now your camera can slide a few feet back and forth along whatever axis you like, and that axis can be tweaked without moving the dolly you've mounted this whole mess on.

What the slider acknowledges is that many dolly moves are short and sweet. *The creep* is a perfect example of this—it often involves traveling only a few inches. Using a slider, a creep, or a *drift* is always right at your fingertips.

Mounted on a dolly or on its own, the *slider* is a super-cool device to enable a short dolly to move in those hard-to-reach places.

THE $30 SLIDER

Since the slider is such an agility-enhancing tool, I wanted to create the DV Rebel version of it. Linear bearings and stainless steel tubes are expensive, though, so I began to despair a bit. Then I realized that I already owned the ultimate DV Rebel slider, and it was propped up right next to my front door.

The DV Rebel slider is also handy for quick runs to the corner store for more corn syrup and red food coloring.

That's right, the perfect slider for the DV Rebel is a skateboard, and while the one pictured here is a deluxe custom-made model (about $150), an entirely suitable version can be found at a local toy store for about $30.

The key to the effective *skateboard cam* is to weigh down the skateboard substantially, so that its hard little wheels can roll smoothly across smooth surfaces. Your camera isn't heavy enough on its own to keep your image from rattling all around, even if you do like I did and build a board with larger, softer wheels than are commonly used. Toss a sandbag onto the deck and use it as a bed to nestle the camera into the desired orientation. Now your little slider should be able to execute creeps and drifts all day long, as long as the terrain beneath is cooperative.

If it's not, you can take this operation to the next level by bringing along a makeshift track for your slider, one that can even be elevated between two supports such as sawhorses or tripods. A simple 1 by 8 from your local lumber store should do it.

Wheelchairs

Using a wheelchair as a budget dolly is a perennial student film technique, and one that has always perplexed me. I always wondered what world these filmmakers lived in that a wheelchair was conveniently accessible at all times. But more importantly, while a wheelchair may well move smoothly along the ground, it lacks a camera mount, meaning the pan/tilt end of the operation, as well as the burden of steadiness in general rests on the operator, who will be handholding the camera while being pushed around.

No one would mistake the results for a professional dolly move, for the reason that the wheelchair dolly breaks the fundamental rule of camera steadying technology. This rule is simply that perceived unsteadiness in a moving image is caused by camera rotation much more than camera translation. When you handhold a lightweight camera, you may well be able to brace its position in space with your elbows, etc., but the smallest twitch of your wrist will translate directly to panning motion in the camera.

Translation Good, Rotation Bad

This diagram shows a normal lens aimed at a subject ten feet away. The double image shows the result of physically moving the camera, or *translating* it, six inches up and down.

This image shows that almost the same on-screen results can be created by only *two degrees* of rotation. Even if you wanted to shake your camera up and down six inches, you could never do so as rapidly as you could rotate it by two degrees, meaning that it's much easier to get rapid and significant motion via rotation than by actually moving the camera. In other words, camera unsteadiness is all about unwanted camera rotation.

And so a sad but important rule emerges for the DV Rebel: Never handhold your camera. The reason is simple: Physics. Have you ever noticed that when a stoplight turns green, a bicycle will beat a Ferrari through an intersection? Lighter objects can accelerate more quickly than heavier ones, and our camera weighs a fraction of a fully loaded Panavision rig's heft. This means your little camera can move in ways that a "real" movie camera just can't. Never is this truer than when a small camera is handheld.

Camera motion telegraphs a great deal to the viewer. The camera is the vessel by which viewers are transported to your cinematic world, and they can tell if they're riding in a Cadillac or a Geo Metro. Big, heavy things feel expensive, and big cameras move in a way that feels expensive, whereas the lighter-than-air motions of your camera remind your audience of their own flimsy camcorder footage. You may be shooting your film with the same camera that one might use to commemorate baby's first steps, but you can't let your audience know that.

Steady That Cam

Garrett Brown understood the translation vs. rotation rule when he invented the device that, more than any other camera support system, changed the look of cinema. Of course I'm talking about the Steadicam, the ultimate camera platform for both freedom and fluidity. The Steadicam works using a clever sprung-arm system attached to a vest to literally float a camera on a shock-absorbing cushion that the operator can guide with one hand.

While the sprung arm absorbs and cancels out translation, the most significant steadying of the image comes from a counterweight that helps eliminate unwanted rotations. It does this by being carefully balanced so there is equal weight above and below the pivot point.

The original Steadicam is still the sexiest camera toy around. Fortunately for us, inexpensive approximations of it abound.

So sure was Brown that this counterweighted pivot system was the key to his invention's success that he developed a lightweight counterpart to the Steadicam for us DV folks, one that lacked any mechanical suspension but featured a gimbaled pivot and a counterweight. The Steadicam JR, which debuted back in the days of Hi8, has since been replaced by the sleeker Steadicam Merlin. These devices rely on your arm to be the shock absorber and focus purely on isolating the camera's rotations from outside forces.

I used a JR on *Birthday Card,* and whole-heartedly recommend Brown's DV offerings. But they are expensive, and several other entrepreneurs have entered this space, further simplifying (and reducing the cost of) Brown's original principles.

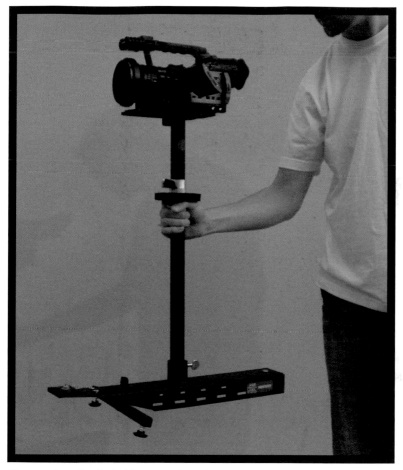

The SteadyTracker looks like a simple stick with a counterweight, but its balancing mechanisms set it apart from cheaper rigs.

Here's my DVX100a riding on the SteadyTracker Xtreme (www. steadytracker.com). The SteadyTracker represents the ultimate distillation of camera stabilizing technology—it works almost entirely by simply making your DV camera heavier (director and Orphanage colorist Aaron Rhodes refers to it as the "Heavicam"), and giving you a place to hold onto right at its center of combined mass. Making it heavier makes it feel more like a bigger camera, because effectively it is. And placing the operator's hand at the center of mass means that even abrupt motions won't result in unwanted sway.

The SteadyTracker Xtreme is less than half the price of the Steadicam Merlin, but it's still a chunk of change for a device with which you should be exercising restraint.

THE $14 STEADICAM

Enter Johnny Chung Lee. Noting that the SteadyTracker and its ilk are basically a pipe with a camera mount at the top and a weight at the bottom, Johnny built his own "steadycam" device using about $14 in parts from the local home improvement store. A list of all of the parts you'll need, along with step-by-step instructions, can be found on Johnny's Web site: www.steadycam.org.

I love the spirit of Johnny's site. Fun, genuinely informative, and DV Rebeliscious. He not only shows you how to build your own device, he also offers kits for the faint-of-tools. However, before you come to the conclusion that spending any more than $14 on a steadying device is a waste of money, look very closely at the differences between the home-brew version and the more expensive systems. The $14 Steadicam doesn't offer much control over balancing your camera on the mount, and proper balancing is the key to effective steady(fill in the blank)ing.

So it boils back down to the old equation of time and money, handiness and hurriedness. Personally, I like the SteadyTracker. It's junky enough that I can throw it in the back of my truck without thinking twice and smooth enough that I'd actually use it in a film. But every once in a while I miss the silky smooth (and difficult to achieve) moves I got from my old Steadicam JR.

THE GHETTOCAM

Garrett Brown simplified the Steadicam into the JR. SteadyTracker simplified that, and Johnny Chung Lee simplified the SteadyTracker. Is there a stopping point?

As you're probably sick of hearing, the common element among all the successful DV camera stabilizing rigs is that they make the camera feel heavier. So if you're stuck in a tight spot without your tripod or Steadicam or SuperTechno Crane, just make your camera heavier any way you can. Like, bolt a 2 by 4 to it.

Eric Maschwitz, brother of the author and Michelangelo with a Makita, demonstrates the 2 by 4 rig that he built in about half an hour with a few dollars' worth of parts.

There are some fancy-pants camera rigs for sale out there that amount to little more than this ultra-cheap contraption. Here are the plans for the DV Rebel GhettoCam, designed by me and built by my brother Eric, who scored all the woodworking genes in the family.

What you'll need:

- A 2 by 4 at least 21 inches long

- At least 17 inches of 1-inch dowel

- Wood glue

- Two 2-inch wood screws

- A ¼-20 thumbscrew

- A ¼-inch washer

- Some adhesive felt, or a small piece of thin rubber (like the things you buy at the grocery store that help you open stubborn jars)

- A drill with ¼-inch and ⅛-inch bits, along with a 1-inch paddle bit

- A saw

- For extra credit, some black spray paint

What to do:

1. Cut the 2 by 4 to a length of 21 inches.

2. At each end, drill a 1-inch hole centered 1½ inches from the end.

3. In the center, drill a 1-inch hole a little more than halfway through the 2 by 4. This is called a counterbore. Drill the rest of the way through the wood with the ¼-inch bit, creating an arrangement like you see in the plan.

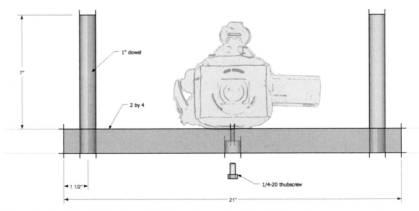

The plan for the GhettoCam. Feel free to modify it to better suit your camera's dimensions.

4. You know you have the right depth of counterbore when your thumbscrew, inserted from the bottom, protrudes about $3/8$ inch out the top.

   Since that thumbscrew is going to get a lot of use, Eric, always the consummate craftsman, recommends rounding the edges of the counterbore with a sharp blade or coarse sandpaper.

5. Cut two $8^{1}/_{2}$-inch lengths of dowel.

6. Slather $1^{1}/_{2}$ inches of one end of one dowel with wood glue and insert it into one of the end holes from the side opposite the counterbore.

7. Drive one of the 2-inch wood screws through the 2 by 4 and the dowel as shown in the photo.

8. Repeat for the other dowel. Note that for the best results, you can pre-bore this screw with your $1/8$-inch bit. Do that before the glue gets involved.

9. You're basically done! Allow the glue to dry and, if you are of the opinion that camera equipment should be black, spray paint your rig.

10. When the paint is dry, adhere your felt or rubber to the top of the plank. Eric also stuck some of the leftover felt to the bottom so my wife would let us set the thing down on the coffee table.

11. Fit the washer over the thumbscrew and feed the thumbscrew into the bottom of the counterbored center hole. This is how you'll mount the camera to the rig.

These photos show that it's possible to make the process of bolting your camera to a plank of wood look much fancier than it actually is.

Think of the GhettoCam as a license to shoot handheld. It's not going to fool anyone into thinking that you've shot with a Steadicam, but I think you will be pleasantly amazed at how much more solid your handheld work will be with this rig. You have to try it to appreciate the difference it makes.

THE AFTER-THE-FACT STEADICAM

The shot that opens Chapter 7 of *The Last Birthday Card* is a slow boom up on Scott's open window. In direct violation of the last few pages (I hadn't read this book yet), I shot it handheld. I stood below the apartment and, as smoothly as I could, lifted the camera straight up towards the window.

This establishing shot from *The Last Birthday Card* required stabilizing in After Effects.

My motion was fairly smooth (I call this kind of thing "Camera Tai Chi," and I've been practicing for years), but of course I wound up with some little rotational bobbles that were revealing my cheapo move for what it was.

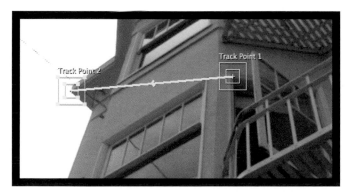

These are the tracking points I used to stabilize the shot.

So I stabilized the shot in After Effects! I tracked two points on the window and stabilized position and rotation. This made the shot a bit too perfect, and started to reveal the edge of the image.

Stabilizing a shot will usually cause it to drift out of your frame, revealing the edge of the layer.

I reintroduced the essence of the old motion with two simple position keyframes, effectively replacing the unsteady pan/tilt motions with perfectly smooth ones. This conveniently works all in one layer, because when you stabilize a layer you place the tracking keyframes in the Anchor Point stream, leaving the position stream free for animation.

If you want to try it yourself, here's the recipe for post-stabilizing of a shot in After Effects:

1. Make sure you're at full resolution and that your layer is at best quality (not draft). Place the current time indicator (CTI) at the first frame of the shot.

2. Select the layer and then choose Animation > Stabilize Motion.

3. The Tracker Controls panel should appear. If your shot has some rolling, i.e., unwanted rotation in Z, check the Rotation check box. Otherwise leave it unchecked.

4. Select good tracking points (see Chapter 8 of Mark Christiansen's book, *Adobe After Effects 7.0 Studio Techniques* for guidance on this) and hit Analyze Forward (the forward arrow).

5. When your track is done to your satisfaction, click Apply.

6. Back in the Comp view, RAM Preview to check your track. If it looks smooth, then watch the shot again to see if the edges of your layer are sneaking into the frame. Chances are they will be.

7. Using as few keyframes as possible, animate the position of your layer to keep the borders of the frame from becoming visible. Don't worry about a little bit of an edge creeping in here and there—if you correct for every little bobble you'll just be back where you started, with a shaky camera move. Try to create a smooth, decisive move that matches the intent of your shaky shot.

   You may find it helpful to select your new position keyframes and press F9 to smooth their interpolations.

8. Or, if you'd like to automate Step 7, skip the position keyframing and simply type this expression for Position:

   anchorPoint.smooth(width = 2, samples = 9)

   This will take out all the high-frequency motion from your move, and will replace it automatically with a smoothed-out version. Just how smooth is determined by the width value (it's actually the width in time of the smoothing operation, expressed in seconds). Larger numbers mean smoother results, at the expense of losing some of your move's original decisiveness. Smaller values retain detail in the move, but some shake as well.

   The second value controls how many steps are used in calculating the smoothing effect. Larger numbers mean smoother, more accurate results, at the expense of a little more computation time. If you increase width, you'll usually want to increase samples as well.

You can usually skip this smoothing altogether for rotation, and just let it remain completely stabilized. But if your shot feels like it's slowly tipping over, then you can reintroduce smoothed roll motion with this expression for Rotation:

rotation - rotation.smooth(width = 2, samples = 9)

Regardless of whether you use keyframes or expressions, do not turn on Motion Blur for your stabilized layer! You don't want to soften the image any more than you have to, and the camera movement already has blur in it. Too much blur, since the camera was moving around more than it appears to be now.

This technique is bound to leave you with some gaps dancing around near the edge of frame. A little of this is OK, as long as it stays inside of Action Safe (press the ' key to see safe guides). If you've shot 4:3 SD for letterboxed output, then you'll have plenty of material top and bottom to account for this. Sometimes adding a duplicate layer under the smoothed layer, one without any animation on it, is enough to fill in the gaps convincingly.

Only use the after-the-fact Steadicam technique as a last-ditch effort to save a shot! It's always better to get your smooth move in-camera than to spend hours futzing with a shot in post. The viewer might feel that there's something "not right" about the results of a stabilized shot. The DV Rebel does not set out to use post to fix her mistakes. You must be constantly weighing your ability to execute a shot in the field against your knowledge of how post can enhance, not repair, your efforts.

Cranes & Jibs

As with the Steadicam-inspired genre, you will find many devices for executing smooth, crane-like moves with lightweight cameras. These range from the flimsy to the substantial and from the expensive to the even more expensive. Most of these devices are technically classified as "jib arms" rather than cranes. A crane usually features pan/tilt operation either via a remote head (i.e., a remote control panel near the base of the crane) or by an operator riding on the crane itself. Both of these things are about as DV Rebel as building your own full-sized Titanic replica.

But a jib arm is a different beast. It looks like a small crane, but the pan/tilt head is operated manually, usually by the same person who is manipulating the arm itself.

Director of Photography David Collier makes a shot for my teaser trailer using a jib arm. The smoke will be color corrected brown to make it appear that the actor (John Tansley) is caught in a dust storm. Photo by Chris LeDoux.

Obviously a jib is limited in that the head cannot stray too far from where a person can get at it. You won't be booming up to a second-floor window with a jib.

With this limitation, it might seem that a jib arm isn't much of an improvement on a good stabilizer such as the SteadyTracker. Both create smooth moves wherever your arm can reach. But they are different beasts. A jib confines your movement to a specific arc about the base. It's counterweighted, so when you stop the camera it can really stop, rather than floating there and getting less and less steady as your arm grows tired. You can shoot an entire dialog scene on a jib arm, maybe only using its boom capability at the very end of the shot, or the very beginning.

But jibs are big and cumbersome. They need to be heavy in order to make smooth moves. When I want to use one, I borrow a friend's. If you find yourself using one a lot, here are some resources:

- cobracrane.com. From the makers of the SteadyTracker, the Cobra Crane is an inexpensive and viable little jib. It offers remote tilt but not pan.

- dvcamerarigs.com. A book devoted entirely to home-built camera rigs.

- skycrane.com, kesslercrane.com, nuangle.com. Various cranes and jibs at various prices. Did I mention you might just want to rent these toys rather than buy? I mean, how many crane shots do you envision in your film? I used about four in *Birthday Card* and then my Cobra Crane sat in the closet for years. On the other hand, maybe you'd rather spend $500 on a jib arm than on Automatic Duck. It's up to you.

Found Cranes

The DV Rebel cannot pass a glass elevator, or an open-air escalator, or a tire swing, without pondering how it might be used to create a smooth establishing shot. I once made a dolly shot in an airport by resting my camera on the rail of a moving pedestrian walkway. If you can ride it, it's a dolly. If you can ride it up and down, it's a crane.

Playing with Time

Whether it's using slow motion, sped-up motion, or a full-on "bullet time" shot, every pivotal action scene has its way with time. There are both in-camera and postproduction techniques to achieving this temporal titillation.

Slow Motion for Me

It would be very difficult to find an action movie without a single slow-motion shot in it. It may be difficult to find a solid minute of a John Woo film with no slo-mo shots. Slow motion is to action films as guitar solos are to rock and roll: intrinsic, indulgent, magnificent, easily overdone, and still kind of great even when overdone.

There are two kinds of slow motion: the slow motion you plan on and the slow motion you decide to do later. Regardless of your original intentions for a shot, you may find as you are editing your film that you want to put it into slow motion. Maybe you want to achieve a more dramatic effect, stretch out a moment in time, or simply make an action appear slower. Whichever the case, you'll be faced with the task of slowing down your 24p footage.

There are basically three "looks" for after-the-fact slow motion. They are step printing, frame blending, and interpolation.

STEP PRINTING

Step printing is the simplest form of slowing down a shot. Frames are repeated as needed to make the action slower. To create half-speed, you simply play each frame back twice instead of once.

Top: A 24p shot at normal speed. Bottom: The same shot slowed down to half-speed using step printing. Each frame is played back twice.

Step printing is the default effect when slowing down a clip in most software. In Final Cut Pro, step printing is what you get when you turn off Frame Blending in the Speed dialog (Modify > Speed). In Premiere Pro, choose Clip > Speed/Duration. In After Effects, if you slow down a clip by selecting Layer > Time > Time Stretch, you will get step printing by default.

FRAME BLENDING

Frame blending is a method of smoothing a speed change by building new frames out of little cross-dissolves between frames.

Slowing down a shot by half with frame blending results in cross-dissolves between the doubled-up frames.

Depending on the content of the shot, frame blending can result in either pleasing or distracting slow motion, but either way it's fair to characterize the results as "softer" and more "dreamlike" than step printing. Frame blending is an option in many NLEs (nonlinear editing programs), including Final Cut Pro and Premiere Pro. In After Effects, you enable frame blending for a layer by toggling the Frame Blending switch to the jaggy-line position:

Note that this switch will only be available for footage layers, not for pre-comps. Also note that you will not see the effect of the frame blending setting unless you switch on the Enable Frame Blending button for the comp:

Note that the way you should be rendering with After Effects, with your Render Setting set to Best Settings, this switch simply controls whether or not you're previewing the effects of frame blending while working interactively. When you actually render, frame blending will be enabled for any layer that has its Frame Blending switched on regardless of this Enable switch's state. This means that you can safely speed up your interactive work by leaving Enable Frame Blending switched off.

Frame blending is a very distinctive and stylized look for slow motion. Experiment with it and use it when appropriate—not necessarily every time, as your NLE's default settings may suggest.

INTERPOLATION, A.K.A. "PIXEL MOTION"

You'll notice that in After Effects 7.0, the process we call frame blending is actually called "Frame Mix," and is one of two options filed under Frame Blending. The second option is called "Pixel Motion."

I think these terms are silly, so I'm going to follow industry standards and refer to AE's Frame Mix mode as *frame blending* and Pixel Motion as *interpolation*.

Interpolation is a new addition to After Effects, and a welcome one indeed. It's one of those technologies that seems too good to be true, and in fact it sometimes is. But when it works, it is nearly magical. Interpolation creates its slow-motion effect by tracking the motion within the frame at the pixel level, and building new frames that attempt to smoothly fill in the gaps, or interpolate, the motion from frame to frame. It's like an automated morph between frames.

Under ideal circumstances, interpolation produces results that pass for in-camera slow motion. Objects move smoothly and lyrically through the frame without betraying that this slow-motion moment was retroactively applied to normal 24p footage.

To enable "Pixel Motion" interpolation for a layer in After Effects, toggle its Frame Blending switch to the smooth line state:

Pixel Motion's relationship to the Enable Frame Blending switch is the same as that of Frame Mix (see Frame Blending above). Pixel Motion can be quite computationally intense, so leaving the Enable switch off while working is very likely something you'll want to do.

SPEED? DURATION? FRAMES PER SECOND?

There are many ways of expressing just how slow is slow. On the set of a film shoot, I communicate my desired slow-motion effect to my camera crew by specifying the frame rate at which I'd like the camera to run. Let's say I ask for 48 frames per second (fps). This is twice my playback frame rate of 24 fps, so it could be said that my shot will be at half-speed or that on-screen events will take twice as long to play out as they did on set.

Different software packages use different nomenclature to express the exact same slowdown. After Effects uses duration, and would describe our 48 fps slowdown as a 200 percent "Stretch Factor." Avid and Final Cut Pro use "speed," and would denote our shot as 50 percent speed. No program I know of helps associate these terms with a shooting frame rate compared with a playback frame rate.

To help you translate between various applications, and to help you translate your experimentation with after-the-fact slomo into informed frame rate selection on your next shoot, I've created an Excel calculator that allows you to translate between speed, duration, and frames per second:

It's called **cameraSpeeds.xls** and you'll find it in the Calculators folder on the included DVD. It's actually three separate calculators in one document, one for each possible bit of information you might know.

For example, if you've time-stretched a shot in Final Cut Pro HD and you want to know how to stretch that same clip in After Effects, you need to convert speed to duration, the first column. The second column reverses this conversion. The third takes a shooting frame rate and expresses it as a time-stretch value.

IN-CAMERA SLOW MOTION

All of the above techniques presume that you are taking regular 24p footage and trying to make it into a slow-motion shot in post. But the DV Rebel plans her shoot and shoots her plan, and this includes knowing in advance that you'd like a shot to be in slow motion, just like our friends who shoot on film must do.

Unless you have an HVX200, your options for overcranking are probably limited to 30p and 60i. In other words, you can shoot 30 fps for 24p playback, for 80 percent speed, or you can shoot 60 fps (effectively) for 40 percent speed on playback. Shooting 30 for 24 is a very subtle slomo—almost imperceptible depending on the subject matter. I know cinematographers who shoot 30 fps material to give a shot a little extra weight or emotion, without actually telegraphing "slow motion" to the audience. This is a fun and powerful technique, one I highly recommend you experiment with.

Jargon Watch

Overcranking is a term for shooting a frame rate faster than the intended projection frame rate, and as you might guess it dates back to the days of hand-cranked cameras.

To shoot 30p for 24p playback, simply follow these steps:

1. Import your 30p footage into After Effects. Since it's 30p, not 60i, make sure After Effects doesn't try to separate the fields of the clip.

Do this by selecting the clip and pressing Cmd + F (Mac) or Ctrl + F (Windows), and then setting Separate Fields to Off. Click OK when done.

When working with 30p footage, you have to manually counteract After Effects' default assumption that DV footage is interlaced.

2. Drag the clip to the Create Comp button at the bottom of the Project panel.

3. In the resultant comp, press Cmd + K (Mac) or Ctrl + K (Windows) to open the Comp Settings window. Replace the 29.97 value in the Frame Rate field with 23.976. Click OK.

4. Now ensure that the Stretch column is visible in the Timeline. Go to the bar above the columns, right-click, and verify that Stretch is checked in the Columns submenu.

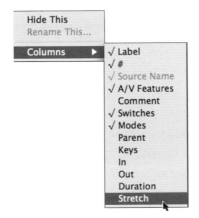

5. In the Stretch column, enter a Stretch value of 125%.

   This will result in the layer stretching by the exact proportion of 24:30. The 30p frames will now match one-to-one with the 23.976 frames per second of the comp, resulting in a smooth 30-for-24 slomo. The term we use here is that we're playing the frames back "1:1" (say "one to one"), just as we would be doing if we'd shot film at 30 fps and played it back at 24.

   You'll notice that the layer has now been stretched beyond the tail end of the comp's duration. Luckily there's a quick fix for this.

6. With the layer still selected, press O (the letter) to go to the layer's out point. The Current Time Indicator jumps to the out point even though it's outside the boundary of the comp. Make a note of the frame number displayed in the Current Time field in the upper left corner of the Timeline panel. Select Composition > Composition Settings and enter this number as the new duration of your comp.

7. Now press Cmd + M (Mac) or Ctrl + M (Win) to add this comp to the Render Queue. Select the appropriate Output Module preset for your offline edit and render your footage. Be sure to decide whether you want to render stretched audio as well.

Yes, this is recompressing your footage to a lossy codec, which, as we will discuss later, is a major DV Rebel no-no. But you're only going to use this footage as offline editorial material. When you conform your film in the onlining process (see Chapter 6), you will use the original footage and redo this time-stretch operation. For the time being, though, you have a nice-looking proxy that you can freely use in your cut.

The process is very similar for 60i material. The big difference is that you do in fact want After Effects to separate the fields of your interlaced footage. To ensure the highest quality when doing so, you'll enable the Preserve Edges option in the Interpret Footage: Main window.

Two Magic Numbers of NTSC Slo-Mo

Even I have trouble remembering these numbers, so here's a handy reminder:

When slowing down 30p material in a 23.976 fps Timeline, the stretch value that causes you to use every frame one-to-one is 125%. For 60i or 60p, the magic number is 250%.

Now add this footage to a 23.976 fps comp and use a Time Stretch value of 250 percent. As before, do not enable any frame blending modes, and expand the duration of the comp to encompass the new layer length.

What you've done in this case is expand the footage such that each $1/60$-of-a-second field is dropped neatly into each 24p frame, playing each field back as a frame one-to-one. After Effects makes a new, full-resolution frame by interpolating between the fields. The Preserve Edges option means that jaggies will be reduced, although we're still basically talking about a half-res image in the vertical direction. Chances are no one will notice, though, and the slow-motion effect will be so lovely that it's worth some small artifacts here and there.

The above techniques generally hold true for both DV and HDV, where 30p and 60i are common options. But if your camera of choice is the HVX200, you have a true plethora of overcranking options, ranging up to a true 60p. If you're shooting 720p, 24pN, then no post processing is required for your slo-mo shots.

Whatever frame rate you're shooting, make sure to always use a 180-degree shutter. You have to be careful because most NTSC cameras will want to use a $1/60$ shutter for 60i material, but that's a 360-degree shutter! Since film cameras don't have that option, the 360-degree shutter is a major no-no. Be sure to use $1/120$ for both 60i and 60p.

Keeping Track of Slo-Mo Shots

Whenever you use recompressed proxy footage in your edit, you must be prepared to revert to the original raw footage for your onlining process in order to maintain the best quality. This means you'll be repeating the time-stretching you just went through when your build your online.

In order to make this process easier (since you're destroying any timecode association with the original footage when you rerender it), you can add a text overlay to your slow-motion proxy footage that will help you line up your shots:

1. In your After Effects project where you're rerendering out your footage at 23.976 fps, add a new text layer.

2. Twirl open the Source Text stream and Option + click (Mac) or Alt + click (Windows) the stopwatch button to create an expression. Enter this text for the expression:

   thisComp.layer(index+1).name + " : x" + (1+(time/thisComp.frameDuration))

This expression says "Take the name (.name) of the layer below me (index +1), stick a colon and an x after it (+ " : x"), and then after that tack on the frame number of the comp (time/frameDuration)."

Assuming your text layer is above your footage layer, and that you haven't renamed your footage layer, you now have a text overlay that displays the name of your footage file and the current frame number. Make this text visible but inconspicuous, and edit away. When the time comes to add this shot to the online, you'll have a handy reference for which shot it was and what frame range you used.

Speed Ramping

Speed ramping, sometimes referred to simply as ramping, is the name for speeding up and/or slowing down a shot while the shot is playing out.

With some cameras this can be accomplished while shooting, by varying the frame rate while the camera is running. There's a nice example of this in *The Game* (Chapter 6 on *The Game* DVD), where Michael Douglas enters the airport and steps into slow motion as he walks. But oftentimes even when such cameras are available, it is a better choice to execute speed ramps in post. For the DV Rebel this is the only choice.

In the world of film, it's common to shoot these ramp-in-post shots at even multiples of 24, so that later you can do a clean speed-up to put part of your shot back to real time. So you'd shoot either 48, 72, or 96 fps, and so on. For the DV Rebel, a speed ramp shot starts the same way a 60 fps slo-mo shot does, with 60i or 60p source footage. With the HVX200 you could shoot 48p, but usually a speed ramp calls for a more profound difference between the slow part and the fast part than two times.

Generally speaking, the idea behind ramping in post is that, for a portion of the shot, you'll take your slow-motion footage and speed it back up to put it into real time. Then you will either abruptly or smoothly transition into slow motion, usually allowing the footage to play back 1:1.

Let's talk about that "abruptly or smoothly" part. This is where you decide if you're making a film that goes on the shelf with the David Fincher films, or with the cinema of McG (director of *Charlie's Angels, Charlie's Angels: Full Throttle*).

If you're going for that cool fast-slow, snap-into-slo-mo, nearly Bullet Time speed ramp, the kind you see in car commercials and almost any time a starlet with a mane of hair pulls off her motorcycle helmet, you are going for the *Charlie's Angels*. This one's easy to do. Let's say you shot your starlet at 60p, and you want her to yank off her helmet in real time, snap into a four-times slomo (the equivalent of shooting 96 fps), and then go back into real time. Here's how you do it:

1. As with overcranking, bring the 60p (59.94 fps) footage into After Effects and add it to a 23.976 fps comp. Since After Effects is a time-based program (rather than frame-based), your footage is now set to play back at real time, regardless of your comp's different frame rate.

2. Select the layer and choose Layer > Frame Blending > Pixel Motion.

3. Find the frame where you want to transition to slow motion and press Shift + Cmd + D (Mac) or Shift + Ctrl + D (Windows) to split the layer.

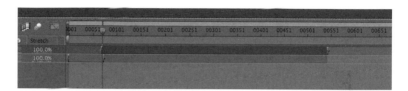

4. Enter a new Stretch value for the top layer of 400% (either using the Stretch column in the Timeline or via Layer > Time > Time Stretch).

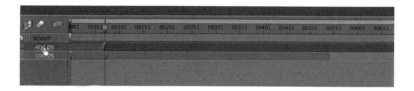

5. Now find the frame in the slow layer where you want to snap back to real time. Split the layer again at this frame.

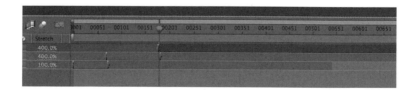

6. Set this new layer's Stretch to 100%. The default is to stretch around the layers in point, which in both cases is exactly what you want.

7. Now turn on the Frame Blending preview switch for the comp and preview your work. If you want to make adjustments, it's often easier to start the process over from the beginning rather than keep track of matching the in and out points of the various layers.

Remember that you can work with the comp frame blending switch off for better interactivity, and when you render your clip at Best Settings the Pixel Motion frame blending will be used.

TIME REMAPPING

That ramping effect is cool, and you see it everyday in films and commercials. But you may want a smoother transition in and out of your slow motion. Or you may want to emulate the gradual transition into slomo that Fincher used in *The Game*. Either way, the answer is time remapping.

Time remapping is where you use a curve to control your clip's speed over time, and it can be a real head-scratcher. But if you follow these simple instructions you can use it to great effect.

Let's say you want to do exactly what you did above, but with smoother transitions in and out of slomo. Start exactly as you did before, by adding the 60 fps footage to a 23.976 fps comp and enabling Pixel Motion for the layer. Then, follow these steps:

1. Choose Layer > Time > Enable Time Remapping. Select the words Time Remap in the Timeline and display the Graph Editor.

   The straight line you see is the graph of your footage playing back in real time. If you moved the last keyframe to the right, you'd be making the duration of the clip longer, or slowing it down. So a shallower slope means slower motion. You need to create a shallow part of the curve in between two real-time sections.

2. To do this, go to the frame where you want to transition into slomo and add a keyframe. Then go to the frame where you want

to revert to real time and add another keyframe. Your Timeline should look like this:

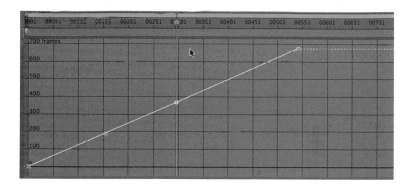

3. Now select the last two keyframes and move them to the right together (hold down Shift to constrain the movement):

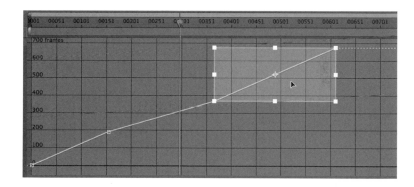

You now have exactly what you did above with splitting and stretching—a slow moment in between two real-time sections, with abrupt transitions. The next step is to smooth out the transitions.

4. Select the second keyframe and right-click to bring up the contextual menu. Choose Keyframe Velocity.

5. In the Keyframe Velocity window, check Continuous. The Outgoing Velocity should change to 1 second/sec. Enter a value of 20% for Influence under Outgoing Velocity:

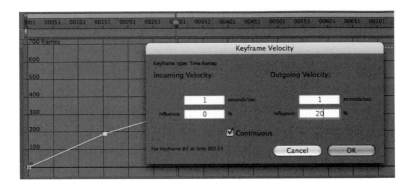

6. After clicking OK, select the next keyframe and bring up the Keyframe Velocity window. Again, check Continuous. But this time you'll have to correct the assumption that you want to continue the incoming velocity. Set seconds/sec to 1.0 and enter 20% for Incoming Velocity Influence. Click OK. If you've done all this correctly, your Timeline should look like this:

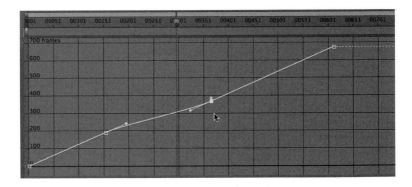

...and your motion should smoothly transition from real time to slow and back.

By using the numeric fields in the Keyframe Velocity window, you carefully avoided messing up the keyframe interpolation in the real-time sections (the parts that were 1.0 "seconds/sec"). You can experiment with different influence percentages and slo-mo amounts. You can always grab the last two keyframes and scoot them left or right to adjust the degree of slowdown in the middle section, even after you've performed steps 4 through 6.

Here are some visual references for other speed changes you can achieve using this basic technique:

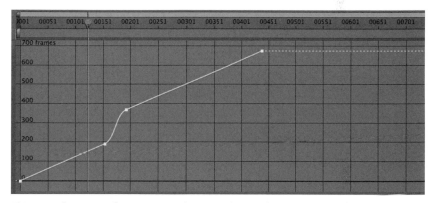

This curve has a very fast section in between two real-time moments.

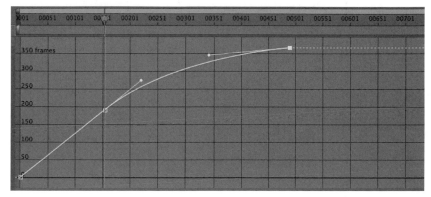

This curve has the footage going real time up until frame 154, where it smoothly begins slowing down, decelerating to the end.

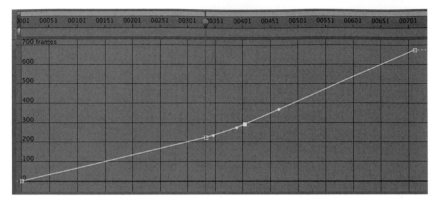

This curve puts the footage in consistent slomo at the head, then at frame 334 it smoothly transitions into real time over the course of about 80 frames.

Undercranking

The obvious opposite of overcranking is undercranking, or running the camera at a slower speed than the projection frame rate, which creates a fast-motion effect. Generally the purpose of undercranking is to lend extra "oomph" to action—to speed up a punch, a fall, or a car chase moment.

This requires a subtle hand. Audiences are very good at spotting sped-up motion, and the idea here is that they buy the speed-up as a legitimately fast event, not any kind of camera trick. So how undercranked is too undercranked? The common wisdom is that 22 frames per second is the ideal speed. Any more undercranked and the audience may spot the gag, and any closer to 24 fps and you're not getting a significant speed-up.

If you are lucky enough to have a Panasonic HVX200, you can simply shoot at 720p22, or 22 fps at 720p. Simple as that. In 720/24N mode, the DV Rebel's HVX200 mode of choice, shooting at 22 fps results in a perfect emulation of shooting 22 fps on film—only the unique frames are recorded, and your fast-motion effect is instantly available for review by playing back your shot from the camera. If there were any questions about the HVX200's qualifications for DV Rebel cinema, this should put them to rest. There's no other camera that offers this feature. You can shoot a take at 22, play it back at 24, see how well your undercrank gag worked, and then try another take at 20 fps and see if you can get away with the additional speed-up.

For those of us with more traditional cameras, the overcranking rules apply. In other words, you'll shoot 60i or 60p, and then speed-change the footage in After Effects. The downside of this is that you have to inter- polate frames, which can introduce artifacts. But the upside is that you can dial in the exact amount of speed-up effect that you want without having to commit to a frame rate on the shoot.

Here's how to speed-change your footage in After Effects:

1. Import your footage into After Effects. If it's 60i, then ensure that After Effects sees the footage as 29.97 frames per second and is properly separating the fields (with Preserve Edges checked). If your footage is 60p, simply verify that it has been imported with the correct 59.94 fps frame rate.

2. Drag your footage to the empty comp viewer to create a new composition.

3. Select Composition > Composition Settings, and change Frame Rate to 23.976 fps. Hit OK.

4. With the layer selected, choose Layer > Time > Time Stretch, or expose the Stretch column in the Timeline.

5. Select Layer > Frame Blending > Pixel Motion to set your layer's frame blending mode.

6. Enter a stretch factor of 91.67%. This is the ratio of 24 fps to 22.

7. Preview your shot and evaluate the speed-up. Adjust the stretch value to taste until the desired effect is achieved.

    Alternately, if you would rather think in terms of shooting in frames per second when adjusting a speed-up (or a slow-down) in post, follow Steps 1–5 above and then replace Step 6 with the following :

8. Enable Time Remapping for the layer by choosing Layer > Time > Enable Time Remapping.

9. When the Time Remap stream appears in the Timeline, select it and choose Animation > Add Expression.

10. Enter the following expression:

```
shootingFrameRate = 22:
playbackFrameRate = 24;
time*(playbackFrameRate/shootingFrameRate)-inPoint
```

To experiment with different speed-up factors, simply enter new values for shootingFrameRate. This allows you to specify your speed-up in more filmic terms. It also has the benefit of providing useful information for your next shoot—if your tests show that you like 20 fps more than 22 fps, you could confidently shoot 20 fps the next time you go out with your HVX200.

Narrow Shutter

Saving Private Ryan started a trend with its gritty, brutal treatment of the Omaha Beach sequence. Spielberg shot much of this scene with a narrow shutter angle, which lends fast moving subject matter a stroboscopic, frenetic effect. Combined with the film's *bleach bypass* look (see Chapter 6), the effect is jarring and memorable. Since then we've seen the technique used in *Gladiator, Mission: Impossible 2,* and *28 Days Later.*

This is one effect that's remarkably easy with video. In fact, we spend a bit of effort trying to avoid our consumer cameras' default tendency to give this effect! Left to their own devices, our cameras will control exposure with the shutter, choosing a fast shutter speed in bright lighting conditions. Generally speaking you don't want this, so you'll manually force your shutter to the correct film shutter speed of 1/48 of a second (NTSC) or 1/50 of a second (PAL).

You'll notice that in video terms, we speak of shutter speed as a fractional value, but in film we tend to discuss it as an angular measurement. If *Saving Private Ryan*'s battle scenes were shot with a 45-degree shutter, what exactly does that mean?

A film camera's shutter is a disk, and that disk has an open and a closed side. It rotates as the camera runs, "opening" as its open side passes in front of the gate and closing as the solid side rotates through. It's during this closed period that the film is advanced to the next frame. All of this happens 24 times per second.

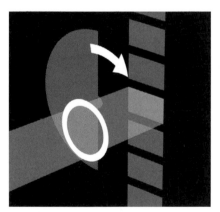 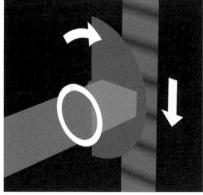

The shutter pictured here is open for half of its 360-degree rotation, or 180 degrees. A 180-degree shutter is the default for a film camera, and results in a shutter speed value of 1/2 the frame duration, or 1/48 of a second at 24 fps. So:

1/shutter speed = frame rate/(shutter angle/360°)

For example:

24/(^{180}/$_{360}$) = 48, or 1/48 of a second

That means that the equivalent shutter speed for a 90-degree shutter is 1/96 of a second, or one quarter the frame duration. See, that disk in the film camera is adjustable, and that 180-degree opening can be narrowed. Here's what a 90-degree shutter looks like:

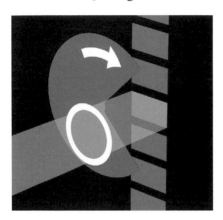

To achieve the *Saving Private Ryan* look, you maintain manual control of your shutter and use an equivalency of a film camera's fast shutter modes. For example, a 45-degree film shutter would equate to a camcorder shutter speed of $1/192$ of a second. Chances are your camera offers a $1/200$ of a second shutter speed, which is close enough.

The visual effect of all this is quite simply a reduction in motion blur. The faster the shutter, the less the blur. This tends to give motion a crisp, brittle look that seems to evoke the adrenalized, hyper-aware state of a warrior in combat. You'll have to adjust your aperture and ND filtration to account for the reduction in light caused by the faster shutter. The nice thing about this effect is that it's entirely in-camera and whatyouseeiswhatyouget.

I suppose you could use just about any fast shutter setting that looks good to your eye, but consider that while video cameras often have shutter speeds as fast as $1/2000$ of a second and faster, most film cameras bottom out at a 15-degree shutter angle, or $1/576$ of a second.

Compare the results of a $1/48$ of a second shutter (left) with an image shot with a $1/1000$ shutter speed (right).

Common Film Shutter Speeds

Here's a quick reference for common movie camera shutter angles and the equivalent shutter speeds at 24 fps. You may need to settle for the closest approximation your camera offers. If you want both a narrow shutter look and overcranked slow motion, you can use the formula from earlier in this section to make your own chart for the frame rate you intend to shoot.

Film Shutter Angle	Shutter Speed at 24fps	Light Loss
180 degrees	$\frac{1}{48}$ second	0 stops
90 degrees	$\frac{1}{96}$ second	1 stop
45 degrees	$\frac{1}{192}$ second	2 stops
15 degrees	$\frac{1}{576}$ second	About 4 stops

Hand-Cranking

From the very first moments of Tony Scott's *Man on Fire*, we are inundated with a jarring photographic technique in which Denzel Washington seems to lurch and pop his way through Mexico City in a kind of otherworldly mash-up of under- and overcranking. This effect was realized through the use of hand-cranked cameras, putting a modern twist on the most ancient of film traditions.

As I mentioned, the reason we use the term *cranking* when we talk about camera speeds is that early movie cameras were actually moved by hand using a crank. The operator had to maintain a steady hand, because if he sped up his cranking slightly he'd create a slow-motion effect, and he'd create the opposite if he inadvertently slowed down. Although camera operators became very good at maintaining a steady frame rate, there would always be slight irregularity to the results in both speed and exposure, which has become part of the charm of the early days of cinema.

Whether you need to create realistic period footage or simply want to experiment like Scott, you can try out the hand-cranked look using the After Effects project file found in the Examples/Hand Crank folder on the DVD at the back of this book. All you need is some 60i (NTSC) or 60p (HD) footage, just like you would have shot for a speed ramp effect.

1. Open the **handCrank.aep** project in After Effects. It contains one comp and one piece of footage, which you are about to replace with your own.

2. Import your own footage. If it's 60i, then ensure that After Effects sees the footage as 29.97 frames per second and is properly separating the fields (with Preserve Edges on). If your footage is 60p, simply verify that it has been imported with the correct 59.94 fps frame rate.

3. Replace your footage into the comp by selecting the one layer and then holding down Option (Mac) or Alt (Windows) as you drag your footage in from the Project Panel. If needed, change the comp size to match your footage, but make sure to keep a frame rate of 23.976 frames per second.

4. Press the zero key on your numeric keypad to start a RAM Preview. If everything worked, you should see your footage playing back with a hand-cranked look. Note that as it speeds up and slows down, the exposure changes as well. This is because cranking slower opens the shutter longer, increasing the exposure.

Pretty cool, but you may want to adjust the results. Select the video layer and expose its Effect Controls panel. There you'll see some sliders to control the hand-cranked look.

The first is called Base Crank Rate (fps). This value is the frame rate that you are trying to crank at, so it defaults to 23.976. If you want a vintage look, you could change this value to 18. You can also freely animate this parameter.

The next slider is called Irregularity. This controls how "off" your cranking is. If you set it to zero, then you've created a perfect camera operator who will crank at exactly the Base Crank Rate. The default value of 30 is an aggressive setting.

Skip down to the slider called Actual FPS. Its name is in parentheses to show that this is not a control you should adjust. It's more of a readout—in fact, it shows the actual frame rate you are cranking at on the current frame. Expose the Graph Editor to understand this better.

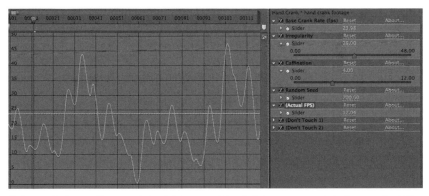

This graph shows the speed at which your virtual vintage camera is being cranked. The crank speed at the current frame is about 12 fps, or halfspeed, meaning the footage at this moment is playing back at about double real-time and will be overexposed by one stop.

The graph shows the camera's frame rate over time. If you set Irregularity to zero, this graph would be a flat line. If you crank up Irregularity crazy high, you might see the graph bottom out. This is because no matter how slowly you crank, you can't crank backward!

The next slider, Caffination, is a tough one to explain, but basically it controls how jittery the effect is. When you watch the effect playing back you will see "pulses" of light and dark, fast and slow. Higher Caffination values mean more pulses per second. Another way of looking at this is that Irregularity controls the amplitude of the FPS curve, and Caffination controls the frequency.

Random Seed is a value you can change to achieve a different randomness with the same settings. If you like the general feel of the effect but wish that your cranking had zigged when it actually zagged, try a different seed and see if you prefer the new results.

One note of caution about this project file: The random effect is based in part on the layer's position in the stack in the comp. So you can't really move this layer into a new comp with other layers unless you're willing to have your randomness change on you. Better to render out the results to a file.

Reverse It

One of the simplest camera effects to execute, and yet the toughest to master, is the art of shooting something in reverse. It's simple because of course you are not actually doing anything special with the camera—you're just going to time-stretch the footage to -100% in post. The difficulty comes from understanding what you can and can't get away with when cutting reversed footage in with normal shots.

For example, a common effect using reversed footage is vines or tentacles that appear to wrap around someone's leg. You wrap the items in question around your actor's leg, and then on action you have someone off screen pull the vine or tentacle away. When played in reverse, this will look like the puppeteered object is wrapping around the leg of its own accord.

Kinda. The problem is that everything looks weird in reverse, even the stuff that's not supposed to. The actor's pants won't look quite right as they pre-act (as opposed to *re*act) to the tentacle. If there's other action in the frame, or if the actor's hair or wardrobe is flopping around, you will face challenges in creating a seamless effect. It's also a bit of a mental tongue-twister to plan a reverse shot. You have to design the continuity with surrounding shots by imagining them in reverse as well.

But if you plan and cut in a reversed shot carefully, you can achieve a very convincing effect. The key is to use as little of the shot as possible, and consider cutting the shot in roughly, using a laptop on the shoot so you can see right away if it worked.

The Coen Brothers are the masters of this technique. They used it to great effect in *Raising Arizona* for a shot of a car screeching to a stop just behind a baby in a bassinet. Turns out a baby that's not doing much looks pretty much the same forward or backward. Maybe today the Coens would do a shot like this as a digital effect, but not necessarily. In *The Big Lebowski* they once again used reversed shots, once for the tossing of the briefcase out the window, and again for the shot of The Dude's (Jeff Bridges) face slamming down onto the glass table in Jackie Treehorn's (Ben Gazzara) Malibu home.

But the greatest reverse shot in action film history has to belong to Mr. Invent His Way Out of a Jam, James Cameron. In *Aliens,* Cameron staged a three-part shot of an alien facehugger leaping onto a rail, then jumping toward the camera. This single action was filmed in three parts, one of which was reversed. The crew thought they had caught Cameron in a mistake when they pointed out that the "rain" falling from the fire sprinklers would ruin the effect by falling "up" during the reverse section. Cameron countered that there would be no problem, because he knew that the motion-blurred streaks of rain would look exactly the same forward and backward. He was right, and the shot works perfectly.

Lighting

The DV Rebel is always trying to do the most she can with what she's got. And what she tends to have least of is lighting equipment. When you see truck after truck lined up outside a location shoot, chances are only one is for camera gear, whereas several are for lighting. Lights are expensive. They require power, which often means a generator. Generators are loud and require permits. Electricity is dangerous, so film lighting, like stunts and practical effects, requires people who know what they're doing.

God Is Your Gaffer

However, you may have noticed a giant ball of burning gas hovering in the sky. This thing is handy for so many reasons. It warms the Earth's surface, keeps us from flinging off into space, provides something to worship if you're just getting your civilization off the ground, and it can light your movie for you.

The sun's position, cloud cover, and recent rain are the reasons this shot looks nice. Taking advantage of these free resources requires planning and a little luck.

When you light a movie with, you know, lights, you control the effect with the position, distance, size, and color of the lights themselves. When you light a movie with the sun, you control the lighting via location scouting and schedule. The same location may look great in the morning sun, but will probably look miserable at high noon. It's common in location work to create a *light study* of a location, which is a series of photos taken at various times throughout the day. The DV Rebel should always be planning around when the best natural light is going to grace his locations, but hanging out at a potential location all day to take a few pictures might seem like a waste of time. Fortunately, there is another way.

The location I found for the teaser trailer I mentioned in the last chapter was a dry field in Northern California. The two significant features of this field were a period-looking barn at one end and an unbroken horizon at the other. I scouted the location and took a ton of photos, but only at one time of the day. I needed to plan my shoot around where the sun was going to be throughout the day, but this location was a 3-hour drive from my house.

Enter Google. I found the location on Google Earth (earth.google.com) and jotted down the latitude and longitude numbers (they appear at the bottom left of the main window). Then I popped open SketchUp (now Google SketchUp—see Chapter 2). There I created a rough representation of the barn and of my lead actor. I entered the latitude and longitude values from Google Earth, and turned on SketchUp's sunlight lighting. When you take the time to enter the correct coordinates for your location (Select Window > Model Info and then Location—you can choose from presets or create your own custom location) and the correct date (the date of your shoot, of course), the time of day slider will animate the sun through an accurate representation of the lighting on the day. How cool is that?

I used this to plan the day's shoot so that my actor would always be backlit or side lit. I picked inserts and other cutaways to shoot during the ugly lighting hours around lunch, and I even discovered some opportunities for cheating my actor's eyeline to get better lighting on his face. The entire shooting order was driven by this SketchUp lighting plan. It's a pretty cool sensation to show up on your location before dawn knowing exactly where the sun is going to rise, and where it will set.

Bounce It or Block It

The other way you control the light from the sun is by redirecting it or blocking it. Usually with the sun as your *key light,* or primary light source, the shadow side of your actors' faces will be too dark. The cheapest and easiest way of adding a *fill light* to correct this is with a bounce card. These come in various configurations, but they all do the same thing: reflect the sunlight in a controllable way.

You can use a piece of white or off-white tagboard or foamcore from an art supply store as a bounce card, but there's a much cooler option. Photography stores sell bounce cards that are made of light cloth stretched over a plastic hoop. Often available for as little as

The flex fill, or five-in-one reflector, packs a light-blocking black surface, a white bounce, silver and gold reflectors, and a silk into one compact package.

$15, these brilliant devices spring open and closed like those sun visors you see in car windshields, making them easy to store and transport.

The coolest ones are sometimes called "five-in-ones," because they have a reversible slipcover that offers four different surfaces (white, silver, gold, and black). With the slipcover removed, the unit's fifth mode is as a diffuser, thanks to its translucent white material. Unlike the bounce surfaces, diffusion is placed in between the light and the subject.

From top to bottom, left to right: Russell the dog with and without some negative fill provided by the black card; with and without white bounce; with and without silver bounce; with and without gold bounce; with and without diffusion.

The Last Birthday Card was almost entirely lit with natural light and bounce. The trick is to make the bounce card someone's full-time job if at all possible. It's not a mindless task, as the sun keeps moving and so do the actors. Don't overdo it—a little goes a long way. And don't bounce light up at your actors from below unless you want the fill to look creepy and unnatural. Try to angle it from about eye level, or from the height of the camera. Everyone looks better with a little *eyelight,* or light bounced in almost directly from the camera's perspective to minimize shadows under the brow or dark circles under the eyes from last night's cast and crew party. Experiment with the silver and the white surfaces. You'll probably find that white works better for close-ups where you can get in close to the talent, whereas silver is good when you need to bounce light in from farther away.

Bounced light doesn't have to be fill. If an actor is in the shade, sunlight bounced in from nearby can provide your key light.

Jargon Watch

A silver bounce card is an *Elvis*, a gold bounce is called a *Priscilla*, and a bounce with alternating silver and gold patches is called a *Lisa Marie*. A piece of foam with some foil pasted to its surface is called a *shiny board*. When you bounce light into the shadows of your shot you are *adding fill* and creating *low key* lighting by decreasing the ratio of key light to fill light.

A diffuser is often called a *silk* or a *soft*. If it's made of muslin it can be called a *muz*.

A flag can be called a *black* or a *cutter*, and if it doesn't have a frame it can be called a *floppy*. When you use flags to cut down ambient fill light, you are *adding negative fill*. You are also creating *high key* lighting, because you're increasing the lighting ratio.

A light-blocking card with an irregular pattern cut in it to cast interesting or mottled shadows is called a *cucaloris*, a *cuke*, or a *cookie*.

OR SMOKE IT

In action movies, you smoke the set. It's just a rule. Maybe not everyone does it, but everyone has done it. You should try it.

What's amazing about filling a room with smoke is that in person it seems so stupid and obvious. But look through your viewfinder and something magical happens. Through your camera, you don't see smoke. You just see a scene that looks more like a movie.

In *The Last Birthday Card,* the one location I knew I could control enough to smoke was Scott's apartment. I rented a smoke machine from a local film supply house and filled Scott's entire San Francisco apartment with smoke.

And then his fire alarm went off. Not just a smoke detector with a 9-volt battery, but one that was wired into the building's power. We had to scrounge around in the basement until we found the right circuit to shut off, but we couldn't leave it off, we could only reset it.

Luckily Scott's place was right next to the fire station. I walked over and explained that it was a false alarm. After I returned we proceeded to cover over all of Scott's smoke detectors with cling film from the kitchen and fire up that smoke machine again.

When the fire alarm goes off, that's just about the right amount of smoke to enhance your production value.

It takes more smoke than you'd think to make an impression on the screen. The amount of smoke in the room when we shot this shot, for example, was so much that you couldn't see the far wall.

Smoke is one of those dirty tricks that really works. It makes things seem larger than life. It gives your images depth. It gives light a physical presence in your film. And perhaps surprisingly, smoke can actually light your scene for you.

The apartment location I used for *Birthday Card* is a classic problem situation for video. I wanted to see out the bay windows of this San Francisco apartment to set the location and establish the layout that would become important for the helicopter scene. Holding exposure outside of an indoor location is difficult on video, due to the dynamic range limitations that I outlined in Chapter 1. But as you add some smoke to a room like this, an interesting thing happens—your shot will begin to overexpose. Smoke absorbs and reflects light and actually lifts the base exposure level of the scene. As I stopped down to correct the exposure, the previously overexposed windows dropped below clipping level. With the room full of smoke I could actually hold exposure on Scott's face and the buildings outside—all without any additional lighting.

There's another option for smoking your set, one that requires no power and might be easier to pull off in a borrowed location. Film expendable shops sell aerosol cans full of some allegedly harmless diffusion material. You can ask for this by the brand name "Cloud in a Can" but there are several manufacturers out there. You spray this stuff into your set and it hangs in the air like smoke. It takes several cans to keep a set smoked all day long, but many people prefer to work with the canned stuff rather than smoke machines because it seems easier on the lungs.

Eventually You May Need, Er, Lights

Even the most rebellious DV Rebel will eventually need to light a scene with actual lights. Rather than use real movie lights that require special power sources and safety precautions we instead use the aisles of our local home improvement store as our lighting department.

BE PRACTICAL

But first we try to do as much as we can with what's already on our set. *Practical sources* are lights that exist in the scene. A lamp, a neon sign, and a fluorescent ceiling fixture are all examples of practical sources. You might be surprised how much lighting you can accomplish by controlling practical sources. Most living rooms can be made to look much more cin-ematic by simply turning off the overhead light and placing an actor near a lamp with a light-colored shade.

Jargon Watch

Color temperature is a measure of the color differences between various kinds of "white" light. It's called temperature because some dude heated up a lump of stuff and noticed that as it got hotter it went from an orangeish color to a blueish one. So higher color temperatures are bluer than low ones, which is confusing because we think of blue as being a cool color and orange as a warm one. When you set the white balance on your camera, you're telling it what color temperature it should think of as pure white.

Color temperatures are expressed in the degrees (Kelvin) that the lump of stuff was heated up to. Daylight is often thought to be 5500 degrees Kelvin (K), where a tungsten light source such as a 200-watt light bulb is 3200K.

The hard part about using practical sources is that they can be all over the map in their *color temperature*. The classic example of this is when you want to use a practical lamp to add fill to a daytime interior. The daylight outside is a cool source, whereas the tungsten bulb in the lamp is warm.

This is one of those times when, as the cinematographer, you have to go to extra lengths to make the movie look as natural as the world does to your eye. The human eye is very good at correcting for the color temperature of a light source, but your camera is not. You might switch on that lamp and fail to notice how much warmer the light is than the daylight ambience in the room, but when you train your camera on that scene the results look accidental and amateurish.

One solution is to replace practical light sources with light bulbs of a known color temperature. In our daylight interior case, we'd want to place a daylight-balanced bulb in the lamp. You can buy these at most photo stores, and the DV Rebel would be wise to bring a few with him in his kit. In addition to being bluer (the bulbs are often actually blue in color even when off), they are also often brighter than standard home bulbs.

The other solution is to gel the offensive light sources. This is sometimes the only way to deal with fluorescent lights, which can be a greenish color that no other light sources, natural or manmade, will match. Magenta gels are made for correcting fluorescent lights towards daylight or tungsten balance.

When scouting locations where you hope to use practical light sources, be sure to bring your camcorder along to record some sample footage. Like I said, your eye may fool you, but the camera will give you the straight scoop on whether you'll be fighting a bunch of ugly, mismatched light sources.

WORK LIGHTS

There are scenes in *Fight Club* that are lit almost entirely with work lights—those quartz fixtures that you get at the home improvement stores that come with their own stands. These things pump out a ton of rather harsh light, but when you bounce them off a wall, or use them as a *rim light* (a light behind the talent that gives them that backlit edge), you can get great results. They're cheap and plentiful, and the quartz bulbs are fairly consistent in color temperature. You must be very careful when changing these bulbs, however, as the tiniest amount of oil from your fingers can cause them to burn out or even explode.

The work light section of a home improvement store, A.K.A. the DV Rebel lighting department. Prices range from $8 to $80.

A great way to control the light that beams out of these work lights is blackwrap. Blackwrap is a heavy-duty aluminum foil with a matte black surface, and you can spend a small fortune on it at camera shops and film expendables stores. You can wrap it around any light and sculpt it into a custom "barn door" that can be tweaked easily with a pair of work gloves. But never cover up so much of a light with blackwrap that the heat from the light has nowhere to escape, or you'll create a serious fire hazard.

CLIP LAMPS

Those tin-pot clip lamps that take a standard light bulb enjoy the same mythical reputation of aptitude for filmmaking as the wheelchair. The truth is, work lights are brighter, sturdier, more controllable, and only a little more costly. Plus, there's a sad fact of lighting, which is that small light sources are ugly, whereas big, soft ones are pretty. So you'd be better off looking into...

FLUORESCENT LIGHTS

If you're willing to get your hands dirty, you can make some very effective lights from hardware store fluorescent lighting fixtures. The process does involve some wiring, and since this book is flammable you won't find any

DIY electrical projects here. But if you attempt to build your own inexpensive fluorescent lights, bear in mind the following:

- The advantages of fluorescents are their low heat emissions, low power consumption, and that they create a large, soft light source.

- Disadvantages include a greenish tint and problems with flicker and hum.

- You can avoid all of those disadvantages by spending a little more on the lighting fixture. You're looking for a high-quality *ballast*, the part that regulates the current flowing to the tubes. If it's a quiet one, chances are it's also flicker-free, even at 23.976 fps.

- Get bulbs that are rated by color temperature. Choose the ones closer to tungsten balance, rather than the "cool white" bulbs that are allegedly daylight balanced. The daylight-balanced tubes are the infamous greenish ones. Although 3200K bulbs may be hard to find, 3500K are common and close enough.

- You'll be taking a fixture designed to be installed in a ceiling and making it into a portable light that you plug into a wall socket. Seek professional electrical assistance with this.

Big fluorescent lights are a DIY project, but little ones are a $10 purchase away. Many small flashlights also have a short fluorescent bulb in them. These are sold as emergency lights or work lights, and they are quite handy for lighting in close quarters. Some even have adaptors for your car's cigarette lighter, which is perfect since these little lights are the ideal in-car lighting solution for nighttime driving shots. You can tuck one in the instrument panel and it will look just like a glow from the dashboard lights.

CHINA BALL

Another small DIY project is the conversion of a round paper lantern shade, the kind you find in stores where everything is wicker, into a movie light. Called a *China ball*, these lights show up on even the most extravagant movie sets, but you can make one for a few dollars.

The main thing you need to do is find an appropriate light socket and mount the shade to it. You can dangle these lights right from their own cords, which is handy because you often need to get them quite close to your actors. The light from a China ball falls off quickly, so you'll often see them manned by a gaffer who can puppeteer the light to follow the talent's motions.

An inexpensive round paper lantern shade makes a lighting fixture called a China ball.

However you choose to light your movie, remember to remain flexible and experimental. Turn a difficult lighting situation into a cool creative choice—maybe shooting an entire dialog scene in silhouette (like Spike Lee did in *Inside Man*, Chapter 15 of the DVD*)*. Go where the lighting is easy rather than spending hours lighting the shot you had originally planned. Light a night scene with car headlights, or entirely with flashlights held by your actors. Lighting is one of the most powerful tools in your DV Rebel arsenal, and yet it can be completely free if you plan well and keep your eyes open.

Movies Referenced in This Chapter

28 Days Later

Aliens

The Big Lebowski

Close Encounters of the Third Kind

Gladiator

Inside Man

Lethal Weapon

Man on Fire

Mission: Impossible 2

Panic Room

The Professional

Raising Arizona

Saving Private Ryan

Se7en

The Shining

The Usual Suspects

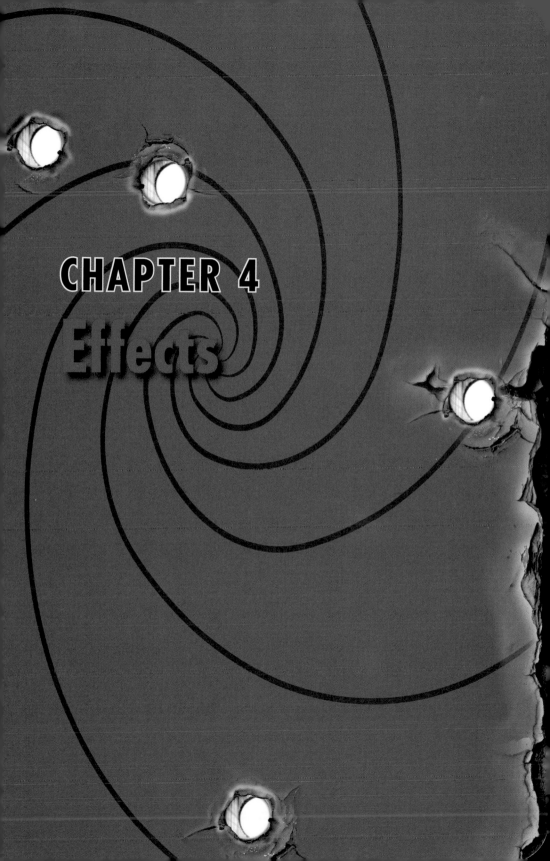

CHAPTER 4

Effects

The DV Rebel must be a visual effects artist. Maybe you won't ever work in the visual effects industry the way I did, and maybe you will not single-handedly execute all the effects work in your own film, but you will need to achieve a comfort level with visual effects. This is because, like Robert Rodriguez, you will be your own visual effects supervisor—the person who designs, plans, and oversees the effects. No one but you will have a complete enough picture of your film to realize all the ways that effects can enhance your production value and save money. Like Rodriguez, it will be up to you to come up with the brilliant plan of building only half a set and simply flopping half your shots to make it look like a massive cockpit (*Spy Kids 2* DVD, 10-Minute Film School). Learning what it takes to put an effects shot together will help you shoot good elements that will make your effects work go smoothly. And a comfort level with 3D and 2D animation software will enable you to not only broaden the scope of your film but previsualize it down to the last detail (as described in Chapter 2) as well.

Special Effects vs. Visual Effects

Those familiar with film effects work know that there is a difference in special effects and visual effects. The term *special effects* generally denotes practical, or on-set, "physical effects" such as blowing up a car or making steam come out of a manhole. *Visual effects* (often shortened to VFX) are things that will be added or assembled later, such as the glow from a lightsaber or a futuristic skyline full of flying cars.

Notice that I did not define visual effects as confined to postproduction. This is a common myth that works to the detriment of the film industry. Yes, a large part of the visual effects work on a movie will take place in postproduction, but perhaps the most critical part, the correct shoot-ing of plates, elements, and reference, is firmly a part of production. Furthermore, as visual effects sequences often require the most planning of any part of a film, they are as much a part of pre-production as anything else.

There's a reason that I subject you to my pet peeve about not relegating visual effects to the postproduction corner of your mind. By integrating visual effects into your planning from day one, you avail yourself of production value enhancing opportunities, and gain a further leg up against the big Hollywood movies that invariably plan too little for, and therefore spend too much on, their visual effects.

Let's look at an example from *The Last Birthday Card*. Throughout my production I was daunted by the task of finding a location for the Nak assassination scene (Chapter 4 of *The Last Birthday Card*, on the included DVD). I wanted to expand the scope of the film by staging this scene in a large corporate lobby of a downtown San Francisco building. But every building manager I queried wanted to charge me an outrageous location fee—$4000 and up for a day of shooting. I tried to explain that I was not a big Hollywood production, that I had a minimal crew and a small camera, and we would cause a student-film level of impact on their space, but to no avail. I was getting sucked into the expensive and inefficient vortex of making movies the "normal" way.

Luckily my producer brilliantly suggested that we investigate shooting in downtown Oakland. The Oakland film commission was very accommodating and understood that we were not working with a large budget. Directly down the street from their offices was a state-owned building with a truly spectacular lobby, and the fees to shoot there were quite reasonable. The only problem was that the vast glass wall of the lobby betrayed that we were not in San Francisco.

Visual effects to the rescue! I shot my scene and made a point of featuring the windowed wall prominently in my opening shot. I then composited a spectacular (and somewhat fanciful) view of downtown San Francisco out the window, tracking it into the motion of the shot. Not only did I reinforce the locale of the film even more than would have been possible in an actual San Francisco location, I got a better-looking lobby for less money. Had I not been thinking of visual effects when scouting this location, I may well have kept on looking, and spent more to put less on the screen.

Visual effects allowed me to turn this spacious Oakland lobby into an impossible San Francisco location.

Because the DV Rebel must always be thinking about how postproduction works hand in hand with production to put production value on the screen, and because so many visual effects work in conjunction with special effects, this chapter covers the entire spectrum of effects work on a budget, from bullet hits to epic space battles, and from practical gags to 3D computer graphics.

It sounds like a lot to ask, that you become an expert visual effects artist in order to be a fully formed DV Rebel. But here's the thing, and I mean this sincerely: You don't really need to be any good to pull it off.

Realism, Schmealism

There is a common belief in the world of film that the principal responsibility of a visual effect is to look realistic. This is quite simply not true. The only important criterion for the success of an effect is how well it helps tell the story. Realism may be a part of this—a completely bogus shot can certainly jar the viewer out of the narrative experience. But as long as the broad strokes are working, the audience has neither the time nor inclination to examine a visual effect for every last detail of perfection.

What is important to the success of a shot is that it "feels" right. A big part of this is editing. If an effect is well integrated into the edit, it will likely sail past a discerning audience even without all its i's dotted and t's crossed.

The other way a shot can function really well is based on its "squint factor." The squint factor is the quality that a visual effects shot has when it is viewed through the veil of squinted eyes. This is literally the way VFX artists look at a shot to gauge how well the color and contrast levels of the shot are working. But beyond that, they also know that this broad-strokes representation of the shot is a better way to fool your brain into seeing the shot in the scrutiny-free way that an audience will when seeing the film for the first time.

When creating the effects for *The Last Birthday Card,* I was far more concerned with the squint factor of my shots than the fine details. My CG helicopter, for example, only needed to look good in a few quick shots, and only from two distinct angles.

The model came from a library, and I didn't do much tweaking to it. It had some funky spots, so I just painted those areas darker in my textures. Check out how sloppy and painterly my texture map for the side of the helicopter was:

In the final shot these mushy blobs of black Photoshop airbrushing wrap around the model and give it a "bite" that it would not have onscreen if I had mapped highly accurate photographic textures onto the low-res model.

Squint factor is something that a good concept artist knows very well. Check out this concept painting by Orphanage concept artist Emmanuel Shiu:

This concept painting by Emmanuel Shiu (www.eshiu.com) is loose and gestural up close, but it has a great *squint factor.*

It's not photorealistic by any means, but it captures a realistic balance of light and shadow. The aerial haze has exactly the right feel. But most important, the image is beautiful and cinematic! If you just used it in your film as a matte painting, without any alterations, composited a few live action guys into the foreground and kept the shot short, you'd have a gorgeous matte shot in the tradition of the great masters of painting on glass, who understood that suggesting detail is better than painting every nut and bolt on the Millennium Falcon.

In the history of visual effects, there seem to be two truisms. The first is that effects keep getting better. The second is that they keep working just as well as they always have to support the storytelling of their films. Do the effects in your favorite childhood movies hold up today? Who cares? Sexy, fun effects with a vibrant, cinematic sense will always look great, even as their technical chops may fade with time.

I'm not saying that you don't need to work hard on your effects to make them great. Just don't get confused about your goal. The audience wants to believe that what they're seeing is real, and all you need to give them is enough of an excuse to do so.

Keep 'em Guessing

Magicians never repeat their tricks, and for good reason. Given enough opportunity, the audience will eventually spot how the trick is done.

The same thing is true with visual effects. You have to keep the audience guessing, keep them off-balance. Just when they think they've figured out how the trick is done, hit them with a shot that proves them wrong. Mix it up!

A terrific example of the mix-it-up technique is the Harrier jet sequence at the end of *True Lies* (*True Lies* DVD Chapter 4). The scene looks great in no small part because we never get a chance to grow accustomed to any one of the techniques used. Had it been all bluescreen, we would have started to notice the processed look after a while. Had it been staged solely on a mockup of the jet, we'd grow suspicious as to the lack of down angles. In fact that Harrier jet with Arnold at the stick is alternately represented by a miniature, a CG model, a fiberglass mockup suspended from a crane off the roof of the actual skyscraper in Miami, *and* that same mockup both bolted to a motion platform on top of that building and shot on a greenscreen stage. And in a couple of shots it's actually a real Harrier with Arnold's head comped in instead of the pilot's. Each shot uses the right technique for its specific needs, and when you cut them all together, the audience can never latch on to any of the artifacts of those techniques. As soon as they might begin suspecting one shot, the next shot clobbers them with living proof that their suspicions must have been wrong. The net effect is an over-whelming sense of realism that no one technique could ever uphold.

I realize that building a fiberglass mockup of a Harrier jet is not in your budget. Sometimes it's all the DV Rebel can muster to accomplish an effect one way, let alone three or ten different ways. Don't think of the mix-it-up technique as a limitation though, think of it as freeing. Mix-it-up can be as simple as following a matte painting with a piece of stock footage, or cutting from a guy getting his spear yanked away by an off-camera PA to the stop-motion creature biting a miniature spear in half. Mix-it-up is another way of reminding yourself that the audience generously fills in the blanks between the shots and creates your film's reality for themselves.

Treat the Fake Like It's Real

When staging an effects shot, the smartest thing you can do to ensure that you get photorealistic results is to create a shot that *could have been photographed* in some way.

When I was an intern at Dream Quest Images in 1993, I found myself dubbing reels for a new visual effects supervisor who had just joined the company. The reel was full of great work from A-list movies, much of it done at ILM. When a shot from *Die Hard 2: Die Harder* came up—the one where Bruce Willis, having just ejected from the cargo plane, flies toward the camera screaming as the plane explodes below him (*Die Hard 2* DVD Chapter 17)—I felt a presence behind me. A voice boomed, "What do you think of that shot?" I had no idea who was addressing me, so I thought for a moment and then answered, "It's the type of shot I imagine every visual effects supervisor hates getting assigned, because it's such an impossible staging that no matter how good a job you do putting it together, it's still going to be tough to win the audience over." The man with the voice stepped into the light and offered his hand. "That was the right answer. I'm Mike McAlister." Mike was the visual effects supervisor on *Die Hard 2* and it was, of course, his reel I was dubbing. A luminary in visual effects, Mike proceeded to confide in me the numerous challenges he faced in creating that shot, all stemming from the simple fact that, regardless of the plausibility of the event being depicted, no camera could have ever filmed it in that way.

Whenever you conceive an effects shot, you must consider how you would go about shooting it if it was not an effects shot. For example, think about the dinosaurs in *Jurassic Park*. The film wants us to believe that the dinosaurs are real. Spielberg accomplishes this by shooting the dinosaurs exactly how he would if they *were* real—even though they are effects. He doesn't change the cinematic style of the film when the dinos arrive simply because he's changing methodologies.

However, Spielberg chose to shoot *Jurassic Park* in his well-known cinematic style of control, grace, and casual confidence in the craft of visual storytelling. There's nothing accidental about this style—it is a highly choreographed one, the cinematic equivalent of impeccable grammar, and perhaps the most effortlessly skillful voice in cinema. By working in this style, whether he intended it or not, he convinced us that not only were dinosaurs real, but they could be trained to perform on cue in a movie! This may sound like a subtle distinction—and there's no doubt that *Jurassic Park* remains one of the most convincing visual effects films in history—but contrast it with the Spielberg's films after his experience recreating the Normandy beach for *Saving Private Ryan. Minority Report* lends *Private Ryan's* gritty, bleach-bypass look (see Chapter 6) to a science-fiction story, and the effects work is all the more believable as a result. But his *War of the Worlds* remake in 2005 stands as a masterful accomplishment in making visual effects look as hazardous and potentially out-of-control as a practically staged car crash or explosion might appear.

Sure, stunts in films are controlled—but when the car bomb goes off in an early scene in *The Last Boy Scout* (*The Last Boy Scout* DVD Chapter 6), it's pretty clear that while the camera operator knew the car was going to lift off the ground, he didn't know *exactly* how high it was going to go. He struggles to keep it in frame as it flies skyward. One gets this same sense in *War of the Worlds*—that the shot with the bridge being torn up as Tom Cruise flees in his stolen minivan *(War of the Worlds* DVD Chapter 7) had to be done in one take, and that the camera operator didn't quite know exactly where the debris was going to fly or where Cruise would swerve. In other scenes, the alien "tripods" fill the frame awkwardly and are often partially obscured by foreground scenery. It's not that *War of the Worlds* was filmed in the same gritty, documentary style as *Private Ryan*—but rather that the massive destruction effects have a messy realism that reflects a physical filmmaking process. This has the effect of subconsciously cueing the audience that they are seeing real stunts and demolitions when in fact they are watching the pixel creations of ILM.

In *Top Gun,* the in-cockpit shots of the Soviet pilots are actual footage of real U.S. Navy pilots flying an F5 Tiger II painted to look like a Soviet jet. Observe how realistic these shots are (you'll find plenty in *Top Gun* Collector's Edition DVD Chapters 2 and 14)—they really sell the credibility of the film. It's interesting to compare them with the cockpit shots of the movie star pilots. These *rear-projection* shots (more about that in a bit) feature our heroes with their masks off giving sync sound dialog—neither of which would be possible in a real jet fighter. It's a concession the audience is happy to make, as they did pay to see Tom Cruise fly a jet, not some faceless pilot with Cruise's voice overdubbed. But ask yourself when looking at these shots—where is the camera? It's floating out in front of Cruise where the instrument panel should be. When the cockpit bobs and twists, the camera does not. Somehow the camera is in the cockpit with Cruise but is not attached to it. It would not be possible to film an actual shot in a jet this way. Go back to a Soviet cockpit shot and see the difference— the camera is tightly packed in over the instrument panel, with a super wide lens to keep the pilot framed properly in the cramped space.

I wonder if the filmmakers ever considered imposing these same limitations on the staged cockpit shots, to try to achieve a little extra realism? *Top Gun* has so much nail-bitingly real air-to-air footage that this creative choice probably didn't impact the audience's appreciation at all, but I can't help but think an opportunity was missed to thoroughly convince viewers that Cruise was flying that plane.

For the DV Rebel, it's not so much about how you shoot Tom Cruise or whether you bolt things to big fake planes you can't afford. Later there's a section on poor-man's process where you'll learn more about staging this type of shot as if it were real. But even in your straight effects shots, you have opportunities to increase the realism factor by considering how you'd shoot them for real.

Sometimes a bit of gritty "realism" is retroactively applied to effects shots. Camera shake, lens flares, and other "dirty tricks" can be very effective, but only if they are a part of a larger plan. When visual effects supervisor John Knoll was designing the effects for the finale of *Mission: Impossible*, he thought about the camera rigs he would employ if he were shooting on a real TGV train. In fact, he was shooting a mock-up on a greenscreen stage. If Brian De Palma needed a shot from seven feet away from the train, he could easily place the camera there on a crane or a scissor lift. But John knew that to achieve such a shot in real life would require attaching the camera to the train with some sort of cantilevered arm, and that arm would probably bounce around noticeably at 200 mph. So he'd add (in post) a bouncy camera shake in the vertical direction to that shot. A shot from the surface of the train car looking back at the (fake) helicopter would get a different shake—a high-frequency vibration from the camera being bolted right to the deck.

In *xXx* there's some excellent effects work by Digital Domain in the avalanche scene. For one shot in particular, the visual effects supervisor filmed an extra element—a bit of snow smacking against the lens. When added to the final shot this little touch of reality is very convincing. The same trick lends a tangible reality to the fanciful "Womping Willow" in *Harry Potter and the Prisoner of Azkaban*.

The problem is that when you are creating something from scratch, it can be very easy to ignore what would be hard and fast physical laws in reality. Back when I was at ILM, I was having a hard time getting a camera move I liked on an all-CG shot for the special edition of *The Empire Strikes Back*. I finally realized that I was trying to mimic a classic crane move that was very simple, but I was doing it by hand using position keyframes. I started over with a new rig for my CG camera—a set of nulls designed to replicate the limited axes of motion of a large camera crane. Within a day I had the animation nailed, and the shot had a familiar cinematic quality to it because of the real-world camera move.

A great way to achieve this kind of realism in an all-CG shot is to poach an actual camera move. Camera tracking software has become very affordable lately (see "Matching Cameras" below), and almost anyone who's done any 3D work has experimented with tracking a CG object into a handheld plate. But what can be even more fun is using your camera tracking software as a kind of "camera motion capture." Shoot the camera move you want—it doesn't matter what scene you shoot as long as it makes for a good track—and use that camera move on your all-CG shot. At The Orphanage we actually keep a library of helicopter footage for exactly this purpose. We use the move data on all-CG matte painting shots, and the subtle dash of realism is a nice touch.

The key with this trick is to keep the scale accurate. The audience knows the "size" of a handheld move, and also of a crane shot. The last thing your CG Titanic needs is a handheld shot circling around it—it'll make your ocean liner feel like a canoe.

Some Effects Basics

In visual effects we make fakery look real. In doing this we consistently run up against the question of why something doesn't quite look believable. How have we fallen short of our goal of realism? What do we need to do to make this shot fool the audience?

Reference Is God

The first answer is always the same: reference. The concept behind reference is simple: If you want to know what something looks like, look at that thing. Sounds simple, but it's amazing how often even the pros need to be reminded of this. Reference can help you understand how things move, how they react to light, how they respond to getting wet, or how fire resistant they may be. You may think you know these things, but trust me: Good reference will always reveal new things about the workings of the real world.

Let's say that for your science-fiction short you will have your main characters pursued by a hovering probe about the size of a basketball. The probe will be CG, and you'll never build a real prop of it. Too bad, because if you could build a prop you could put it on a stick and fly it through the scene after actors had been shot. This is called shooting *reference pass*. This pass would show you exactly what the probe should look like—how it passes through light and shadow, what reflections it receives, and what shadows it casts on the set. But even without a probe prop, you can still shoot great reference. Just use a basketball, a bowling ball, or anything else about the right size, shape and color.

If you're adding a CG helicopter to a scene (like some people I know), you should look at real helicopters. Easy enough, but what if you're adding a CG dinosaur? Hard to come by a real dino for reference, but walking an alligator purse through the scene's lighting may be just as good.

The more reference you can shoot along with principal photography, the better. Even little things help. When preparing the splitscreen demo you'll read about in a little bit, I shot two plates: a background and a foreground. I knew that when I comped the foreground over the background, I'd need to have the actor (me) cast a shadow on the background plate. This shadow would very likely be generated in the comp, and when adding in shadows there's always the simple question of how dark they should be. Rather than guess, I shot a reference pass of me casting a shadow on the background location:

When putting the shot together this simple bit of reference allowed me to set my shadow darkness with confidence. See the completed comp in the "Stunts" section later in the chapter.

Matching Cameras

Fundamental to almost all visual effects is the idea of matching a camera. Any given shot in a movie is made with one camera. Visual effects shots, on the other hand, can be composed of elements shot with many cameras, some real and some virtual. You need to make the final shot look like it was filmed with one camera, as if no funny business was going on. For this to work, these cameras need to match, and to ensure that you need to know a few basics about how cameras work.

As I described in The World's Most Skipped Over Sidebar ("AOV, DOF, WTF?") in "The Camera" chapter on the DVD, the primary characteristic of a lens is its angle of view, or its place on the spectrum from wide-angle to telephoto. This measurement is in degrees and is usually expressed in relationship to the horizontal axis. In other words, as viewed from above, the camera sees a triangle-shaped slice of the world:

The angle near the lens is the angle of view or AOV. Now, you may be thinking that focal length is the more common measure of a lens's view of the world, but the problem is that focal length is only half the equation. Different cameras with different-sized film or digital imaging surfaces will produce different results from the same focal length lens. The simplest and most reliable way to describe a lens is by its horizontal angle of view, or hAOV.

You need to know the hAOV of a lens when you want to add CG to a shot, because inside the computer you will also be using a lens, albeit a virtual one. That virtual lens works just like a real one, though—it sees the world in a triangle slice. If you try to add a CG element to a shot and you use the wrong lens to render it, you'll wind up with a mismatched and unconvincing scene.

Three attempts to integrate a CG cube into a scene. On the left, the computer camera has too large an AOV, or too wide a lens. On the right, the virtual lens is too long or has too narrow an AOV. In the center, the correct AOV has been used. The perspective lines in blue match the surrounding buildings. This cube alone appears to be sitting in the photographed scene.

FINDING THE hAOV OF YOUR CAMERA

You may be asking how you go about measuring the AOV of your camera. But that's not fair for you to ask because you just read in the heading above that I'll be showing you how. Don't try to fool me.

You'll recall that in "The Camera" chapter I beseeched you to restrict your zoom lens usage to a few choice focal lengths, in the spirit of emulating a set of prime lenses. One of the many reasons for doing this is that it gives you a finite number of lenses to match in the virtual world. When you slate a visual effects shot (visually with a clapperboard or piece of paper, or audibly with your voice), note the focal length you are using and whether or not you had a wide or telephoto adaptor on the lens. Then, in post, you'll be able to correlate your shot with the appropriate hAOV.

For each of your common focal lengths, do the following:

1. Aim your camera as perpendicularly as possible at an object of known width. This object should be big, like a car or a sofa or an aircraft carrier.

2. Using an external monitor that has an underscan feature, position the camera at the proper distance so that the object perfectly fills the frame edge to edge.

3. Now measure the distance from the camera's lens to the center of the object. You should measure from the *nodal point* of the lens

(see "Matching a Real Camera" below), not the front element. Note that if you selected the aircraft carrier as your object, you will now find yourself in need of a very long tape measure.

4. Open **FindYourCamAOV_02.xls** in the Calculators folder on the included DVD. If you don't have Excel, you can open this document in Google Spreadsheets instead—it's free!

5. Enter your two measurements in the appropriate fields.

Find the AOV of your camera
Frame an object so that it just touches the left and right edges of frame.

width of object: 100   (any units)
distance to object: 200   (same units, measure from lens nodal point)

horizontal AOV = 28.072487°

Included on the enclosed DVD is an Excel calculator (also compatible with Google Spreadsheets) that derives your camera's Angle Of View from two simple measurements.

The yellow number is your hAOV. Rejoice!

When matching a CG camera to a real one, starting with a correct, measured hAOV is the best possible thing you can do for yourself. Whether you plan to use 3D matchmoving software such as Boujou or Syntheyes, or you intend to match the camera by eye, you will want to start with a CG camera that has an accurate hAOV.

MATCHING A REAL CAMERA

Back in the '90s there was a great music video for the Rolling Stones' "Love Is Strong." Directed by David Fincher, it features the Stones romping through New York as Godzilla-sized giants, stepping over bridges and between skyscrapers.[1] The concerns involved in placing giant rock stars into cityscapes are the same as placing miniature elements into background plates, or adding an exotic background to a shot from your backyard—and they start with matching the camera used to shoot the initial plate.

---

[1] At press time this video is available on YouTube: youtube.com/watch?v=4_a3NUeowcc

Jargon Watch

Matchmoving is the name for creating a 3D camera inside your computer software that matches the movement and other characteristics of a real-world camera. Once a painful, manual process, this important step in any 3D visual effects shot is now somewhat automated, thanks to software that tracks hundreds of points in your footage to deduce how the camera must have been moving.

If you're on Windows and want to try a free camera matchmoving application, try the Voodoo Camera Tracker by digilab (digilab. uni-hannover.de/docs/manual.html).

Matchmoving is too deep a subject for this book, but there's a great book devoted entirely to the topic called *Matchmoving: The Invisible Art of Camera Tracking* (Sybex). The author is the matchmoving supervisor at The Orphanage, so you can bet that he knows what he's talking about!

In addition to hAOV, which is much easier to match with real cameras because you can simply use the same focal length (assuming you're using the same camera, which you should), the following list describes everything there is to know about a camera's location in the world and what it will see: Tilt angle, roll angle, and height.

That's right, only three additional things. Now, you may be thinking that there's much more to be known about a camera. What about pan? What about horizontal position? F-stop? Believe it or not, those things don't matter. Or another way of putting it is, those things fall into place easily once you nail the top three.

So as you shoot your background plates in New York for your own personal "Love Is Strong" video starring you and your dog, you need to jot down only your camera's height and tilt angle. You write these in a little notebook along with your shot numbers from your storyboards. This documentation is called a *visual effects camera report,* and a handy side benefit of maintaining such a document is that you really look like you know what you're doing.

The reason that a video like Fincher's works is that cameras don't care how big something is. Large and small objects photograph exactly the same way with only one exception: depth of field. Everything else about how you frame up a shot of a real object stays the same when you shoot its miniature equivalent—as long as you put the camera in the right place.

So how do you do that? You measure!

Let's say you're lining up a shot for your homebrew "Love Is Strong" video. You start with the background plate, which you will shoot from the roof of a parking garage. You line up a lovely shot looking down a street, a perfect framing for the prancing of your surrogate Mick Jagger.

Your BG plate shoot for your homebrew "Love Is Strong" video. The orange outline indicates where your giant rock star will appear.

As you shoot, you jot down the focal length and the three important bits of info you'll need later for your Jagger element: height, tilt, and roll.

Focal length you can read off your lens barrel (and later you'll translate this value to the hAOV you measured). But how do you measure height? You could measure the height of the tripod, but that's not all that useful. Later, you're going to measure your miniature camera height off the floor, so you should do the same now—the "floor" being the street below. So you need to figure out the height of the building you're on, plus the height of your tripod.

Chances are your camera isn't Dutched (see "The Camera" chapter on the DVD), so write down zero degrees for roll. How do you measure tilt? The answer is an inexpensive tool available at any hardware store, an inclinometer.[2]

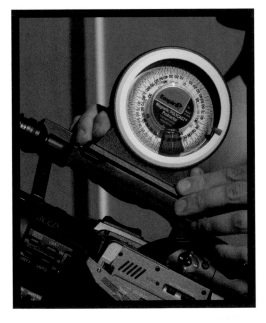

A carpenter's protractor or *inclinometer* is the perfect tool for measuring camera tilt. In this example the camera is tilted about 27 degrees.

---

2 If you search online for "inclinometer," you'll probably find products costing $50 or more. But at a hardware store, you should look for a carpenter's protractor. It's the same thing and they go for less than $10. Most have magnetic bases, which can be handy but means you'll want to keep them safely away from your DV cassettes.

Hopefully your camera has a nice, flat horizontal surface somewhere on it that you can place the inclinometer on to get a measurement of the camera's tilt. If not, that surface might be on your tripod head. Either way, your goal is to record the angle of tilt in degrees. It's helpful if your tripod has a ball level, so that you know you're measuring from a neutral basis.

Leveling your tripod ensures that your subsequent measurements will be accurate.

Because that's really the whole point—hAOV, tilt, height, and sometimes roll are the only measurements that you can make in relationship to something meaningful. You can measure pan, for example, but only based off of some arbitrary zero mark. The truth is that any angle of pan that works for your Mick Jagger element will look correct in the composite as long as your tilt and height are correct.

OK, so now it's time to shoot Mick. You've got your greenscreen set up, and you've got your measurements handy. Now, obviously your measurements need to be scaled. Your camera was maybe 30 or 40 feet off the ground, but now you're shooting your "miniature," so the camera's position must be miniaturized as well.

The rule is that you scale linear measurements, but not angle measures. So leave tilt alone and multiply height by your scale factor. Our mini-Mick is 1:12 scale, so we'll do a little painless math here:

30 feet $\times$ ($^1/_{12}$) = 2 feet, 6 inches

That makes our Mick shoot look like this:

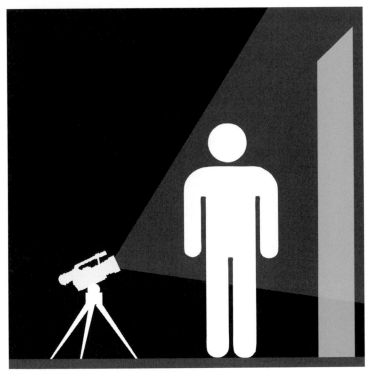

The miniature shoot uses the same focal length and tilt, but a scaled-down height, ensuring a perfect perspective match with the background plate.

When you're measuring the height of your camera in miniature photography, sometimes the numbers don't make a whole lot of sense. What if your background plate had been shot at street level? The height may have been something like 3 feet. Three feet scales down to 3 inches at 1:12 scale, but how do you get your 7-inch-tall camera 3 inches off the ground? The key is that you need to know what part of your camera you're measuring from. There's a center point to your lens called the nodal point. This is the point in space where the triangle of your camera's vision comes to a point.

Finding the nodal point requires some experimentation. The trick is that when you pan around the nodal point of your camera, you don't get any parallax, or crossing motion of foreground and background elements in the shot. The easiest way to test this is to set your camera on some kind of pivoting platform, like a lazy susan. Aim it at a scene that has both foreground and background elements. Pivot the lazy susan as you watch the viewfinder. If panning left causes foreground objects to slide right, push the camera back. If panning left causes foreground elements to slide left, push the camera forward. When there's no more sliding, the nodal point of your camera is now directly above the pivot point of the lazy susan. You'll need to measure this point with and without any wide-angle or telephoto lens adaptors you might be using.

Given that the nodal point is going to be buried within your camera and near the front, it's impossible to put your tilted-up camera 3 inches off the ground. The solution is of course to raise the ground. Have Mick stand on a platform, and measure your camera's height relative to the platform's surface.

In order to get the *nodal point* (black crosshairs) of your camera at a miniature height, you might need to raise the floor.

Matching Lighting

Of course, there's another important factor that makes the gigantic rock stars look like they belong in the Manhattan background plates, and that's lighting. It's crucial to match lighting between foregrounds and backgrounds, and it isn't all that complicated. The trick is that you don't have to get it exactly right. Get your key light coming from the right direction, get your fill level just right, and you're golden. If you watch the "Love Is Strong" video closely, you'll see some moments where buildings maybe should cast shadows on people but they don't or vice versa, but it doesn't really change your impression of the reality of the scene. Of course, you should do your best to match these things. Just know that if it looks right, it is right.

VIRTUAL GAFFER

Then there's the fine art of matching the lighting of a scene inside the computer. This used to be my job back at ILM—I'd get handed a background and a CG character animation take, and I would be tasked with lighting the character within the computer to match the scene.

Remember a few paragraphs ago when I said "reference is god"? There's no better example of this than in trying to match lighting. Documenting how real light hits a similar surface to the one you're trying to fake is the best leg up you could possibly give yourself when you're sitting in front of a computer weeks after you've forgotten all the details of principal photography.

This also reinforces the first thing mentioned in this chapter, which is that visual effects is as much a part of production as it is post. Since the DV Rebel is most likely both shooting the plates and creating the CG, she's already thinking about the kind of reference that might be useful later when staging the backgrounds.

On-set lighting reference has, in recent years, moved from something that is consulted when creating CG lighting to something that is directly used to create it. I'm talking about the infamous "chrome ball." If you haven't seen the chrome ball, then you've managed to stay blissfully far from the world of computer graphics. But even if you've seen it, you may not have a complete understanding of how it can be used in lighting CG objects and scenes. While I don't have the space to give you a complete how-to, I can give you an overview and some pointers.

The basic idea is that a mirrored sphere, believe it or not, reflects back to the camera not just 180 degrees of the world around it, but a full 360-degree view. Even objects directly behind the ball are visible reflected in the ball's surface. This means that clever computer programs can "unwrap" the reflected image and create a complete panorama of the scene.

This factoid works in conjunction with another cool trick, which is that you can combine a bunch of photographs taken at various exposures into one image that contains a faithful record of all the light in a scene, no matter how bright. Called HDRI, or High Dynamic Range Imagery, this technique overcomes the limitations of today's digital cameras, which tend to allow bright highlights to blow out to flat fields of white. By merging several exposures into one HDR image, you create not only a really cool image that can actually be exposed up and down like a real scene, but also a lighting map that can be used by 3D software to light a scene. If this sounds like the coolest thing ever, it's because it just about is.

There are as many handy online tutorials for HDR lighting as there are 3D programs, so I'll leave you to your Googling, but only after a few handy tips for recording HDR on the set:

- Tip #1: The mirrored balls most people use are "gazing balls" from garden stores. They are big, beautiful, and very fragile. Skip 'em.

What sound does a glass "gazing ball" make when snugly tightened into a C-stand clamp? Answer: "Crunch."

- Tip #2: For most HDR work, you don't want a super high-detailed image. So a steel ball bearing an inch or two across is just as good as a gazing ball.

If I can't get the high score at pinball then nobody can!

- Tip #3: Use the shutter of your camera, not the aperture, to bracket the exposures. Software exists that automates this process for many cameras, as long as you're willing to tether the camera to a laptop.

- Tip #4: Use a tripod and mount the ball securely. This way you don't need to realign the images before merging them.

- Tip #5: Photoshop CS2 introduced a Merge to HDR option that does a decent job of creating an HDR from bracketed photos. But unwrapping the spheres into usable lighting maps still requires specialized software such as HDRShop, version 1 of which is available for noncommercial use from hdrshop.com (Windows only), or Photosphere (anyhere.com, Mac only).

- Tip #6: Scale the HDR lighting map down to a small size, like 64 × 32 pixels, before using it in your 3D software. You'll remove a lot of detail in the process, but this is a good thing. Most ray-traced renderers respond to all that detail in light maps by creating noise. Save the high-res light map for reflections.

- Tip #7: Remember that using HDR lighting doesn't take the art out of the process. You still need to use your eye to tell you if the shot looks right or not. Computer graphics for film has never been, and will never be, a by-the-numbers exercise.

The Blue Screen of Death

A necessary evil: the bluescreen.

The bluescreen. So synonymous with visual effects is the mighty cobalt backdrop that you'll actually hear people use "bluescreen" as a verb, as in, "you can just bluescreen that in later, right?" The same thing applies to the sister of the bluescreen, the greenscreen. Together they are seen as the panacea of post, the enabler of visual effects, and a prerequisite for perfect composites.

Nothing could be further from the truth. I hate greenscreens and bluescreens. They contribute to bad-looking visual effects under the best of circumstances, and those of us using consumer digital video equipment are actually in the worst possible situation for taking advantage of green-screen's few appropriate uses.

And yet, begrudgingly, I must admit that sometimes there is no other choice but to join the crowd and shoot against one of these ubiquitous backdrops.

WHY YOU SHOULD NOT SHOOT BLUE/GREENSCREEN

If the above diatribe has you envisioning the author being abused by a greenscreen as a child, you wouldn't be that far from the truth. I've been doing visual effects professionally since child labor laws would allow, and in that time I've seen nothing but confusion and misinformation surrounding green- and bluescreens.

I blame *Forrest Gump*. We all saw *Forrest Gump* and were blown away by all the amazing visual effects: the insertion of Tom Hanks into historical footage, the vivid period reconstructions, and the removal of Gary Sinise's legs.

So revolutionary were these effects at the time that the TV news did stories on them. People all across the world saw before-and-after shots of Sinise with his blue stockings on, and then with miraculously amputated legs. Suddenly, everyone from my grandmother to my letter carrier knew that blue things magically disappear when they get near a computer.

Now this common knowledge permeates every movie set. No one need know anything more about visual effects than "green things go away." If a prop or setpiece has anything to do with visual effects, ten people will immediately pounce on it and paint it green.

There are two big problems with this. First of all, green isn't such a great color for props or rigging that need to be removed. It's a bright, unique color, and it has a way of reflecting its light onto nearby surfaces. Anything near a green stocking will have a greenish cast to it, a cast that will need to be color corrected away.

A more insidious disadvantage of green stuff is that it makes people stupid. People who don't understand visual effects will assume that simply because something is green, it will go away all by itself in post—even if it's directly in front of something really important, like an actor's face.

The alleged benefit of painting things green is that a visual effects artist could extract the green using keying software, making the removal process easy and saving the labor-intensive process of rotoscoping, or tracing mattes by hand. But this is a myth. Those blue stockings on Gary Sinise's legs become every color but blue on film. They have bright highlights and deep, black shadows. Every single frame of those legs needed to be rotoscoped—almost no procedural extraction was done. Had the stockings been gray or black, the job would have been much easier, since no nasty blue spill cleanup would have been necessary for the adjacent surfaces.

Even under the best of circumstances, with a perfectly lit foreground and clean, well-exposed greenscreen, keying is still an imprecise science. Computers don't know the difference between a pixel that's greenish-pink because it's a blemish on the backing and one that's greenish-pink because it's a hand motion-blurring over a greenscreen. That keying works at all is a minor miracle, but even when it works well, it's not perfect.

The truth is, a little roto is a good thing. A lot is bad, but a little is great. You'll wind up doing it anyway. And when you shoot a view out a car window, for example, shooting against black instead of green allows easy recovery of reflections and other lighting details that make the shot look real.

HOW TO SHOOT BLUE/GREENSCREEN

Having said all that, there are times when blue/greenscreen is necessary. Most of the time, the thing that pushes me away from black and toward green is hair. You don't want to roto hair. Nor do you want to roto a full-body character running and jumping around for hundreds of frames.

So greenscreen is occasionally necessary. There, I said it. Now, let's talk about how to do it.

The key is that you need to keep the screen far, far away from your actors or sets or whatever it is you're shooting in front of it. This is to avoid that bounced green or blue light that we call *spill*.

However, not all spill is bad. Some traces of your greenscreen look like spill but are in fact reflections, which are great records of where your foreground element should be reflecting some of the background color.

Four easy steps to put your dog on Mars. At the far left, the original photography reveals ample blue spill on the seat. If you work around that spill and suppress it, you get the first comp (second from left), which looks flat and fake. The next image shows the spill extracted as a separate step. Using that matte, I added background color back in to the composite to create the realistic image on the right.

Use as small a screen as you can get away with. "Wing in" a small screen just behind the area you need. A perfect example of this can be found on the behind-the-scenes DVD material of the 1998 movie *The X Files*. As David Duchovny approaches the bombed-out building, visual effects supervisor Mat Beck placed a small bluescreen just where Duchovny's head would cross over the building, and nowhere else. Brilliant.

There are no technical advantages to green over blue for digital video. The myth is that, since green is the channel with the most detail in it (that part is true), you'll get a better extraction than you would from blue. But in truth all color keys are based on comparing the differences between the various channels, so blue and red factor just as much into a greenscreen matte as does green. Choose your backing color based on the characters' wardrobe. Got blue jeans? Use green. Making a Godzilla movie? Use blue. Look out for actors' eye colors, as well as hair. Wispy blonde hair keys better on blue than on green, but Caucasian skin tones suffer more under simple green spill suppression than blue.

When extracting using your keying software of choice, do not expect to get a perfect key with one simple application of the plug-in. You will need to combine multiple keys to get good results. At the very least, expect to create an edge matte and a core matte.

An edge and a core matte were required to preserve both the reflections in the glass and the furry edges of the talent, while avoiding the blue reflections on the black shiny surfaces.

DV, DVCPROHD, and HDV all decimate color information in their compression processes. In Chapter 6, I describe in detail how to recover lost color information without the use of any third-party plug-ins. You'll want to do this before you apply your keying plug-in.

If you're setting up to key a car interior, keep the windows clean or rolled down. Then sandwich in a light layer of window dirt between the car and the background. This will be much easier than keying through all that schmutz.

If you have any camera movement at all, place tracking markers on the screen.

DV is tricky to key due to chroma subsampling, an artifact you'll learn how to combat in Chapter 6.

Most of the bad bluescreen shots you've seen are that way at least partially because the background is moving separately from the foreground.
Markers on the screen tell you how to track in the background believ-
ably, as well as other useful things like how out-of-focus the background
should be.

Tracking markers made from one-inch tape will save your butt when your camera
moves.

The world is full of free blue and greenscreens. If you live near an Ikea
store, you live near a bluescreen. As you drive around your 'hood, keep
your eyes peeled for blue or green walls facing parking lots.

On this street in Emeryville, California, a free greenscreen is only two doors down
from a free bluescreen! I actually used that blue building at the end of the street for
the examples in this section.

Miniatures

There was a time when visual effects and miniatures went hand in hand. Whether you were creating a flying DeLorean, an evil castle, or even a bloodthirsty monster, you were working with miniatures. Although much of that kind of work has gone to computer graphics lately, there's still a significant amount of miniature work in major Hollywood movies. Miniatures look great and do certain things, such as explode or collapse, better than their computer-generated brethren. Even when miniatures don't look 100% real, they still look real in the sense that they have a real physical presence, whereas when CG falls short it loses all corporeal credibility.

Note the perplexed look on my face as I actually touch a visual effects element.

While some of the large-scale miniatures from films like the *Lord of the Rings* trilogy and *Titanic* require a huge budget and legions of skilled craftspeople, there's plenty of miniature work that is well within the means of the DV Rebel. While few of us will ever become journeyman 3D artists capable of creating a photorealistic image from scratch in Maya, most people find X-Acto knives and paint brushes approachable if not downright fun. And as if this wasn't enough temptation to put down the mouse in favor of the model glue, there are some high-end toys that look pretty good right out of the box.

Scale

The single greatest determining factor in whether or not a miniature looks real is its scale. The scale of a miniature is expressed with two numbers that represent, in one way of looking at things, how many of the miniatures you need to line up to measure the real thing. So a 1:18 scale model is 1/18 the length of its real-world counterpart.

If your miniature is 1:12 scale, that means it would take 12 of them lined up to measure the same as the real world object.

Walk into any hobby shop and you'll discover that there are several standard scales. Your Dad's HO train set in the basement is 1:87 scale. Those big, fancy dollhouses that take up half a kid's room are 1:12 scale. It's difficult to find a rule of thumb about how small is too small to look real on screen. While a 1:12 scale battleship might look just barely credible in the water, an evil starship might need to be 1:1000 scale just to fit through the stage door.

Speed

Godzilla, depending on the film, stands about 164 feet tall. The guy in the Godzilla suit is about 5-foot-5 inches tall. If Godzilla were to pick up a Tokyo subway car and drop it from head height, it would take over 3 seconds to crash to the street below. But if the guy in the Godzilla suit drops a model train car 5 feet, it will hit the ground only half a second later. Gravity, it would seem, is unwilling to cooperate with your need to make monster movies.

For this annoying reason, miniature photography is almost always overcranked. And if you sense more math coming, you are correct—there's a formula for how fast you need to run film through a camera so that when you play back footage of Godzilla chucking train cars around, they fall at a realistic speed.

Since I noticed that you didn't pick up the book for a week after the last time I subjected you to mathematical formula, I'll simply direct your attention to the Excel document (**miniatureFPScale_2.xls**) in the Calculators folder on the included DVD.

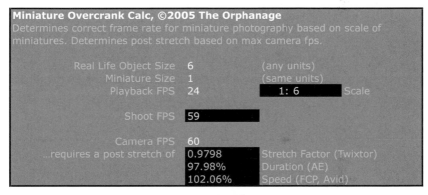

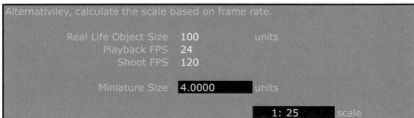

This Excel calculator, included on the DVD at the back of the book, tells you the frame rates for shooting your miniatures. Remember, should you find Excel evil, this file can also be opened in Google Spreadsheets.

You can enter the actual sizes of your miniature and the object it represents, or just enter the scale if you know it by using 1 for the Miniature Size and the number on the other side of the colon for the Real Life Object Size. Check the scale field (in yellow) to ensure you entered the correct values.

So, for example, if you had a 1:18 model, you'd need to shoot it at 102 frames per second for it to look real when played back at 24p.

"Great," you say, "but my camera only goes up to 60 frames per second." We love you, digital video, but overcrank excessively you do not. Luckily there's a field in the Excel thingy called Camera FPS, and you will note that it defaults to 60. This maximum value is used to calculate the speed change values below it. So if you shoot your 1:18 scale miniature at 60 fps, you will have to stretch it to 170% in After Effects, preferably with Pixel Motion frame blending turned on, in order for your trains to fall on time.

It's at this point that I should mention that the formula used in this spreadsheet, while sizzlingly accurate, is widely regarded by industry veterans as a rule of thumb only. Most visual effects supervisors start with the math, shoot some tests, and then use whatever frame rate looks best to them. This is why they're visual effects supervisors and not NASA engineers or cardio-thoracic surgeons. So if, say, you have a 1:10 miniature, you may well get away without performing the 126% stretch in After Effects—your 60 fps footage might look just fine played back at 24p (following the overcranking method from Chapter 3). Or it could require a 200% stretch—only your gut can tell you.

Another way to explore the possibility of using miniatures is with the lower portion of the Excel calculator. Here you can enter the maximum frame rate of your fastest camera and derive the scale from there. As you'll see, the ideal scale for 60 fps is about 1:6. As such, for those of us in NTSC countries, 1:6 represents an ideal miniature scale. Although 1:6 miniatures and toys are rare, when you do find them they usually look great. Google around a bit and you'll find some amazing model military tanks, for example, crafted by hand in 1:6 scale. Often the builders of these beasts are delighted to hear from an Internet fan who wants to feature their hard work in a film project.

Remember, the overcranking rule only applies if your miniature is actually doing something like falling or swinging or exploding. If your miniature is just sitting there, you may not need to overcrank at all. And often just sitting there is all they have to do.

Hanging Foreground Miniatures

One of the best things about working with models is that you can some-times get a completed visual effects shot entirely in-camera, without any post work. One of the coolest ways to pull this off is with a hanging foreground miniature.

A $30 visual effect and worth every penny—the "hanging" foreground miniature.

There's a hysterical shot in *Top Secret* where a military officer steps forward to answer a ringing phone. Only when he grabs the handset do you realize that the phone is huge. Right up until the moment he touches it the illusion is that the phone is normal size. The gag works both because we have certain expectations of how big a phone is and because, as I mentioned in the "Matching Cameras" section, there's no difference in how a camera sees a large object and a small one. The same rules of perspective apply.

In other words, a 1:12 scale model placed 1 foot from a camera will look exactly like the full-sized object at 12 feet away. What this means is that you can actually line up a miniature that is very close to the camera to look as though it occupies a scene many feet away. As long as you can keep both the model and the background in focus, you can have a con-vincing scene in which people and other full-scale items appear to stand right next to your miniature! You're effectively doing both setups from the "Love Is Strong" foreground/background example at once.

To create the example on the previous page I bought a 1:48 scale toy Black Hawk helicopter online for $30 including shipping. I took it out to an open area and set up the following arrangement:

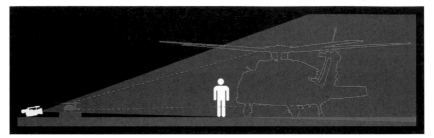

The side view of a hanging foreground miniature shoot. The outline shows where the 1:48 scale toy helicopter will appear to be—exactly 48 times as far from the camera as the toy.

The trickiest aspect of this kind of shot is lining up the camera and the model. The tiniest change in camera or model height will wildly throw off the apparent depth of the helicopter. If I were to boom the camera down only 1 centimeter the helicopter would appear to rise in the frame and would suddenly seem way too big and far away. Lower the helicopter a hair and it instantly appears too small for the car parked alongside it.

Lining up the camera for the foreground miniature effect.

The only rule to guide you is that the miniature should be the correct scale distance from the nodal point of your lens. In my case, the model was about 8 inches from the nodal point, which makes the helicopter appear to be 32 feet away (8″ × 48′). After that, you can measure to find a point on the ground that is 32 feet away and then line up the model vertically so it appears to sit on that point.

Once you have this setup, you will have the distinct pleasure of watching your completed visual effects shot live, through your viewfinder. This is especially handy if you want to make it look as though people are interacting with the model, because you will need to guide your actors to cast their gazes into the empty air where the miniature appears to be.

So why is it called a *hanging* foreground miniature? Often the miniature must be suspended in some awkward way in front of the camera, especially for a high angle looking down. There are some impressive alien landscape shots done this way in *Dune*. In recent cinema, some of the best use of foreground miniatures has been in *The Lord of the Rings: The Fellowship of the Ring*. Many of the shots featuring hobbits interacting with full-sized people were executed in-camera using miniature foreground sets correctly aligned with a full-scale background.

A foreground miniature is a fragile setup that only works within a limited set of circumstances. But with planning, it's a finished effects shot right out of the camera!

This all might sound like a lot of work, but all told this helicopter example cost me $30 and took about an hour to complete, a feat that no CG effects shot could easily claim!

Using miniatures and in-camera techniques doesn't mean that you can't use any computer effects at all. Sometimes a simple composite can make a miniature shot sing. For example, I took that same helicopter model and lined it up on a small platform so that it appeared to have landed on an industrial building.

Upper left: Placing the 1:48 scale miniature on a small platform inches from the camera. Lower right: Removing the platform for the clean plate. Lower left: The matte generated from the blue sky in the clean plate. Upper right: A shadow matte traced around the toy's shadow on the platform.

Of course the platform was in full view, but once I had the helicopter element shot, I simply removed the platform to record a pass of just the building. In After Effects I used Keylight to key out the sky from the clean pass and composited the building back on top of itself, hiding the platform on which the miniature rested. Best of all, the shadows that the model cast on the platform provided the perfect reference for the helicopter's shadow on the building.

In the completed shot, the helicopter appears to rest atop the building. The spinning blades were shot at 60i and slow-mo'd to 24p using the overcrank technique from Chapter 3.

Cleveland for Paris

Matte paintings. The very term conjures up nostalgic images of Michael Pangrazio dabbing paint onto a giant pane of glass. Imagine my shock when working with Michael on *Sin City*—today he uses Photoshop, just like the rest of us. Matte paintings have slowly morphed into a larger category that is sometimes called *digital environments*. They're no longer so different in technique than other visual effects, or at least they don't have to be.

Matte Paintings for Nonpainters

Not many people can sit down with some brushes and paint—or a Wacom tablet—and create a photorealistic scene from scratch, but that doesn't mean you can't use digital environments in your films. The truth is, few digital matte artists (as they are still sometimes called) paint their way to success one brush stroke at a time. Matte paintings these days, for better or worse, tend to be artful collages of photography, stolen bits of media, reprojected plates, and some clever compositing to tie it all together.

Copy Paste

Earlier in this chapter I mentioned that I used a digital backdrop to make a *Last Birthday Card* location look like San Francisco instead of Oakland. This is a perfect example of a "matte painting" that required no painting. There are a couple of others as well. That same location was a state gov-

ernment building; a sign out front proudly proclaimed "State of California." I digitally replaced that sign with the name of the architectural firm in the film.

Another "painting" became necessary when I could not secure permission to shoot on the Golden Gate Bridge. In particular, for my all-important lines of action, I needed to shoot from the West sidewalk, usually closed to pedestrians. What I did was to steal the shot I needed from the East sidewalk, and add a digital image of the Marin Headlands to the background.

A 2-minute matte painting of the Marin Headlands turned this south-facing plate (left) into a north-facing shot (right). The final touch was to remove the telltale tourists.

If you'd like to use this technique as a method for simulating an exotic location, all you need is a good image to steal. Luckily for you, there's Stock.XCHNG (www.sxc.hu). Stock.XCHNG is an online stock photo service, and it is free as long as you play by the rules. The rules include uploading some of your own photography to give away—it's like karma-based stock photography. For the DV Rebel, though, it's a free library of digital backlots.

A Stock.XCHNG pyramid photo (middle, by Andrea De Stefani) turns a bluff into an otherwise expensive Egyptian location shot. (Desert conversation photo by Mira Pavlakovic.)

Virtual Worlds

Another cool way to create digital environments is with dedicated "virtual world" software. Certain 3D applications have focused their efforts on generating realistic landscapes from nothing but a ton of math, and in recent years these systems have become realistic enough that they've seen use in some big movies.

A very capable example is e-on software's Vue series (e-onsoftware. com). Available in a range of pricing options, Vue allows you to create spectacular vistas that you can fly through, animate, and even integrate with other 3D projects.

On the free side, there's Terragen (planetside.co.uk/terragen). While not as deluxe as Vue, it's free, so you can download it and play with it as you wish, and decide for yourself if it's up to the task of creating that opening shot for your desert island adventure.

Both Terragen and Vue are available for Mac and Windows.

POV Shots

I don't know why, but action films seem to require unique POV shots. Whether it's "Terminator vision" or the fluid perspective of an animate water tentacle, at some point you'll find yourself needing a cool post treatment for some POV shots. *On the DVD, in the supplemental material for this chapter (**Chapter4/POV.pdf**), you'll find some tricks to try for three common types of POVs.*

The Scope template project on the included DVD allows the easy creation of that all-important sniper POV shot.

Guns Guns Guns!

Your film has a gun in it. Probably several. And finally, at long last, you are reading a book that will not try to persuade you that this is a bad idea.

Action movies and guns go hand in hand.

A Little About Real Guns

Most of the guns that you see in movies are real, working firearms that have been modified for film use. When they are fired, you are seeing specially prepared blanks being discharged. Due to a small number of tragic accidents on film sets, most people have been cured of the belief that blanks are harmless. In truth, they are extremely dangerous. They are also loud, meaning that they are impossible to use in a "creative permitting" situation. They absolutely must be handled and supervised by a trained professional, and they require special permits and insurance. For all of these reasons, the DV Rebel is better off avoiding real guns.

There are numerous other options, and with varying degrees of post-production manipulation, they can look as good as the real thing. All enjoy the benefit of being cheaper and safer than the real thing.

What Guns Do

*For a detailed description of how real guns work, including pretty pictures, see the supplement to this chapter on the included DVD (**Chapter 4/Guns. pdf**). There you will also find a bit about the electric gun, a film-industry alternative to using blank-firing guns.*

Blank-Firing Replicas

There are some fairly realistic blank-firing replicas of well-known automatic pistols available by mail order. I used two of these on *The Last Birthday Card* for Scott's signature pair of Beretta 92FS pistols. But I did not ever fire a single one of the 8mm blanks that came with the guns.

Although they must be treated with all the respect of any firearm or pyro effect, these replicas are pretty darn safe—principally because they have no barrel. The body is cast from a solid piece of metal, and the muzzle opening in the front is shallow and not connected at all to the chamber.

This important safety feature is, unfortunately, the Achilles heel of this otherwise ideal movie gun. When you fire it, the 8mm blank discharges as would occur with a real gun. But since there is no barrel, the exploding gas emits out of a hole on the top of the chamber—a hole that the real gun obviously does not have. In other words, there's no muzzle flash. You get the kick, the smoke, and you certainly get the sound, but no muzzle flash.

Did I mention the sound? These things are *loud,* every bit as loud as a real gun. The sound that blanks make is not only an impediment to creative location usage (the one time Scott fires his Beretta in *Last Birthday Card* is in a San Francisco hotel room, the status of our permission to shoot in which is left to the imagination of the reader), it is a legitimate safety hazard. You would not want to spend time at your local firing range without hearing protection, and the same holds true for film sets with blanks being fired. Actors must wear "invisible" hearing protection when performing in a scene with live fire. Just what you want, your star running around with a loaded gun, unable to hear you scream "cut!"

You might put up with some of this under the right conditions, but only if you were getting a badass muzzle flash out of the deal. Consider the blank-firing replicas a great option for a realistic-looking pistol that doesn't need to fire.

Toys & BB Guns

There was a time when toy guns could be mistaken for the real thing. A plastic cap gun would be black or silver, not red or green. Again, time and tragedy punishes the low-budget filmmaker, and maybe for good reason. Plastic guns now look fake because it keeps kids from getting shot. Reasonable enough.

You can paint a toy gun black and be off to the races, but you're still going to have a nonfunctioning prop that can't survive a close-up. Let's pause for a moment and discuss the broader strategy for guns in the low-budget action film.

Your guns may be worn, brandished, fired, reloaded, thrown, swallowed, or baked into a cake. The prop you require will vary depending on the on-screen requirements for your gun. A painted plastic toy might suffice for a brief appearance at a distance. If you need to see your gun go boom, you are looking at some digital effects. A muzzle flash and maybe a hint of an ejecting shell are about to be easy effects for you to create (stay tuned!). So let's consider the ideal working gun prop, one that does everything detailed on the book's DVD (*see the supplement—"What Guns Do"—to this chapter on the included DVD*) short of create a flash and eject a shell.

THANK GOD FOR JAPAN

I'm going to tell you how to get this ideal gun prop for $40. Hold the applause, though, because in doing so I will expose you to the option to spend a little more and get an even better gun prop, and before you know it you might have what I call an *Airsoft problem*.

What's Airsoft? *Airsoft* is a delightful Japanglish term for a type of BB gun that fires a (relatively speaking) soft, plastic BB using some form of compressed gas. In Japan, real guns are so rare that these BB guns (notice that I am not referring to them as toys) are able to take the form of highly realistic replicas of actual firearms. Being Japanese, the degree of realism is astounding, and through some glorious loophole in international copyright law, they bear all the logos and markings of their real-life counterparts.

Airsoft guns are meticulous Japanese replicas of real firearms. Shown here is a Tokyo Marui replica of the FN P90—street price about $210.

SPRING GUNS

There are four types of Airsoft guns that interest us. Least expensive are the spring guns. These fire a single shot at a time, and you cock them manually to generate the compressed air that expels the BB. The firing action isn't of any use to us, but they make great static props. A submachine gun, which has very little external physical animation when fired, can be doubled well by a spring gun (and an enthusiastic actor). "Springers," as they are dorkily called, range from $20 to $75 and more.

This spring gun cost me only $40 on sale from a U.S. dealer. It doesn't look nearly as nice as the expensive auto-electric guns, but it would survive a longer shot with a little black spray paint on that muzzle.

Springers can be totally realistic on the screen, but one good trick is to find some way to add weight to them. Fill them with fishing weights or pennies or something—anything to make them heavier. Audiences can tell just by the body language of your actors how much a prop actually weighs.

ELECTRIC GUNS

Next up are electric guns. These use electric motors to compress air to eject the BBs, and can therefore be fully automatic. There are electric Airsoft pistols that have a lovely blowback action on their lightweight, plastic slides. They go for about $40 and run on standard batteries.

AUTO-ELECTRIC GUNS

There are electric submachine guns as well. These full-auto beasts (known as AEGs, for "Auto-Electric Gun") look much more realistic than their springer counterparts, since they are made from top-quality plastic and often have metal parts where appropriate. I used AEGs in *Birthday Card* for Scott's sniper rifle (a Steyr Aug) and Nak's briefcase-enclosed MP5 PDW. Expect to pay top dollar for these replicas—$200 to $300.

GAS BLOWBACK GUNS

Also expensive and alarmingly realistic are gas blowback (GBB) Airsoft guns. These are most often automatic pistols, and they have a look, feel, and blowback action that vastly exceeds the electric blowback models. They operate on compressed gas and cost a couple hundred bucks or more. GBB pistols are the ultimate DV Rebel gun prop.

So while a $40 BB gun that answers all of our needs exists, you have now been exposed to the tantalizing world of Airsoft, which can become for action film guys what Manolo Blahniks are for Sarah Jessica Parker's character in *Sex in the City*. Still, a gas blowback Airsoft with gas and shipping can cost less than a week of renting an electric gun. And between you and me, they are kind of fun to play with in their actual intended role as the bane of stacked Styrofoam cups everywhere. Before you know it you may be an Airsoft *Otaku,* the Japanese word for a chronically obsessed hobbyist!

The prop on the left is a $40 plastic spring Airsoft gun. On the right is a gas (GBB) Airsoft with a metal slide, realistic blowback action, and a price tag in the hundreds. In person you can easily tell which one's the big-ticket toy, but on video the difference is harder to spot.

GUNS FROM THE FUTURE

There are kits available that convert Airsoft guns into popular science-fiction gun designs. For example, Robocop's gun is a modified Beretta 93R, and that modification is available in Airsoft. The gun pictured below is the "Seburo" from the Manga series Appleseed, and I bought it on eBay (in slightly beat-up shape) for less than the price of the working gun inside it.

This futuristic-looking gun is a model kit assembled over an Airsoft gun.

GREEN PLASTIC GUNS

Mere paragraphs ago I lamented that toy guns have come to look nothing like the real thing, bedecked in neon plastic colors rather than silver or black. But there is a way to turn this disadvantage into an asset—as long as you are willing to get arrested and possibly shot.

As you can imagine, this is another opportunity for a little disclaimer. I don't recommend trying the Green Gun technique. I describe it here merely for your entertainment, and that you may chuckle at the author's commitment to guerrilla filmmaking to the exclusion of all sanity.

Would you call the cops if someone ran by your Chinatown souvenir store waving one of these? I decided to find out the hard way.

Every year, San Francisco's Chinatown holds a massive street fair to celebrate the Moon Festival, one of the biggest Chinese holidays. One year I decided that it would be really smart to shoot a foot chase amidst the crowds at this fair without a permit or a crew.

My plan was to have my actors shove their way through the actual crowds, wielding green plastic guns. I would then digitally color-correct the guns black in post. I reasoned that the festivalgoers would react to the guns, but would recognize after a moment that they were plastic and not call the cops.

Actor Mike Murnane brandishes a green plastic gun in a crowded Chinatown street as onlookers provide exactly the reactions I'd hoped for. Footage from this project can be found on the book's DVD, and you will color correct this project yourself in the onlining tutorial in Chapter 6.

As it turns out, I was right—but I hold this as a prime example of the unique demands that truly guerrilla film production places on the on-screen talent!

Unfortunately, for the reasons mentioned in the section on blue/greenscreens, it's not easy to color-correct a green gun black. It's not impossible, it's just not as automatic as I'd hoped. Footage from the green gun project makes up the mini-movie you'll work with in Chapter 6, so you can see for yourself how well it worked!

Digital Ordnance

The success of your low-budget artillery lies in the artful blending of well-chosen prop guns and a bit of compositing in post. The elements you'll be adding digitally are muzzle flashes, smoke, and ejecting shells. Only the first one is mandatory, and that is usually a one-frame event, so the compositing demands of gunfire arc pretty low.

To make things easier on you, the DVD included with this book features a template project that will generate an infinite supply of muzzle flashes based on rough paint strokes you provide. More on that in just a bit.

First let's talk about "brass," the gun-guy term for the casings left behind when the bullet leaves the building. Many filmmakers contemplating sidestepping the blank-firing gun route are concerned about the lack of ejecting shells in their shots. In truth, brass often flies out of the ejection port so fast that a film shutter barely catches it. When you do see the flying shell, it's often just a blur.

Of course, there are shots in films where the brass streaming out of a machine gun is a featured element. These shots are often in slow motion and found in films that are taken to task for being too "celebratory" of their violence. You may have trouble creating this shot, but then again your film might be better off without it.

What works just as well is to create the spent shells using editing. A shot you can easily accomplish is an insert of shells hitting the ground. You can find spent shells at any shooting range. They won't be free for the taking—ranges are able to sell them back to ammunition manufacturers to be recycled. Explain to the nice man behind the counter full of real guns that you just need a handful or two and you'd like to give him a Special Thanks or Executive Producer credit in your film. I find it particularly worthwhile to be polite around people who sell guns for a living.

The DV Rebel may want to keep a handful of spent brass around to dump on the ground for the all-important slow-mo shells bouncing around shots. Those are 9mm on the left, and .45 calibre on the right.

It is not the easiest thing to add ejecting shells into a shot in post, but if you simply must have brass in a shot that you didn't shoot an element for, you can synthesize some in the compositing environment. How do you create 3D spinning, flying shells in a compositing program? What I did for *Skate Warrior* was to pre-render a looping animation of a 9mm shell spinning in space. I then hand-animated this as a 2D element, tracing its trajectory from the ejection port. This was back in the days before After Effects had 3D and expressions, so this by-hand animation was painfully time-consuming.

Animating something flying through the air is a classic case where the path animation method favored by After Effects breaks down. What I really needed for this kind of animation was a particle system. After Effects ships with a couple of nice particle tools, but the effect that really does this job right is the amazing Particular from Trapcode. With Particular you can animate an emitter and assign a looping texture as the particle sprite. It's pretty much the perfect tool for the job of spewing out massive amounts of shells. But it's not so easy to use a system like this to emit particles one by one on specific frames, and I'm trying to avoid suggesting any solutions that require buying third-party plug-ins.

So, with a little help from my friends,[3] I built you a custom particle system in After Effects and crammed it into the same project that makes muzzle flashes automatically for you.

THE GUNFIRE PROJECT

On the included DVD, you'll find an After Effects template for creating muzzle flashes and ejecting shells. The how-to for this monster of a project is included in the supplemental material for this chapter (**Chapter4/Gunfire.pdf**).

The gunfire template project on the DVD turns simple Vector Paint brush strokes into detailed bursts of fire, and includes a complete particle system for ejecting shells.

MUZZLE MATTERS

When using the gunfire template project, you create the shape of your flashes by painting simple white blobs using the Vector Paint effect. The shape of the blob dictates the shape of the flash. Your entire DVD library is fair game as reference to guide you in this process. As I mentioned at

---

3 Anyone who's snooped around the online After Effects community should be familiar with the contributions of Dan Ebberts. Dan is one of those crazy people who deeply understands the dark recesses of After Effects' expressions capability—the feature where you can create little mini-scripts to drive parameters in the Timeline. Dan has always been very generous with his knowledge—a great example is the tutorial he published at www.creativecow.net on how to create your own particle system using After Effects 3D and expressions. My shell ejector project owes much to Dan's example.

the start of the chapter, reference is your trusty ally when navigating the murky waters of making something look real. In fact, reference is the only thing you can trust—what you really can't trust is your brain! In other words, you might think you know what a muzzle flash looks like, but actually your mental picture of a muzzle flash could be quite inaccurate.

For example, I've seen a lot of digital muzzle flashes that last longer than one frame. People seem to want to fade the flash out over one or two frames. But as you've learned, muzzle flashes last far less than 1/48 of a second. You're lucky to get one on film at all! So you should comp yours in for just one frame, and vary the intensities from one blast to the next to simulate the effect of the flashes occasionally slipping out of sync with the camera's shutter.

Many people advocate compositing muzzle flashes in as static elements, and in fact that's what I did for *Skate Warrior*. I had a library of a few flash elements that I recycled. But with some of the fancy new features in After Effects 7.0—most notably 32-bit floating point color, I can make a much smarter and more flexible muzzle flash system now than I ever could then. What to me is a dead giveaway of a digital muzzle flash is a static element comped in at a reduced opacity or faded off over a few frames. The muzzle flash system in the sample project is designed to prevent those issues.

Another thing to be aware of while looking at your reference material is the wide variety of muzzle flash shapes out there. Some are teardrops, others have giant spiky protrusions. How do you know which to use? The key lies in the muzzle itself.

Different gun muzzles produce different muzzle flash shapes, depending on how the exploding gases are shaped.

Each of these three guns has a different exit path for the gases exploding out of the barrel. On the left is an MPK, the pistol-like SMG that Neo (Keanu Reeves) made fashionable in *The Matrix*. Its barrel is unadorned and short, resulting in a bright and amorphous flash that represents the simplest muzzle flash option:

The next gun is the Styer Aug, the gun wielded with panache by Karl (Alexander Godunov) in *Die Hard*. Its barrel ends with a flash suppressor, one with a unique three-groove design. Those grooves actually shape the flash, and you can see this in *Die Hard* when Karl fires. The result is a sort of triangular shape to the flash:

Last up is the MP5 PDW. It's the same basic gun as the MPK, but with a folding stock and a flash suppressor with six notches. Each notch allows a little gas to come through, resulting in that super cool star pattern. Note that the star may change in intensity from one shot to the next, but it never changes orientation, since it's tied to the position of the gun:

The last thing I'll mention about muzzle flashes before someone suggests that I write a separate book on the subject is that you should match their exposure level to that of the scene. In a very dark scene, it stands to reason that the flashes would be among the brightest things in the shot, probably blowing out the exposure and reading as pure white shapes. But in a daylight scene the flashes may just barely read. Adjust your Flash Exposure slider in the Main Comp appropriately.

A muzzle flash in bright daylight should be less bright than one in an otherwise dark scene.

Handling the Guns, Handling the Gun Handlers

I've blathered on enough about guns that I feel I should clarify my position on them. Guns scare the crap out of me, and at least for the purposes of your filmmaking endeavors, it would do you well to feel the same. Even Airsoft guns should be treated with the ultimate caution and respect, on the set and off.

GIVE A SAFETY BRIEFING

At the start of any day that you'll be shooting with your gun props, call everyone together and give a quick overview of the events of the day. Explain that you'll be using gun props, and that while they are not real guns, you'll be treating them just as seriously as if they were. Show how the safeties, clips, and accessories work, and save time for questions at the end.

DESIGNATE A HANDLER

If at all possible, devote one crew member explicitly to wrangling the guns. At the call of "cut" this person should collect the props and store them in a safe place between setups.

HANDS OFF THE TRIGGER

The rule is, don't touch the trigger unless you're going to pull it. When carrying a gun, your finger should rest alongside the trigger guard. Show this to your actors and get them in this habit—it will have the side benefit of making them look more like pros.

LOAD ONLY WHEN NECESSARY

If you're using Airsoft or BB guns to create squib effects (as you'll read about in a bit), make sure you only load them immediately preceding a take and unload them immediately afterward.

Have your actors follow proper gun protocol and keep their fingers away from the trigger until they actually intend to fire.

NO GOOFING AROUND

Making movies is fun, and making action movies is the kind of fun that allows people to live out their fantasies of being their favorite action hero. But playing around with toy guns can be dangerous in many ways, from potential injury to arrest. If you take this stuff seriously your crew will too. Set the proper tone and have a safe and fun set.

Guns Shoot Things

Faking realistic firearms, muzzle flashes, and shells is only half the gun-fight equation. What happens when things (or people) in your film need to get shot? On a "real" movie, bullet impacts, or *hits* are usually effected with the use of pyrotechnic charges called *squibs*. Squibs can be strapped to actors and layered under blood packs to create bullet hits on a person, or they can be wired into walls, props, or dirt—pretty much any semi-destructible surface.

The other popular way of creating bullet hits is with an air gun shooting a sort of modified paintball. The gun is almost identical to a paintball gun, but the rounds it fires are not filled with paint. Instead they are rigid and brittle little orbs that pop open like those plastic domes that vending-machine toys come in. Inside, the effects technician will either load a fine dust-like dirt or a mixture of magnesium and zirconium. The dust balls create a nice little poof of dust when they impact, and the zirconium rounds, called *zirc hits,* actually make sparks on impact. Most of the time when you see sparking bullet hits ricocheting off of concrete or metal surfaces, these are zirc hits fired from an air gun.

Squibs and zirc hits fall neatly into that category of effects that some low-budget filmmakers will attempt on their modest budgets and varying levels of experience. But not the DV Rebel. Squib crafting is a time vortex that I've seen too many friends disappear down, and the results of their efforts always scare me. Homemade squibs and Zirc hits are dangerous, expensive, and unreliable.

But don't think that the DV Rebel approach will be all digital either. There are some safe and effective ways of getting ballistic mayhem on your shoot that, when used in combination with judicious digital enhancements, can create a very exciting shootout scene safely and cheaply.

Light Fuse and Get Away

If you live in or near an area where fireworks are legal, you can stock up on that childhood favorite, the firecracker. While not exactly "safe," firecrackers are one of the safest unsafe squib alternatives out there.

Photo by Dain Hubley.

The thing is, you can't time them (their fuses are unreliable) and you don't want to be near them when they go off, so reserve these for shots that don't have actors in them. They're perfect for an insert of a bullet hitting a flowerpot or a bowl of cereal. Put them under something that will react to the blast and give you more bang for your buck.

I recommend lighting the fuses on these things with a long match or one of those fireplace lighters with the long neck. One out of every 50 or so of these things seems to have a lightning-fast fuse!

BB Guns

Along the same lines of the firecracker is another semi-safe solution that only works when there are no people in the shot: Shoot stuff with a BB gun.

Flip back to the introduction to see this approach combined with the delightful fragility of breakaway glassware in *The Last Birthday Card*. To show Scott's apartment getting riddled with bullets from the helicopter's Gatling guns, I lined up breakaway glass bottles and pint glasses and picked them off with my trusty CO_2-powered BB gun. Not the gentle little Airsoft one, but the good old American one that shoots the tiny metal BBs. These guns will put a BB through a full can of soda,[4] a technique I utilized in *Skate Warrior* (shake the can first for maximum effect, of course).

As the soda can proves, you don't need expensive breakaway props to pull off this effect. Lots of things react well to BBs, such as balloons, dirt, water, cheap glassware from a thrift store, and, unfortunately, the windows in Scotty's apartment.

Again, safety goggles and generally safe practices are important for this kind of thing. On *Skate Warrior* I had a BB ricochet off the dirt I was "squibbing" and hit one of my actors. He was, um, slightly unhappy about that. Clear the set before you BB the living hell out of it and reserve this trick for actor-free inserts.

---

4 It is with heartfelt apologies to my Minnesotan heritage that I refer here to carbonated, sugary beverages as "soda" rather than "pop." I've just been living in California for too long. Please don't kick my ass the next time you see me having breakfast at Bryant Lake Bowl.

Blood Hits

Blood hits in movies are not realistic. The explosive chest squib that sends blood and bits of shredded shirt flying is nothing like what really happens when bullets and people meet. But it is what your audience has come to expect, and so you may have to produce something along those lines should your script call for someone to get shot.

There's a cool Hollywood trick for bullet hits to the head that can be expanded into a safe and reliable blood hit under clothing. It's called a wire-pull gag, and it's cheap and fun.

Wire-pull gags are used when squibs cannot be used, for example when a bullet hit needs to happen on bare flesh. Skip to chapter 20 on your *Blade Runner* Director's Cut DVD and watch the demise of Leon. If you have a good player you can pause on the frame right before his forehead blows out and see a bit of blurred wire leading off-screen to the right. This is a piece of thin piano wire being used to yank a plug out of a built-up mound of mortician's wax and makeup on actor Brion James's head. The force of the plug pulling out creates the violent appearance of the wound, which is simply stage blood and more wax under the plug.

You can do the same thing with a zip-lock bag of blood under a shirt if you practice and experiment. Tape down the bag (maybe to a form-fitting undergarment rather than the actor's skin) and Superglue a wide button to the surface. Run a wire from the button out through some fine slits in the garment and to the end of a broom handle. Using a lever like this to help you yank the wire is the key to getting some good velocity, as you can swing that broom handle harder than you could ever tug the wire directly. Good old physics.

The key to success here lies in the prescoring of the garment to be squibbed. Don't expect the force of the yanking to break the fabric—define how you want the fabric to give way by gently running a razor blade across it several times until it's barely holding itself together. I hasten to point out that this should be done before the garment is placed on the talent.

This technique requires some experimenting and some willingness to make a mess, but the results can be worth it. And unlike the filmmakers of

1982, you'll be able to digitally paint out any part of the wire that's visible before the yank!

Squib That Which Is Squibable

With all of these homebrew solutions, you must give thought to what on your set you would like your missed rounds to hit. If it's a person, you set yourself up for more success with light-colored wardrobe that's cheap and easy to replenish. With bullet hits on props and set pieces, you'll get more visually pleasing results if you squib something fragile and light-weight than if you simply tape a firecracker to a metal pole. Watch the amazing tearoom shootout in John Woo's seminal *Hard Boiled* (Criterion DVD Chapter 3). You'll notice that every squib seems to be set under a stack of napkins or a deck of playing cards. The debris from these charges hangs in the air much longer than heavier material would, increasing the on-screen mayhem and making the most of each squib, even ones that detonate off-frame or before the shot begins.

52 Card Pickup

In fact, so inspired by this observation was I that I implemented a pyro-free variation on it for the helicopter scene in *The Last Birthday Card*. At the call of action, my producer Jacqui and my crew-of-one Dav Rauch would each throw into the air one pile of 3-by-5 index cards and one handful of broken plaster mixed with scraps of breakaway glass. For some takes we'd even toss a whole sheet of breakaway glass at the ceiling of the apartment, where it would shatter and rain down onto poor Scotty. After each take we'd sweep up all that debris and dump it into buckets from which future handfuls would be procured. Everyone but Scott (sorry, buddy) wore safety goggles and stylish bandanas during this process, and although we made quite a mess we had a great time and produced dynamic on-screen results. The key lies in always having something going on in the frame—it doesn't even matter what. Why would stacks of index cards be sitting around in Scott's apartment, much less a Hong Kong teahouse? Who cares—just fill your frame with motion and mayhem and you'll have an action-packed shootout scene, even without any real pyro.

Digital Squibs

When embarking on the digital post for *Skate Warrior,* a project that predates DV, I was faced with several scenes of gunplay that had precious few practical elements to help me sell the mayhem. In fact I had tried to use firecrackers where I could, but doing so one late night in a "borrowed" location resulted in a long and complicated conversation with a police officer during which I agreed to remove the pyrotechnic component of my shoot plans. As I later assembled these scenes I knew I would be compositing digital bullet hits into a great many shots.

Although today there are libraries of stock elements for muzzle flashes and bullet impacts, at the time there were none. So I decided to make my own. I borrowed a sheet of *duvetyn,* which is the black, felt-like material that soundstage curtains are made of, and draped it over my sofa to create a black backdrop. I set up my camera facing this backing and recorded several takes of firecrackers going off. I'd just tape the firecracker to the center of the duvetyn. The whole process took no longer than a long lunch break. I digitized[5] these elements and cleaned them up, using the slow-motion technique from Chapter 3 to convert them to 24p. They worked out so well that I still use them to this day, and I have included them on the DVD so that you can use them as well. Find them in the **Elements/couchSquibs** folder.

Each element is a 23.976 fps lossless QuickTime movie. PAL users will want to reinterpret them in After Effects to 25 fps. They have no alpha channels, so you should composite them using an additive Blend Mode such as Add or Screen. You can see these elements at work in the *Green Project* movie on the video portion of the included DVD. On

---

5 Back in the Cretaceous period, people *digitized* rather than *captured* video, because it wasn't digital to begin with. The process of getting these squib elements into a digital format back then was so cumbersome and Byzantine it pains me to even think about it.

the data partition of the disc you'll find the raw footage for the shot at **Examples/Green/Footage/greenShot05.mov**—you can use it to follow along with this tutorial.

1. First, look through the six elements and pick the ones you think might work well for this shot. I settled on a combination of two: **sw_Squib_13.mov** for its bright flash and **sw_Squib_E1.mov** for its falling debris. These elements are simple enough that you can often get better results by stacking two or three together.

2. The next step is to place the elements in the shot, setting them to either Add or Screen mode. Line up the elements on the impact frame and dial in their position and rotations.

3. I parented one to the other and did a rough track to lock the parent element in to the camera move. The move is fast enough that I did this with hand-placed keyframes rather than motion tracking, but for most shots you should probably use the 2D tracker built into

After Effects. Create some keyframes to keep your element locked in. Don't worry about being rough—you can refine the track later.

4. In your comp with the two squibs added or screened over the plate (whichever looks better), duplicate the plate layer. Select the duplicate and make it into a Guide Layer by right-clicking on it and selecting Guide Layer from the context menu.

A Guide Layer is a layer that is only visible in the comp in which it lives—it doesn't render into any downstream comps. You'll see in a moment how handy this is.

5. Select the squib layers and the Guide Layer plate and choose Layer > Pre-compose. Name the new comp Squib Animation, and leave the option to open the new comp unchecked.

You should now have a two-layer comp, with Squib Animation over the plate. The Squib Animation layer needs to be set to Add or Screen to preserve the look you've already established. Once you set that, your comp should be right back where you started, but with the important distinction that the squib's motion and placement is now a precomp, which allows you to perform the next step.

6. Select the plate and duplicate it. Select the top plate layer and apply the Compound Blur effect by choosing Effect > Blur & Sharpen > Compound Blur. In the Effects Controls pane, set Compound Blur's Blur Layer to the Squib Animation Layer.

   Now you should see something pretty cool. The luminance values of your squibs now drive a blur effect on the plate, giving the impression that the heat and smoke from the squib are distorting the background and taking some of their color from it. Cool! But the effect is probably a little over the top. You could reduce the Maximum Blur amount, but what you really want to do is "mix back" this effect a bit. That's where that bottom, effects-free layer comes into play.

7. Expose the Opacity stream for the layer with the blur effect by pressing the T key. Experiment with reducing the opacity until you have a good balance of blur effect behind your squib.

   This is the basic recipe—it boils down to blurring the background to some degree wherever the squib is bright. This technique is useful for any kind of fire element you might need to composite.

8. Remember when you made the plate into a Guide Layer? You did that so you'd be able to easily refine the tracking of the squibs. Open the Squib Animation comp and you'll see your simple composite, including plate. You can continue to edit the motion and choreography of the squibs here with the background as a visual reference, and you don't need to worry about remembering to turn it off when you're done. Guide Layers are cool.

Left: A simple Screen or Add composite of the squib elements included on the DVD looks unconvincing. Right: The same composite with a Compound Blur effect to smudge the background under the squib looks photographic and believable.

I hope you have some fun using the squib elements—they've served me well for many years. Here are some tips to bear in mind when putting them to work:

- Tip #1: To make these six squib elements look like more than six, remember to mix it up by using them in various combinations, and flopping them left-to-right occasionally.

- Tip #2: If my couch squibs have given you the taste for pyro elements, you can find a ton more at Detonation Films. Many are free, and the rest are only a few bucks (www.detonationfilms.com).

- Tip #3: Like any effect, this trick works better with some interactive light already present in the plate. One really cool way to create this on your shoot is with a remote slave flash. Available from any photography store for around $40, a remote slave flash is a small, battery-powered flash that is triggered either by the push of a button or by, get this, seeing another flash go off. That's right, these things flash when everything else flashes. This means you can set this tiny box anywhere in your scene and set it off remotely by simply triggering a flash from your digital camera. Because light moves really, really fast, they will appear to go off simultaneously. In a dark scene, this lighting will look impressive and will provide a perfect accompaniment to your digitally added squib elements.

Tinfoil Bullet Hits

A fun trick I used in *Skate Warrior* was to create a handful of small bullet-hit stickers from aluminum foil and black gaff tape. I decorated one of our picture vehicles with these and digitally removed them from the shot, revealing them in sync with my composited squib elements.

What's nice about these is that they aren't a digital effect, so once you've made them appear, they're "real," requiring no digital trickery.

The (Nearly) Free Blood Hit

The DV Rebel is always pre-editing his film in his head, and finding efficiencies in the process. You could spend all day setting up squibs on your actors, but that doesn't necessarily mean they'll all wind up in your movie. Watch any randomly selected movie shootout and you'll see that only occasionally does a squib play a large visual role. Oftentimes it's more about the actor's reaction and the sound effects than about spurting blood. Or, when editing, you might find that seeing the shooter's face is more important than seeing the bullet's impact. If you know this in advance, you can arrive at your location with two shirts for your victim—one clean, and one prestained with fake blood. Swap shirts and grab a quick shot of the victim slumping over. Your audience will think they saw someone shot when in fact all you showed them was the aftermath!

Splitsville

Some wonderful effects can be accomplished using one of the oldest tricks in the book—the splitscreen, or soft split. This is where you use a simple matte—so simple it can be a wipe or other transition in your NLE—to split between two different shots. Usually the two shots are different takes from the same camera angle. The multiple Michael Keatons in *Multiplicity* and the many characters played by Michael J. Fox in the *Back to the Future* sequels are extreme examples of this type of shot.

Creating a digital "twin" of an actor with a split is the most obvious use of this technique. For the DV Rebel, the more interesting use of the split is in enhancing the production value. By cleverly using splits you can make a crowd of several look like several thousand, or turn one expensive costume or prop into several.

The only trick is not moving the camera. Use your tripod, and weight it down good so no bumps or jitters blow your gag.

For this example, I've constructed a shot that requires a little more planning. The idea is that you have one really killer SWAT costume, not four, for a sequence where a SWAT team storms a building.

One SWAT guy (Andrew Dunn) becomes four, thanks to some planning and simple splitscreen compositing. Big thanks to Andy and Augustine Chou of Bay Area Airsoft Hobbyists (baash.com) for helping out with this shoot!

This shot requires a little planning, since my "twins" are crossing over each other. I needed to matte my four takes into one. This means moving from simple soft splits to more articulate mattes. In other words, roto. The good news is that often a little bit of roto goes a long way with a shot like this. You only need to do perfect roto in the areas where the twins overlap. In the other areas you can get away with simple soft splits:

Here's the basic workflow for a twin shot:

1. Start with your layers blended together in After Effects using simple opacity. All you're trying to do is line up your clips for timing purposes.

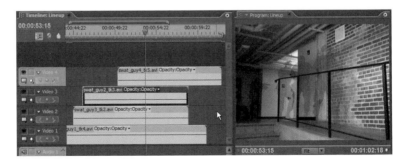

2. When you have the timing working, switch to soft splits using the Rectangular Mask tool. See how far you can get with only soft splits. Use the softest mattes you can and remember to preserve the actors' shadows and reflections.

3. If you see areas where the soft splits are failing, address them with rough roto. You can add hard-edged spline masks right onto the layers with the soft splits.

4. Refine the roto until the shot looks clean.

5. You may find that you need to color correct the layers just a bit to account for variations in lighting between the takes.

Stunts

This book is committed to the rebel spirit, and we've already talked about the fact that I'm not here to absolve you of your principal responsibility to the safety of your cast and crew, but it would be wrong to begin a section on stunts with anything other than a somber precaution that no film is worth a serious personal injury.

Avoid Killing Your Friends

Yet there's no question that stunts represent managed risk, much like driving your car at 70 miles per hour or going outside when the sun is shining. Some of our favorite movie stars do in fact believe that a managed risk of personal injury makes for a unique and thrilling brand of entertainment. No one can say that Jackie Chan always took the safest option in his Hong Kong heyday. But no one has ever been killed on the set of a Jackie Chan film, a record Hollywood cannot claim. And, most importantly, few people are placed as much at risk as Chan himself!

In this spirit, I've (very) occasionally done my own (minor) stuntwork. My philosophy is that I should not ask of my cast what I would not be willing to do myself.

Sometimes the DV Rebel does his own stunts.

I've also staged some zero-budget stunts of questionable safety. My gut continues to be at odds about the ethics of these endeavors. For *Skate Warrior,* I asked my lead actor how he felt about doing a couple of car-to-car transfers. He agreed to them, we rehearsed them, and did three takes of the first and two of the second. The results were nothing short of spectacular to us when we viewed the dailies, but now every time I watch that footage all I can see is me putting my dear friend's safety at risk, and my stomach takes the down elevator a few floors.

When you put violent or dangerous scenarios up on the big screen, you are engaging in a pact with the audience. In order to enjoy them-selves, they must trust that what they are seeing is truly a fantasy. A film that wears its low budget on its sleeve and then suddenly presents a dangerous-looking stunt may be more likely to have the audience cringing than cheering. Remember that the audience will be generous with their suspension of disbelief, and remember the effectiveness of the Ollie-to-Edit cheat (see Chapter 1).

Don't do this.

What Professionals?

There's an argument that, aside from all the obvious safety reasons one should leave stunts to the professionals, it is also good to do so because to do otherwise takes a job away from a working stunt performer. We DV Rebels aren't paying anyone and couldn't afford a professional stunt performer if we were married to one, so we can respectfully dodge this criticism as we search for creative and safe ways to get stunts on the screen.

LOTS OF THINGS ARE STUNTS

Stunts are not confined to high-falls and rappelling. Anytime an actor does something physical, it can be considered a stunt, and can require precautions to that effect. I keep a simple set of knee and elbow pads in my ditty bag in case an actor needs to bang around a bit in the course of an ordinary day. These are cheap foam and elastic things available from any martial arts supplier. The kneepads are also handy for groveling to local law enforcement to please let you bang out just one more shot before they kick you out of your creatively acquired location.

Don't underestimate the demands you put on your talent when simply asking them to be physically active, take after take. But don't underestimate the on-screen impact of this either. The protracted foot chase in *Point Break* is not something that would be particularly expensive to shoot (assuming the number of homes and pit bulls you decide to burst through is equal to the number of favorable replies to a blanket email to your friends and family), but the energy level of the performances is so high that I imagine shooting it must have been exhausting. This energy is picked up on by the audience—I get tired just watching that scene. Plan on providing rest breaks and gallons of whatever bright green sports beverage your stars prefer when asking them for this kind of performance.

THE TEXAS SWITCH

One ingenious stunt concept is the *Texas Switch*. This is where the stunt double does something dangerous, like a fall, but he falls behind a part of the set and out of sight. The camera keeps rolling as the identically dressed star, who had been hiding there all along, hops up into view and dusts himself off. The illusion is that the star did the stunt himself.

If you don't have a stunt double, you may wonder how you can take advantage of this cool idea. My favorite way is with the absolute best kind of free labor: a dummy. In two separate occasions in my student films, my cohorts and I dressed a dummy up as our lead, threw him ungracefully through the frame, and then had the actor pop up into the shot. It's an idea that's so unbelievably stupid that it works every time.

DIGITAL DUDES

The Lord of the Rings: The Two Towers delighted audiences with a sort of digital Texas Switch. When Legolas effortlessly mounts his galloping horse after the battle against the Wargs, he begins as live action footage of Orlando Bloom, but in midshot is replaced with a digital stunt double.

Creating a photo-real *digital double* requires a full set of computer animation skills, from modeling to animation to cloth simulation to rendering. But there are ways to shortcut this process. Almost anyone can create a human figure in e frontier's Poser (e-frontier.com), for example, and while you may not get that figure to do much beyond stand, walk, and run, that might be enough if what you need is a very distant shot of your character running along a high ledge, or across the rooftop of the Vatican.

WIRE/RIG REMOVAL

One common stunt requirement is the removal of wires and other rigging used to either ensure a performers' safety or lend them a superhuman ignorance of gravity. While there's not much to say about this process other than it's always a lot more work than you think it will be, there's a similar technique that can be used without needing to be an expert in harnesses and wirework—the old remove-the-safety-pad technique.

The idea here is that you have your actor take a fall onto a nice padded surface, then you remove that surface and shoot a clean plate. You either rotoscope or extract the actor from the shot and place him over the matching clean plate, and you have a believable shot of your actor hitting the deck hard.

MORE SPLITTING

One great use of the soft-split technique outlined a few pages back is to make a small stunt look big, or a big stunt look enormous. For example, check out this not-so-amazing jump over a parking garage wall that the author was willing to attempt.

Thrilling it is not, but I then walked my camera 40 yards to the left and set up a matching shot of a ledge with a perilous drop-off. The best part about this is that by walking the tripod over without adjusting it, I knew that the camera angles and lighting would match perfectly. Unfortunately a little rotoscoping is necessary to bridge the two shots, but the result is a very convincing, if quick, shot. In the spirit of "mixing it up," the following shot that would naturally follow this one could be executed with another technique entirely—perhaps using my old favorite, chucking a dummy off the building!

Upper left: The background plate shot on the roof of a parking garage. Upper right: Without changing the tripod configuration, I walked it 40 yards to the left and shot the foreground plate. Lower left: The lineup between the two plates is shown here in this 50/50 dissolve. Lower right: The rotoscoped matte for the jumper.

On that same parking garage I created another example of splitting two shots together to create the illusion of danger. I clambered up a small wall separating two levels of the roof, and then shot a matching angle of a more vertiginous wall in the same lighting.

As I was working on this chapter I stumbled across an example of stunt enhancement so inspiring that I contacted the filmmaker to request permission to feature it. *The Other Side* (www.EnterTheOtherSide.com) is a film made in the true DV Rebel spirit, even if director Gregg Bishop shot 16mm film instead of a digital format! The story follows a guy who escapes from Hell to track down his murderer. In one scene, he has to jump from a three-story building into a fast moving pick-up truck in a last-ditch effort to escape a team of invincible bounty hunters sent from the Netherworld to bring him back.

This shot from *The Other Side,* a film by Gregg Bishop, is an example of using simple compositing to enhance an already cool stunt.

The shot is based on a professional stunt performed by stuntman Frank Fearon. Fearon jumped the 35 feet and landed on a thick pad covered with a greenscreen. Bishop filmed this from above, using a wide-angle lens to enhance the distance of the fall.

Immediately after the stunt, the pads were quickly removed and the landing position was marked with an "X." Using the exact same camera angle, Bishop then filmed the truck driving over the mark.

The final shot, composited in Combustion by Matt Shumway, shows Fearon landing in the bed of the truck, with helpful touches such as motion blur and some 2D animation on the impact to lend him some of the motion of the truck.

This stunt is, of course, not something you should attempt without the proper training and supervision, but it stands as a great example of using simple compositing to enhance the production value of whatever kind of stunt you can muster. You can see this shot and a bunch of other fun stuff in the trailer at EnterTheOtherSide.com.

Cars

Action films and cars go together like vinyl and Armor All. Chances are, as you compiled your Rodriguez List, it was your distant friends' cool cars that you listed first. *On the PDF supplement on the included DVD is a massive section on cars (**Chapter4/Cars.pdf**), covering everything from shooting them correctly to creating a realistic computer-generated car paint look.*

This shot from the short film *Similo* uses *rear-projection,* a technique discussed in the "Cars" section on the included DVD. Image courtesy of Macgregor.

You've now been exposed to a torrent of techniques for creating visual effects on a tiny budget. I hope within the range of expert to basic visual effects challenges you've found a few ideas that inspire you. What inspires *me* about these techniques is that they almost all deliver a terrific on-screen punch for a modicum of effort. In the visual effects industry, it's not uncommon to slave for weeks or even months on an effects shot that blitzes past an audience without leaving a mark. Most of the effects in this chapter are projects you can attempt in a single day, from shoot to rough comp to potential final. The nimbleness you prize on your DV Rebel shoots also stands you in good stead when crafting your effects. Remember, they don't have to be perfect—they just have to *feel* perfect.

Movies Referenced in This Chapter

Back to the Future

Bad Boys 2

Beverly Hills Cop 3

Blade Runner

Collateral

Die Hard

Die Hard 2: Die Harder

Dune

The Empire Strikes Back

Forrest Gump

Hard Boiled

Harry Potter and the Prisoner of Azkaban

Jurassic Park

The Last Boy Scout

Lord of the Rings trilogy

Minority Report

Mission: Impossible

Multiplicity

The Other Side

The Rock

Saving Private Ryan

Similo

Sin City

Spy Kids 2

Titanic

Top Gun

Top Secret

True Lies

Underworld

War of the Worlds

The X Files

xXx

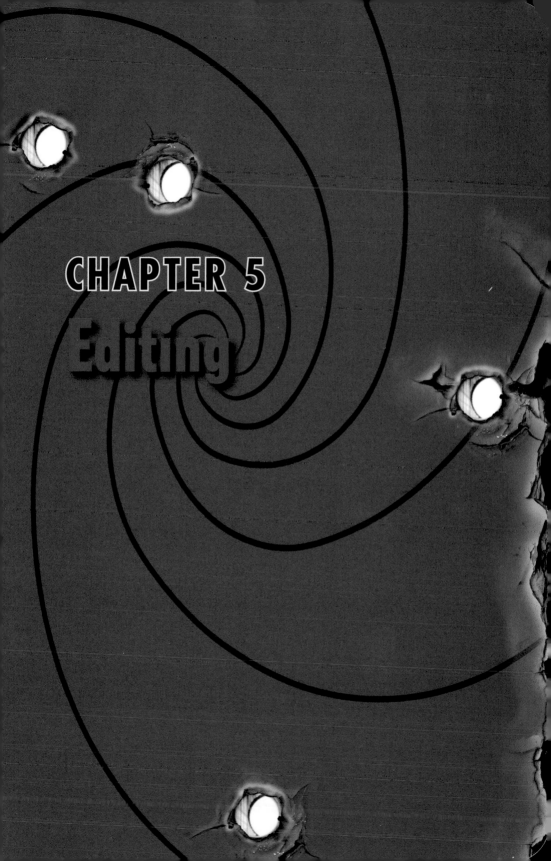

CHAPTER 5

Editing

This is a short chapter. It used to be longer, but I edited it. Boom! Thank you, I'm here all week.

OK, seriously, what am I going to say about the craft of editing that hasn't already been perfectly expressed by Walter Murch in his must-have micro-tome *In the Blink of an Eye*?

Why, this:

Cut Like a Pro

Editing is everything. It just is. Editing is filmmaking. Filmmaking calls upon many disciplines, from photography to theater to music to knitting, but only editing is actually film *making*. Follow me?

You can have the biggest engine in your car, but if you have bad tires you go nowhere. Editing is where the filmmaking rubber meets the road. I've seen excellent footage cut poorly, and conversely, jumbled messes of awful coverage cut masterfully into a salient story.

If you follow the DV Rebel strategy outlined in Chapter 1 you may think that editing will be a paint-by-numbers affair. You planned your shots, you shot your plan, now it's just time to insert tab A into slot B.

But any filmmaker will tell you that you make three films: the film you plan, the film you shoot, and then the film you edit. It's fairly obvious which of the three is the film your audience sees!

Yes, you shot according to a strict plan. You efficiently picked off your boards one by one and shot exactly what you needed to craft the film you envisioned. But a funny thing happened on the way to the edit suite. *Reality* happened. Timings got messed up. Brilliant inspirations were had. Actors got sleepy. Happy accidents occurred. And hey, you can admit it, maybe the plan wasn't, you know, *Plan of Arabia*. Maybe it wasn't quite *Citizen Plan*.

Your responsibility in the cutting room is simple and pure: to make the best possible film, using what you've got. Throw the plan out and make an effort to see your footage with fresh eyes. It's all too easy for a director to cut in a dysfunctional shot because of the storytelling beat it was originally supposed to have contributed.

In fact, an objective eye on the functionality of your footage is so important that I must ask you:

Who Shaves the Barber?

Should you cut your own film? Or should you find someone to do it for you?

I must confess that I weave back and forth on this question. Two of my heroes, John Woo and Robert Rodriguez, have edited many of their own films. I like editing. I like getting my hands on my footage—rolling up my sleeves and getting into it, trying different things, and watching my plan come together.

With some of my short projects I've taken a hybrid approach. I'll find an editor friend, always hungry for a challenge, and have him or her cut a version while I work on mine. Every time I've done this I've wound up using some combination of my cut and theirs.[1]

When you make a film the DV Rebel way, you call in a lot of favors and ask your friends to do a lot of unglamorous things in the name of show biz. But when you ask an aspiring editor to cut your film, you are doing them a favor. Those learning the craft of editing live for opportunities to cut cool little short film projects. They can't hone their craft without your footage. It's a symbiotic relationship and a free resource that you'd be foolish to ignore.

Kill Your Babies

And what's going to happen when your editor friend gets her hands on your footage is that she's going to cut it all wrong. In particular, she will

---

1 I should point out that professional editors really frown on the "horse race" approach to editing, where multiple editors are assigned the same scene. I can sympathize with that, but I think it's a different matter when a director uses her familiarity with editing tools to communicate ideas to her editor.

utterly fail to use your favorite shot. That brilliant, perfectly executed crane shot that you made with your homebrew GhettoCrane2000™ at 2 a.m. just when half your crew (one person) quit the production and took half your gear (one ditty bag) with them.

There is a well-known axiom in film, and that is that you must kill your babies. What that means is, take a look at your cut, pick your favorite shot, and cut it out. The film will get better. Why? Because you had used that shot not because it worked well, but because you love it so. You love the lighting or the perfect teardrop on your actor's cheek, but you love those things so much you can't see that the shot's not working. So whether you cut your own film or work with an editor, be prepared to kill your babies.

Manufacturing Reality

What did I mean above by saying that editing is filmmaking? One might suggest that editing is simply assembling the pieces of a film according to a blueprint (the script). Sure, you improvised here and there, but editing is really just executing a plan, right?

To see how wrong this is, direct your web browser to the following YouTube URL:[2]

youtube.com/watch?v=XHtyAoqTnTE

What this is, if you haven't seen it already, is a re-edit of *The Empire Strikes Back* that makes it seem as though Darth Vader is being a total jerk to General Veers. Using material from two separate scenes, the anonymous creator of this remix used only the power of editing to completely recharacterize the Dark Lord as a petulant brat. What's of particular interest is how he or she was able to generate reactions from actors Julian Glover and Kenneth Colley. You'd swear they are struggling to maintain their composure and professionalism in the face of Darth's behavior.

---

2 If that link is broken, do a search for "Darth Vader Jackass."

Of course, their performances are no different than they were in the original film, but the context has changed substantially. This *Star Wars* retooling is a modern version of an experiment conducted by Russian filmmaker Lev Kuleshov in 1918. Kuleshov intercut the same shot of a man staring intently with various reverses including a bowl of soup, an attractive woman, and a coffin. Audiences interpreted his performance as hungry, amorous, and contemplative respectively—never once suspecting that it was the same footage each time. The shot didn't change, but the context did, and along with it the nature of the performance.

Your job as an editor is to manufacture an emotional reality in the viewer's mind. Never underestimate the power of juxtaposition, and never catch yourself thinking there's no way out of a jam. Editors routinely rescue bad performances and under-covered scenes, or work miracles such as cutting an entire character out of a movie or joining two scenes into one. Great performances are always a tag-team effort by an actor and an editor.

Everything Is Fair Game

Hard drives are so cheap now, you should capture every last bit of footage you shoot. As you capture, watch it all. Every last second of it, including the mistakes, outtakes, and five minutes of the tops of your shoes in between handheld shots.

This is the strict policy of editor Gregory Nussbaum, with whom I've worked on several commercials. One, a spot for Toshiba's first HD DVD player,[3] features a classic action movie scenario: a beautiful woman dangling from a helicopter as a rugged hero tries to hoist her to safety. The spot takes a surprise turn as the woman (Tracy Campbell) does something quite unexpected. Somehow in the chaos of a very challenging one-day shoot, I neglected to cover a decent reaction shot of her would-be rescuer. Actor Jason Maltas was hanging from a helicopter mockup with fans blowing and

3 The spot, called "Chopper," is available in HD QuickTime on the Orphanage Commercial Productions site (theorphanage.com).

Actors Jason Maltas and Tracy Campbell prepare for a shot in my Toshiba HD DVD commercial, "Chopper." (Photo by Paul Grimshaw.)

lights flashing and me shouting instructions at him, and somewhere in that footage Gregory found a tiny moment of Jason trying to hear what I was saying over all the racket. In this half-second of footage Jason appeared vulnerable and genuinely confused (probably because I wasn't making any sense), and Gregory cut this in as a reaction to Tracy's mischievous maneuver.

Had I been cutting the spot myself, chances are I'd have never noticed that this shot was needed, since I didn't plan the script around having it. Even if I'd discovered the need for the shot, I certainly would not have had the presence of mind to suspect that it might be lurking in between takes. Had Gregory not fastidiously studied every last inch of my HD footage from that day, he might have missed this bit of good fortune.

Invisible Cuts

Editing is a craft that's at its best when it goes unnoticed. It's amazing when you think about it—one might think there could be nothing more jarring than instantaneously changing everything on the screen, transporting the viewer to a completely different location. And yet we don't notice editing unless it's particularly bad. For the most part, edited sequences wash over us as effortlessly as a story being read aloud.

It turns out that editing works because it mimics the way we perceive the world. When you shift your attention from one thing to another, say, from a person shouting "Stop!" to a car peeling away, you may in literal terms execute a pan as you turn your head and shift your gaze, but inside your head it feels like a cut. You don't notice the irrelevant details in between the shouting and the car. And when you see the car, you don't notice much else, which is why it feels right when the shot of the car doesn't include much else in the frame.

POINT OF VIEW

So in one way, editing is the process of simulating the audience's natural tendency to look at what's interesting. But whereas people can look wherever they please, and ten different people follow the same situation in ten different ways, by editing the scene you are enforcing one particular way of observing the events—one particular *point of view*.

For example, imagine a scene in which a man explains to a woman that she may never see her son again. You, the editor, have ample coverage of both sides of this heart-wrenching exchange. How do you approach the process of cutting the scene? One way is to imagine the backstory of the imaginary viewer whose point of view you want the audience to take. Someone who knows the woman well, for example, may only occasionally glance at the man. He's of little interest—what the audience really cares about is her friend's feelings about this horrible news. From her point of view, entire sections of the man's dialog may take place "off screen" as she studies her friend's reaction. But a person who knows the man might view the scene the exact opposite way. Maybe the man is an FBI agent facing his first kidnapping case. He's never had to face a distraught parent before. The agent's friend will primarily be interested in how he delivers this difficult news.

Now here's the interesting part: By editing the scene in one of these two ways, you tell the audience which of these people they are. You actually change the virtual personality of the audience by dictating what's interesting to them.

This truly represents the power that the editor holds. You control the eyes through which the viewer experiences the film. You not only are telling the story, you are controlling the eyes and ears the audience uses to experience it.

You have to be careful with this power. You may gently nudge the audience's attention in a particular direction, but you can't force it. If you are constantly failing to show them what they truly want to see, they will become impatient with you and lose interest. This can happen in horror films when characters archetypically go off by themselves with the flashlight that barely works to check out that noise they heard coming from the shed full of rusty farm tools. It may delight the audience that the camera fails to show what's behind the character as she backs up into the shadows, or it may annoy them. It's a delicate balance.

CUTTING ON ACTION

When editing a conversation, you must be aware of your subconscious desire to shift your gaze from one participant to the other. But there are times when editing is not so empathetic a process. There are times when editing is mechanical, guttural. These are the times when you cut on action.

Cutting on action means placing an edit during a moment when something is moving decisively through the frame. On the B side of the cut, you pick up that same action from another angle. The cut disappears because the motion is continuous. If you followed the stir-stick-to-the-head example in Chapter 2, you've seen the power of cutting on action.

As you learned from that example, cutting on action has much more to do with on-screen lines of motion than with reality. You proved that getting the screen direction right makes the event seem real, even if it's not credible. Conversely, you may find that an edit may be a perfect cut-on-action in the 3D space of the scene, but the camera angles involved prevent it from working. This is a common problem if you've crossed the line, another concept from Chapter 2. But even when screen direction isn't an issue, sometimes an intellectually perfect edit still doesn't work.

CUT LIKE KIRK, NOT LIKE SPOCK

In other words, cut shots so they *feel* right, not so they "are" right.

All it takes is a visit to the Internet Movie Database (imdb.com) to see how many people feel that edits must be factually perfect. Listed under "Goofs" for any given film will be any number of continuity errors, where things don't match up between shots. A cigarette changes length, a glass contains different quantities of wine, or, most famously, a car enters an alleyway on two wheels and exits on the other two wheels *(Diamonds Are Forever)*.[4]

So vocal are these persnickety viewers that one gets a sense that this stuff actually matters. It doesn't. Factual continuity is totally unimportant unless it's so egregious that it distracts a properly immersed viewer from the story.

Notice that I say "properly immersed." What the continuity hounds forget is that movies are for people who like movies. Which is to say, people who allow themselves to be swept up in the moment.

Because, see, I have terrible news for the continuity police: There is no such thing as a technically correct edit. Not unless you have footage of the same scene from multiple cameras, which, while possible, is an even better illustration of the point because even when multiple cameras are used, editors rarely cut between them in perfect sync with reality as they would if editing a live event. Most explosions in films are shot with multiple cameras, and in the final film you tend to see about as many beginnings of the explosion as there were cameras on the set—see the "Double or Jump" section below.

Anyway, the point is that all edits are imperfect, but factual perfection is not critical to their success. Instead, it is simply important that they feel right. As an example of this, watch *The Green Project* on the included DVD.

---

4 This example, by the way, *must* be a playful joke. You don't just accidentally pop a car up onto the wrong two wheels. What's interesting is that the filmmakers must have thought this joke would be blatantly obvious, but in fact it seemed to largely go unnoticed until it became the *cause célèbre* of pedantic cinephiles everywhere. Just goes to show you how powerful lines of action are that audiences didn't chuckle as planned at the "obvious" discontinuity.

This is the sample material that you'll use in the next chapter to practice the process of mastering your movie, but for now just watch it and marvel at the stunt work performed by my brother Eric. I asked Eric to vault over the police barrier, not knowing that he'd knock it over in the process. It was one of those happy accidents that I was hoping would happen (and Eric was not).

Once I got that delightfully destructive moment in the can, I knew I would need a good shot to follow it, so I convinced Eric to fall on his face right in front of some lion dancers. The result is what you see in *The Green Project* movie.

This edit from *The Green Project* sample movie on the included DVD looks like it shouldn't work, but it does.

This edit has almost no factual continuity whatsoever. I cut from Eric still airborne to him already on the ground. His body is in a completely different position and the barrier that he knocked over has disappeared in the second shot. Yet the edit works because of the strength of left-to-right motion and because the landing *feels* like the right landing for the jump.

MAKING LEMONADE

While continuity is not of paramount importance when editing, it is very important when shooting. The job of the *script supervisor* is in part to be the continuity watchperson on the set, and when he does his job well, editing becomes a joy. There is in fact such a thing as a continuity error so noticeable that a cut simply won't work, and the set is the place to prevent this. Consider making one member of your crew (preferably the one whose socks match) your deputy script supervisor, and give him a digital still camera to take pictures of the scenes so he can help you match shots across a sequence.

Despite everyone's best efforts in this area, continuity mistakes still happen. They happen on every film from the big to the tiny. And it falls to the editor to deal with them.

When issues of factual continuity get you in a jam, you must lean even harder on what you know about the other important qualities of a successful cut. For example, if you find yourself stuck cutting from a person holding a football in his right hand to holding it in his left, you'd be much better off cutting during a fast motion that is continuous through the frame. If you make the cut while the ambidextrous quarterback is lining up his throw, it probably won't work. Cut on the motion of the throw, and you'll be surprised how well it works—as long as both shots feature the ball traveling in the same screen direction.

But what if screen direction fails you? Despite your careful planning, you will eventually find yourself staring down the barrel of a pair of allegedly complementary shots that cross the line.

One strategy for dealing with this comes by process of elimination. What I mean by that is, if left-to-right fails you, try up-and-down. It's very hard to place cameras such that vertical motion is different from one angle to the next. If you're faced with a scene with two people eating at a table, and the master crosses the line from the over-the-shoulder coverage, then the only time you may be able to cut is when one of the diners stands up to leave, or sits down. The vertical motion will count as cutting on action and bridge the mistake in screen direction.

In *The Last Birthday Card*, I somehow managed to cross the line shooting simple matching reverses for Scott's conversation with Baxter about facing Nak. My solution was to "flop" the shots of Scott—mirror them left-to-right—reversing his eyeline to one that worked. Seems like I'm in good company with this trick—a great number of the continuity "goofs" listed in the IMDB for the *Lord of the Rings* films are reversed wardrobe details, indicating flopped shots.

Jargon Watch

Dictionary definitions aside, in editing-speak, *flopping* a shot means mirroring it left-to-right, and *flipping,* if anything, means mirroring it up and down.

DOUBLE OR JUMP

After all this talk about continuity and seamless cuts, it may shock you to discover (or you've been waiting for me to admit) that sometimes the best cuts make absolutely no sense at all from a logical standpoint. When you need to go beyond editing like Kirk and start editing like Khan, reach for the *double cut* or the *jump cut.*

Action films are littered with these two devices, but you can witness them back to back to magnificent effect in the film *X-Men.* Chapter 5 introduces Logan/Wolverine (Hugh Jackman) having a rough go of things in a Canadian cage fight. As he is pummeled by his opponent, note the cutting structure. The editors do not show the contender rearing back to throw his punches, but instead they jump cut straight from one brutal blow to the next. By excising the bits in between, the editors create the unmistakable impression that Logan is being beaten within an inch of his life. Had they instead opted for a more literal, continuity-based approach, the scene would not have nearly the impact it does.

Then, of course, Logan turns the tables. Just when the opponent seems about to deliver the crushing blow, Logan stops his punch cold with an outstretched hand, and I'm pretty sure we hear some breaking bones there. This lightning-fast action plays out over several shots, each of which overlaps the others in motion continuity. This is the double cut, where you actually see something happen twice or more on screen, and yet somehow *feel* it happening only once.

Jackie Chan's fight scenes are full of double cuts. For some reason, doubling up the action on a punch or kick seems to enhance the power of the event. Jump cuts are the stock in trade of directors from Tony Scott to Steven Soderbergh. As popular as they are, these tricks must be used sparingly and where appropriate. As with any edit, double and jump cuts only work when the audience doesn't notice them happening. If you can make them feel right to your eye, then chances are they'll glide right past your audience unnoticed and deliver their desired impact.

ASK, ANSWER, ASK, ANSWER

As you follow the above advice, there's a governing principle that you can use to help you gauge the emerging structure of your film. In any sequence other than a montage, it is often the case that each shot both answers a question put forth by the one before it, and asks a question to be answered by the subsequent shot.

Here's an example from *Birthday Card:*

Scott peers into the scope. What does he see?

His target. How does he feel about that?

He looks serious. Will he pull the trigger?

Looks like he's about to. But he stops. Why?

He hears something behind him. He turns—what does he see?

A yellow truck! Who could be behind the wheel?

It's Nak!

You can keep that game going throughout the entire sequence, and indeed through the entire film. Sometimes the questions and answers are obvious, sometimes more subtle. Sometimes the nature of the question isn't fully clear until the answer is given, like when you cut to another location—in that case you're reminding the audience that they might be curious to catch up with the parallel events.

Verifying this relationship of one shot to the next is a great trick when you're trying to figure out how to hone the structure of your film—if a shot doesn't contribute to the ask/answer flow, maybe it can be removed or placed somewhere else.

Pacing

Get to the point!

I made this analogy already in Chapter 3, but it's worth making again: Film is a language, and it's just as possible to have poor grammar in film as it is in English. In fact, it's much possibler. It's also just as common in film to be overly verbose, wordy, redundant, and repetitive. Consider the following sentence:

"He thoughtfully contemplated the many options that lay before him, hesitating before finally making the agonizing decision."

You can say the same thing much more simply like this:

"He contemplated the options before finally making his decision."

Now you could argue about including the word "agonizing" or not, but the point is that by removing excess words, the sentence makes its point more efficiently and clearly.

Half of my editor's job on this book is to trim out my careless attempts to overemphasize my points. It's funny how words often have the exact opposite effect than what their dictionary definitions would indicate. For example, when you say "I'm *sure* I left my car keys on the cabinet," what you really mean is that you're not so sure. And when I write "Watching the playback of your first pass at a color-corrected online is really, really exciting," it has less impact than if I were to simply describe the moment as exciting. The same is true in film grammar. You may feel that inserting a snippet of a key turning in the ignition between shots of a person entering a car and driving away would enhance the feeling of urgency, but it will probably have the opposite effect. If it goes without saying, then let it. Your audience knows how a car is started, and they want you to get on with the story.

Do Over

Sometimes while editing, you get in a jam that you just can't get yourself out of. You are missing one crucial piece of footage, one tiny morsel of action that would bridge things just perfectly, or a story beat that would help immerse the audience deeper into the film.

This, my friend, is why there are reshoots.

Reshoots, or *pickups,* are nothing to be ashamed of. They are a big part of the reason I suggest you own rather than rent your camera. To fully embrace the power of pickups, I recommend that you dive into the supplemental material that accompanies the Special Extended Edition of *The Lord of the Rings: Return of the King.* On disc 6, there's a bit about the editing process, and Peter Jackson describes how the reshoots worked in conjunction with his editorial process. Even after the scheduled pickups were wrapped, he found himself missing critical inserts of some baddies jumping at Orlando Bloom. In order to ensure that the next round of pickups would yield the material he required, he grabbed a video camera and shot some quick *videomatics* of editor Jamie Selkirk jumping at the camera with a broom. Selkirk and Jackson were immediately able to drop those into the cut, and send the rough edit to the pickup unit as reference.

This edit-as-you-shoot, shoot-as-you edit approach used by Jackson on his back-to-back *Rings* sequels is the kind of thing the DV Rebel can do better than anyone. It's easy to catch yourself thinking that the only tool available to you as an editor is your NLE software, but try to keep an open mind—sometimes the best way to fix or find a shot is to reshoot it.

Sound and Music

While I am consciously staying away from a discussion of final sound design and mix (in much the same way that I avoid advising NASA on the design of Mars rovers), sound does play a critical role in editing.

There are some editorial decisions that simply cannot be made without some kind of temporary (often shortened to *temp)* sound design. Every editor should keep a library of sound effects to help "sell" the cut. Take another look at *The Green Project* movie on the DVD. That edit I discussed earlier—where Eric jumps over the gate—works as well as it does in no small part because of the sound of the gate falling. The sound bridges the cut and carries the motion of the A side into the B, even though the shots have little to do with one another visually except for their left-to-right motion. Until I laid that sound effect in, I didn't think I could get away with this edit, but once I added the sound I knew it would work.

How far do you go? A good rule of thumb is that you should confine your temp sound effects to the number of tracks that your NLE can mix in real time. As soon as your software starts beeping in protest or demanding that you render your audio before playing back the sequence, you should back off, both because your editing process is about to get slow and painful and because you've started putting too much work into what should be a simple temp track. The number of tracks you can mix in real time will depend on your hardware, software, and quality settings, but even two laptops ago I had no trouble creating rough sound mixes to help me gauge the efficacy of my edits.

Locking Your Cut

There's a mental shift that you should be prepared for as you complete your edit. Editing is one of the freest, most open-ended processes in film-making. There are no rules. Everything is possible. The film is gelling before your eyes and your lifestyle becomes one of waking up at four in the morning stricken with the immutable desire to slip a shot by three frames.

And then you finish. Kinda. Ending the editing process is sometimes difficult. Without a deadline or any other outside forces dictating that you must someday stop tinkering with your film, the impulse to continue to hone it is overpowering. But someday, at the time of your choosing, you must stop tweaking.

This time is much, much earlier than you think it is. In this day of nonlinear editing, with penalty-free readjustments of your cut being only a click away, it is all too easy for films to get overworked in the edit room. You get used to a particular pause and after three weeks of seeing it ten times a day you suddenly think it needs to be half as long. A continuity error that you thought was negligible when you first saw it now grates on you.

But you must remember that you are editing your movie for an audience that will never scrutinize your film to this degree. Some of your early, off-the-cuff decisions came from a place of fresh, unsullied inspiration. Some can be improved with time. Knowing which is which is a big part of maturing as an editor—and imposing a deadline on yourself, arbitrary as it may be, is a great way to encourage yourself not to edit your film to shreds long after it was working just fine.

The day that you *lock your cut* is a momentous occasion. Celebrate. Take a day off. Screen your cut for a few people and absorb their comments. Some of these comments will be valuable, some will be worthless. A DV Rebel film often looks quite messy as a rough cut, with missing shots, slap-comps of effects shots, and a rough sound mix. Some audiences won't be able to see past this to give good feedback. Ultimately only you can decide which comments make sense to you. You may find yourself tweaking a few cuts as a result of these screenings, and then celebrating the second locking of your cut.

Prep the Effects

One of your side jobs while editing is acting as your own visual effects editor. On a movie with a sizable number of effects shots, the VFX editor has both the fun job of slap comping stand-in versions of visual effects shots and the rather tedious job of preparing the effects plates and elements.

A good example is the shot from Chapter 4 where a single actor poses as all four members of a SWAT team. This shot would start life as a *slap comp* (see sidebar) of four layers in the NLE software. In the fast and fluid environment of the editorial timeline, you'd experiment with the timings and cut length until you had a shot that felt like it worked, even though the split screens might be hasty soft splits rather than elaborate roto.

When the shot is "locked," which is to say you don't plan on doing any more tweaking to its timings, you need to export your plates.

Slap Comps

Slap comps are composites that are quickly "slapped" together as a rough stand-in for the eventual effects work. It would be impossible to edit a film like *Multiplicity,* with its numerous Michael Keatons, without slap comping the various split-screen shots. Slap comps are often done right in the NLE Timeline, although you can break them out to After Effects as well. The LiveLink feature of Adobe Production Studio is perfect for slap comps. In addition to helping you and your trusted preview audiences visualize how the completed film will look, slap comps also inform you of the editorial information relevant to creating an effects shot—how much of which plates and elements you'll need. For this reason, you should slap comp a shot even if there's no question in your mind about how it will eventually be put together.

Remember the cool stunt shot from *The Other Side* in Chapter 4? Here's what the slap comp looked like. Image courtesy of Gregg Bishop, www.EnterTheOtherSide.com.

One theory in exporting VFX elements is that you don't create any media at all, but rather create a *line-up sheet* that describes how you're using the clips. A line-up sheet is nothing more than a document defining how elements relate to each other in a shot, using explicit frame counts.

This works well if all your media lives on one hard drive, or if you are using Adobe Production Studio and keeping live links between your After Effects projects and your Premiere Pro Timeline.

But the truth is, even if you're not exporting plates for someone else, it's kind of nice to provide yourself the luxury of a properly trimmed and exported plate. When you're working in After Effects, it's inconvenient to be working with long, unwieldy clips. And who knows, maybe you'll hit up your friends for some help, in which case you owe it to them to make their lives easier with plates trimmed to the proper length.

Most NLE programs have the option to export some kind of lossless media, like an uncompressed AVI or a TIFF sequence. Oftentimes, this functionality is not as obvious as the numerous ways of exporting heavily compressed media such as MPEG. Still more nefarious is the customary default of most NLEs to re-render to the compression format (codec) of your Timeline. This obvious feature is the single most treacherous characteristic of your NLE and you must always be on the lookout for it, as you will learn in the next chapter.

It is possible to export media in its native codec without recompressing it. This would seem to be the obvious choice for exporting effects plates, as the resultant file would be as high in quality as is possible, but no larger than it needs to be on disc. Perfect, if it weren't for one little problem: the problem of the top ten percent.

The Top Ten Percent

On the left is a DVX100 clip that showed no zebra when it was shot. But after exporting from Premiere Pro to After Effects, the highlights are badly clipped. On the right, the important highlight detail has been recovered using the techniques described in this section.

It turns out that your DV, HDV, or DVCPRO material is stored in YUV space, or YCrCb to be annoyingly accurate. Either way, it's the Y that we're interested in here. Y stands for luminance, of course, and it is measured in IRE values on a scale of zero to 100 percent, a scale that you will recall from your waveform display described in "The Camera" chapter on the DVD. But users of some NLEs may notice upon closer inspection that their waveforms are more than happy to display Y values well above 100 percent. There's another rung in the ladder above 100. The luminance signal of your digital video does have a limit, but that limit is 110 percent, not 100 percent.

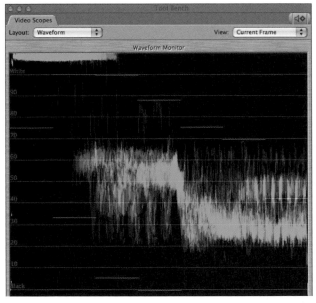

The waveform scope in Final Cut Pro HD shows that luminance values can range as high as 110 percent.

If that sounds like a good thing, you're right. But here's the problem: When you export to an RGB format, or for any other reason convert from YCrCb to RGB, you'll most likely be clipping off everything above 100 percent.

Clipping, as you'll recall, is bad. You went to a lot of trouble to shoot without clipping. Maybe you even used your camera's zebra display to help you avoid losing detail in the highlights. But your zebra doesn't start zebraing until the Y values go above 110 percent, which means that you could be shooting exactly the way you're supposed to be, riding right up against that zebra, only to find yourself with clipped highlights in your edit because your highlight detail all lives between 100 and 110 percent.

The 16–235 Club

If you use a third-party video card and/or codec, you may have another way of dealing with this clipping problem. Some codecs map the entire range of YCrCb video's luminance to fit within the 255 values of an 8-bit RGB image. Folks familiar with these codecs know that this results in black mapping to a value of 16 instead of zero, and white mapping to 235 instead of 255.

After Effects ships with an Animation preset that corrects this (Levels > video to computer), and even has an Interpret Footage option for mapping 16 back to zero and 235 to 255. But if you're trying to preserve those whiter-than-white values you only want half this equation. Apply a fresh Levels effect to your footage and set RGB Input Black to 16 (on the 0–255 scale, which you can set in the Info palette) and you're set—a perfect full-range image with no clipping.

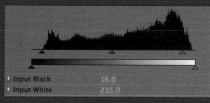 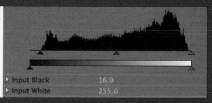

Left: The traditional way of expanding 16–235 video to full-range can actually clip important image detail from a camera original. Right: Remapping only black preserves the highlight detail.

Even if you don't do anything to instigate this clipping in your NLE, After Effects will do the clipping for you[5]. When you import a clip from your NLE into After Effects, it gets converted to RGB, and clipped at 100 percent in the process. Ultimately, this is the reason why exporting native media is not a good way of getting images out of an NLE for visual effects, or, as you'll discover in the next chapter, for onlining.

While no NLE provides an automated way of extracting the full luminance range from a clip, most will let you retrieve those values through the use of color correction effects. The trick is that you must use effects that operate in the native YCrCb color space. Most of the basic filters in Final Cut Pro and Adobe Premiere Pro work this way, but some don't. Those that don't will clip off the highlights in the same way After Effects would.

IN FINAL CUT PRO

In Final Cut Pro HD, there is no effect that performs a simple gain on the image's Y values. How this can be, I am not sure, but no matter—there is a workaround. See, fading a layer's opacity over a black background is the same thing as gaining down its values, and Final Cut Pro's opacity fades are processed in native YUV. So the process for extracting the full luminance range from a clip in Final Cut is as follows:

1. Create a video track under your clip in the sequence. Add a black slug to the new track.

2. Double-click the top layer and select the Motion tab in the viewer.

3. Set the Opacity to 90%, or whatever value causes all the values to drop to no more than 100 percent.

---

5 In truth, the clipping is mandated by the codec and its treatment of luminance values, not by After Effects. You can blame Apple for this problem in Final Cut Pro and Adobe for the same problem in Premiere. Or, if you use a video card or codec that maps video to 16–235 RGB, then you can ignore this whole section and head straight to the sidebar.

The cleanest way to uniformly reduce the luminance of a clip in Final Cut Pro HD is to fade its opacity over a black slug.

Since you'll be darkening the video, you run the risk of damaging the quality of your image. You should take two steps to prevent this:

1. First, choose Sequence > Settings and go to the Video Processing tab. Check the option called Render all YUV material in high precision YUV. This option makes Final Cut do its image processing at its highest quality setting (32-bit floating point).

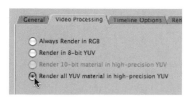

Why wouldn't you select this enticingly named option in the Sequence Settings dialog?

2. When you export your shot, you'll need to select a format. The ideal format would be a TIFF or PNG sequence, but unfortunately those image sequence formats are not options because of a little bit of stubborn confusion on the part of Final Cut Pro. See, if you choose to export to an RGB format, Final Cut will render all of its effects in RGB, disabling the high quality setting you chose in Step 1 and bypassing its own ability to extract the values above 100 percent! The only way to render in YUV is to specify a YUV codec as your output format. Luckily, Final Cut comes with one

that's perfect for the task: Apple Uncompressed 10 bit. Export to this codec and you'll have nice, uncompressed plates with the full dynamic range of the source material.

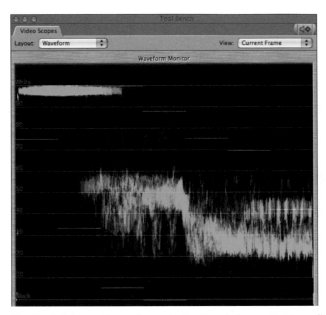

The Final Cut waveform after reducing the clip's opacity. Now all the values fall between zero and 100 percent, so they will all be represented in subsequent RGB conversions.

IN PREMIERE PRO

In Premiere Pro, the process is similar. It's easier in some ways and trickier in others. The first trick is that the waveform displays don't seem to show you the same units as Final Cut. If you look at the YCrCb waveform, for example, you'll see that it tops out at 100 percent. So does the RGB waveform, but that's the one you want to use, because it's there that the

100 percent line actually means what we think it does—anything above it will get clipped.

Although you won't see any values above 100 percent, they may well be there. The only way to know is by darkening the image. There are a hundred ways to do this in Premiere Pro 2.0, but you'll recall that only methods that operate in YUV space will work in Final Cut, and the same rule applies here.

Unlike Final Cut, Premiere won't even think about those greater-than-100-percent values until you switch on the fancy rendering stuff. Find that in File > Project Settings.

In Premiere Pro 2.0, the key to extracting the full dynamic range of your footage lies in the Maximum Bit Depth check box.

The steps in Premiere Pro are as follows:

1. Enable Maximum Bit Depth and click OK. Nothing will visibly change, but now the next step will actually work.

2. Apply the effect called "Proc Amp" (found under Video Effects > Adjust) to your clip.

3. In the effects controls, grab the Contrast slider and lower its value slowly. You should see whatever values might have been lurking above 100 percent drop into view at the top of the RGB waveform display.

    Stop moving the slider when no new values appear in the scope. Generally speaking you shouldn't have to set Contrast any lower than 90 percent to recover all the values.

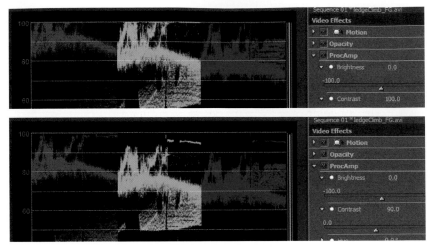

In Premiere Pro, the Contrast slider in the Proc Amp effect can be used to recover highlight detail from YUV sources. Note the additional values that have appeared in the waveform on the bottom screenshot.

When it comes time to render, you do not have the same restrictions that Final Cut imposes—you may render directly to an RGB format such as a TIFF sequence or a QuickTime movie with the animation codec set to 100 percent quality, which is a lossless compression setting.

Of course, you can and should ignore all of this madness for shots that don't have any values above 100, but it's probably still a good idea to maintain a consistent pipeline and export all your plates to the same format.

Getting a Handle

When you export plates and elements for your visual effects work, you must decide how much *handle* you want to include. Handles are extra frames at the head and tail of a shot, and they serve multiple purposes.

Principally, they provide a measure of safety and protection against slight changes to the edit after effects work has begun. This isn't just to protect you from changing your mind—the truth is, a completed effects shot may not sit in the cut in exactly the same way that its animatic or slap comp did. This doesn't represent any kind of failure, it's just the sensitive nature of editing. Subtle characteristics of the animatic may be ever-so-slightly different in the final shot, enough so that a slip in sync, a trim, or a lengthening of a few frames may be required.

Handles also provide extra material for things like speed changes and motion effects that build up over time, like an echo effect. If you try out the night vision template file on the included DVD (see **Chapter4/POV. pdf**), you'll want to feed it at least a second of head handle so that the motion trail effect will work properly.

Handles are reassuring because it's inconvenient to lengthen an effects shot after you've done a great deal of work on it. At the same time it's no fun killing yourself creating extra frames that will never be seen, so you must strike a careful balance when choosing how many handle frames you wish to work with. Eight-frame handles are common in the professional visual effects world, although 10- and 12-frame handles are not unheard of.

Accounting

In addition to exporting and naming visual effects shots, there are a couple of other things you should be keeping track of as you edit, because they create special cases when the time comes to online your movie. These include time stretches, dissolves, or other layered transitions, repos (repositioned or blown-up shots), and minor effects that you'll handle in the online, such as boom mic paint-outs or other cleanup.

As you use your slow-mo, hand cranked, or other pre-rendered material, you must be sure to keep track of the After Effects project files that created them, so that you can revert back to them to create the lossless versions of the sections you used.

As you work on effects shots, make a habit of cutting them into your master Timeline in their own layer, riding above the slap comp, plate, or animatic they replace. This may be the context in which you *final* your effects work, or you may still be working on it even as you begin to online your film.

Jargon Watch

The visual effects industry has turned the word *final* into a verb. As a visual effects supervisor, when I declare an effects shot completed, I am finaling it. Then I send that shot to my clients hoping they will final it as well. It's still a noun too—a shot that has been finaled is, of course, a *final*.

Ultimately, all this work builds up to that moment that you stop editing your film and start thinking about finishing it. If editing is building the house, onlining is painting and decorating it. I find each of these stages extremely satisfying in different ways. In editing you see the film take shape, and you interact directly with the storytelling machinery. In onlining, you take a cobbled-together mess of shots and stand-in effects and polish them into a seamless film. Go ahead and be messy during the editing process, but stay just tidy enough so that when you finish, you can focus more on the creative aspects of onlining, color correction, and look, and less on the massive organizational effort it represents.

Movies Referenced in This Chapter

Diamonds Are Forever

The Lord of the Rings: The Return of the King Special Extended DVD Edition

Multiplicity

Star Wars: The Empire Strikes Back

X-Men

CHAPTER 6

Onlining

You've been a rebel all throughout writing, planning, shooting, and editing your film. You've even been a rebel as you've done your visual effects. But now, I'm sad to say, it's time to put a bit of that rebel spirit aside. The way you're going to get beautiful images out of your home setup is by following some hard and fast rules. Fail to do so and you risk degrading the already fragile quality of your digital video and betraying the true budget of your film.

The Rules

In Chapter 5 you got a taste of the image quality pitfalls lurking throughout your workflow when you learned of the perils of luminance clipping. You must simultaneously avoid these issues and avail yourself of the powerful range of tools available to the desktop artist.

But hey, before we talk about that, let's talk about something else essential for a successful filmmaking experience: coffee.

A good espresso machine in a busy coffee shop probably costs more than the car driven by the barista operating it. For home use, you can buy coffee machines ranging from 50 bucks to $5,000.

But the best cup of coffee you can make at home is with a $4 coffeemaker.

Don't believe me? Read the excellent article at coffeegeek.com/guides/howtouseapourover. OK, there's a little catch—you'll need a really good grinder and some fresh coffee to go with your $4 coffee filter holder. But with those items you can make a truly stellar cup with an $80 investment in equipment—a cup of joe that will have you tossing your $200 digital timer combo coffeemaker in the trash.

What's the point of all this coffee talk? Well, first, if you're at all like me, coffee will play an important role in your ability to complete the postproduction of your movie. But more importantly, the myth that an expensive coffeemaker makes better coffee is a perfect analogy for modern digital postproduction.

In high-end post, real time is king. A Da Vinci 2k color corrector does its work in real time. This means it needs something real-time to record to—usually either a Digibeta deck or an HDCAM deck. Both of those formats are lossy, compressed digital formats. So the mandate of real time has already resulted in a quality compromise in a room that will cost you $1,000 per hour.

Then you take your tape to a slick post house with leather couches and a receptionist who will make you coffee on demand using a $5,000 coffeemaker. You load the tape into a Flame, where you do a bunch of compositing work in either 8-, 10-, or 12-bit color. You record the results back to tape, losing another generation of quality.

Lastly, you online your spot in a real-time suite. That's one more generation loss back to tape. Your high-end, expensive, latté-drenched workflow has caused you to recompress your original imagery three times at the very least. Each of those stages has required a conversion from YUV to RGB and back, hopefully with 10-bit processing but maybe not.

On your own home computer, the one that costs less than the push-button LatteTron2000™ at the post house, you can do so much better. You can take your actual original image data from your DV tape, HDV tape, or P2 card, convert it to RGB only once, and work with it in 16-bit color throughout. You will never touch tape and never recompress until you're finally ready to output.

The DV Rebel can, with some care, produce better looking images in his home studio than a seasoned pro can in an expensive post environment.

To make good on this potential, you'll need to resist some temptations and often take the slightly less-trodden path. With the same confidence that lets you walk right past the expensive coffee machine, you will come to embrace the first and most important rule:

No Mastering in the NLE

Your NLE is designed for speed and interactivity. The trade-off is quality. While video cards exist that allow you to edit with "lossless" video codecs, the truth is those codecs aren't actually lossless. They're usually 4:2:2, just like digibeta tape, or compromised in some other way. Besides, converting DV to a near-lossless codec is a bit like carrying around a golf ball in a steamer trunk.

When you cause an NLE to render something, such as a color effect or a transition, it recompresses the video to the codec you're working in, which is usually a heavy compression. Trying to do any kind of effects or color work in your NLE is signing up for recompressing your precious images, which is such a no-no that it's a rule unto itself:

No Recompression

As in, not ever. You compressed the living heck out of your image when you shot it to a consumer digital video format, but you don't need to do it again anywhere in your workflow until you create a tape or a DVD for playback.

For example, in the last chapter you learned how to retrieve errant luminance information from your YCrCb video files and I emphasized picking a lossless output format for the newly rescued files, such as a TIFF sequence. Although a TIFF file may be compressed, that's *lossless* compression, which is OK. But if you went to all that trouble to rescue your image's upper ranges and then rendered back out to DV, you'd be compressing your image twice and drastically reducing the quality for no reason.

So be careful and always use lossless file formats when moving images between applications. That's it, right?

Not quite. Think back to the first rule for a minute. You can't online in your NLE, which means that you need to somehow get your edited clips into After Effects. You'll read more about that later, but take a moment to embrace what a pain this could be. Everything you've done in your edit needs to be reproduced in After Effects. In the case of cuts, this is easy enough. But what about dissolves, repos, color effects, titles?

You cannot let your NLE render these effects. If you do, you will not only recompress your images, but you'll also take flexibility away from the online. For example, if you render a dissolve between two shots and export the results to After Effects, you no longer have the ability to color correct each shot separately.

So the first two rules are really one—you can't master in your NLE because it requires recompressing, and in avoiding recompressing you'll be redoing all the work you did in your NLE, but in the high-quality world of After Effects.

High quality? What does that mean anyway? Well, one thing it means is the last rule:

No 8-Bit Processing

After Effects has three project-wide color modes: 8-bit, 16-bit, and 32-bit (float). Of these three, only the last two are acceptable choices for your onlining work.

For many years most of us thought 8-bit color was all there was—255 shades of gray sounds like more than you'd ever need, as does "16 million colors." And it's true, for most types of images, 8 bits per channel is plenty to store a high-quality image.

Unless you want to do anything to it.

To see what I mean, you can do a simple experiment with any 8-bit image you have lying around. Pop it into After Effects (a new project should default to 8-bit—leave it that way for now) and apply two Levels effects to it, one right on top of the other.

You should see that both histograms look identical. If yours look anything like mine,[1] there's some room to *optimize* the image by bringing

---

[1] If it doesn't, mine is on the included DVD in Examples/Eight Bit Image.

in Input Black and Input White to surround the extents of the histogram (in case you didn't rush out and read Mark Christiansen's book, you'll learn more about that in a bit). Do this now, on the first Levels.

You'll notice that the second histogram shows the results of your correction. As expected, the color range has been expanded. But what's with all those gaps? That shows the results of color-correcting in 8-bit. What started as a perfectly lovely image is now lacking color fidelity, simply because of a basic color correction.

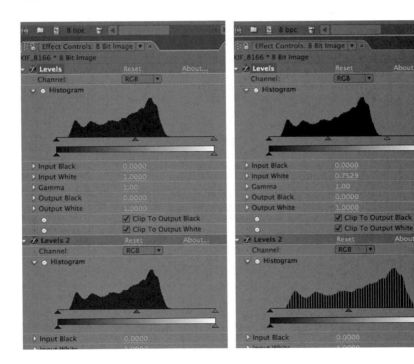

Think of it this way: Imagine you have ten cars in ten parking spots. Each car fills a spot. When you pulled in Input White, you clipped off some of the upper range of pixel values, or drove away with the last three cars. Now you have seven cars, but still ten spots. How do you distribute seven cars evenly into ten spots?

The answer is, there's no good way. You wind up with gaps. The same thing happened to your image, and that's what the histogram shows.

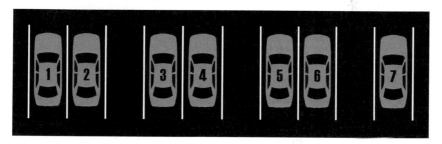

But if you switch your project into 16-bit mode (File > Project Settings), you'll see something miraculous happen:

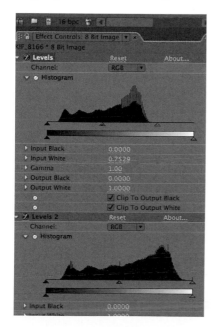

The gaps have been filled in! What's happened is that your old color values have been freed from the restriction of needing to fit into those same ten parking spots. They can meander freely, evenly distributing themselves within the new range.

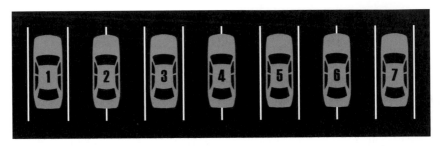

By working in 16-bit you've actually created a higher-fidelity image out of your 8-bit source. This fidelity can make quite a bit of difference as you stack multiple color corrections on top of each other, which is exactly what you're about to do. And even when you ultimately render back to an 8-bit format, the results will be noticeably better than if you'd worked in 8-bit throughout.

Be a Pixel Purist

The easiest way to hurt an image is to scale it. Whether you scale an image up or down, you are softening it in the process. If you scale your NTSC material up to HD with the idea of creating an HD master, and then scale the results back down to NTSC to make a DVD, you'll wind up with an image of lower quality than if you'd stayed at NTSC resolution the whole way. Let your shooting format drive the mastering resolution and scale up or down for various distribution formats as a very last step.

So that's it—four rules, all designed to help you extract the best possible image quality out of your footage. Following them doesn't guarantee good results, but failing to follow them guarantees that you've missed an opportunity to add production value to your film.

Getting Your Movie into After Effects

Based on the first rule, you have a little work ahead of you. Once you've locked your cut, it's time to move the party from your NLE into After Effects. Depending on what software you used to edit and/or your willingness to spend some serious money on one of the excellent products from Automatic Duck, this can either be a one-click operation or a lengthy manual process.

If you edited in Premiere Pro, you probably already know how easy it is to open your cut in After Effects. Go ahead and grin smugly while the rest of us muddle through. If you edited in something other than Premiere, you can buy the appropriate product from Automatic Duck and use that software to transmogrify your edit into After Effects. I love these products, but I have to acknowledge that they are high-end tools, priced appropriately for professional users who expect good, personalized tech support. Which means that some DV Rebels will be looking for more cost-effective solutions.

That was certainly the case for me when I found myself done with my edit of *The Last Birthday Card*. There was no such thing as Automatic Duck back then. All ducks were strictly manual in 1999. So I borrowed from my 16mm film-editing education and created a way of getting my cut safely out of Final Cut Pro while following the crucial "no recompression" rule. *You can read about it in the supplementary section on the DVD* (**Chapter6/Exporting.pdf**).

Color Correction

While there's quite a bit of information out there about the technical, video engineering side of color correction, little has been written on the creative aspects. Color correction is viewed as a black art, and its premier practitioners enjoy rock star status.

And rightly so. The telecine *colorist*—the one behind that daunting control board, wielding those mysterious black knobs with deft precision—is much like the film's editor. They have the power to make everyone's good work look great—or terrible. The sets, props, makeup, and of course cinematography all owe their final polish to the color correction.

Color correction is also like the musical score of a film, in that it is a direct psychological device for eliciting an emotional response in the viewer—one that works better when it operates at a subconscious level.

How does the image on the top make you feel? The image on the bottom?

The product Web page for a popular film grading system suggests that you can make your film look "better than real," and that's a great description of the power of color. A good color correction can make film look sexy, HD look like film, and a beginner's cinematography look expert. Best of all, it enhances production value. The DV Rebel should plan on color correcting every shot in his film individually, using off-the-shelf tools in Adobe After Effects 7.

Jargon Watch

Grading or *color grading* is exactly the same thing as color correcting—it's just the British term for it (so I guess it would be *colour* grading). *Telecine* refers to the process of transferring film to tape, inevitably involving color correction in the process. *Datacine* is the same process but the destination is digital files, not tape. A *DI*, or *Digital Intermediate*, is both the result and process of color correcting a movie shot on film and scanned to a high-quality digital format (although watch that term get commandeered by filmless projects). Color *timing* is a term that refers to the photochemical process of color correcting film by exposing it with colored lights for varying amounts of time.

Grade in Layers

When color correcting, you are concerned both with making your shots consistent and giving them a look. The first part is why it's called color *correcting*—it's not the creative part of the process, it's the technical exercise of taking shots staged at various times and circumstances and making them look like one continuous scene. This isn't easy. It requires a good eye and an adept command of the tools. But the fun part, and the part that has turned colorists into a unique creative breed, is the part where you develop a signature look for a shot, sequence, or entire film.

In a traditional DI, both of these concerns are handled at the same time, using the same tools. Quite frankly, this is because many elaborate, real-time systems found in DI suites allow only one channel of color correction at a time. After Effects may not be a real-time program, but its infinitely flexible architecture allows you to separate the tasks of grading for consistency and grading for look. The result, as you'll see, is a much simpler process, and a more flexible one, allowing you to achieve professional results without years of experience.

In *The Last Birthday Card*, there's a scene I intended to take place in warm afternoon sunlight. Shot over the course of one day, this scene has setups with direct overhead sunlight cut right up against shots with low morning or afternoon sun.[2] Here are stills from three shots in the sequence:

Note that they vary quite a bit in color and tone.

Here are those same three shots after color correcting for consistency:

And here they are with the overall look of the scene applied uniformly to all three corrected frames:

2 I shot this long before Google SketchUp existed, so I had no tool to plot my sun's path throughout the shoot day.

Each shot gets a specific color correction that brings it into line with the others, creating a seamless sequence rather than a disjointed collection of shots. Then the look is applied as an adjustment layer over all three shots—in fact, all the shots in this sequence. The wonderful thing about this technique is that you can make a change to the look and it will automatically apply to all of the shots, without affecting the work you did to even them out. You can also continue to refine issues of consistency without worrying about messing up the overall look.

Here's what that looks like in the After Effects Timeline:

Each shot has a color correction adjustment layer over it (read on to discover why I didn't simply apply the color correction to the layers themselves), and then the overall look is created with a single adjustment layer at the top called "look."

Remember, this multistage color correction process is safe because I did it all in 16-bit color rather than in 8. In 8-bit, multiple color corrections can introduce artifacts such as banding and noise, but by working in 16-bit color you can almost completely eliminate that risk.

So your basic workflow in After Effects will be to grade your shots first for consistency using effects applied directly above the individual shots, and then again for look using adjustment layers spanning entire sequences.

Not So Secondary Corrections

Traditional color correction systems have a tool called a *secondary correction*, or simply *secondary*. As the name implies, it is performed after the initial or *primary* correction. A secondary is often confined to a certain range of values in the image, such as skin tones. In extreme cases secondaries are used to completely change the color of an object or piece of wardrobe, but contrary to every software demo you've ever seen this is not the best use of a secondary. A secondary is best used with a light touch. And oddly enough, a secondary color correction is often better done *before* the primary. This flies in the face of every million-dollar grading suite in the world, so I need to explain myself well here.

Most of what you will do with secondaries is localized correction. Make the sky a little bluer, or tone down the redness in an actor's face. You might darken an area of the frame to make the lighting moodier, or brighten a face that wasn't hit by as much light as another. You may also simulate lens effects such as a vignette or a gradient. These corrections are all either attempts to "fix" the scene or in some way alter the impression of how it was filmed. In other words, your relighting correction should look like it's a part of the footage, not like a postproduction effect. The key to pulling this off is doing these corrections first, before any other color work.

To see what I'm talking about, compare the two images below. The one on the left has a color correction that makes the shadows blue and the highlights warm. Over the top of this creative grade, I've added a masked adjustment layer in After Effects that brightens up the face of actor Billy Brooks. Unfortunately, this attempt at relighting the scene reads as exactly what it is—an after-the-fact digital correction.

Many look corrections achieve a cinematic feel by pushing shadows to a different color than highlights. This look has bluish shadows and since Billy's face was in shadow, it got tinted blue. Brightening his face after the look has given him a blue complexion that is not only unattractive, but it fails to fit in with the rest of the shot, making it painfully obvious that some digital tomfoolery is afoot.

To create the image above, all I did was to reverse the order of my two corrections. I moved the adjustment layer with the brightening effect below the creative look adjustment layer. The difference is profound— not only is the brightening effect less conspicuous, Billy's flesh tones are now an appealing tone appropriate for the look of the shot.

Giving yourself this flexibility requires only a little more legwork in After Effects. Since I wanted to apply masked corrections first, I had to be sure to put my color correction effects on an adjustment layer. That way I could sandwich the relighting in between.

There's another reason for placing all your color corrections on adjustment layers. I often find myself wanting to dial in individual elements of a color correction as I'm tweaking the sequence, and an easy way of doing that is by adjusting the opacity of an adjustment layer. You can easily select all of the adjustment layers associated with a shot, press the T key to reveal their opacity streams, and scrub their individual values until you're happy with the result.

Doing spot corrections before overall looks is just one example of an important structure to follow when mastering your film: the *order of operations*.

Order of Operations

No, that's not the title of a new Tom Clancy novel. *Order of operations* is a term used to describe the sequence in which things occur. For example, unless you are Superman, you generally put your underwear on before your pants. In visual effects, you base the order of your image processing operations on the way light behaves in the real world. For example, you never comp anything in front of a lens flare, because the lens flare happens inside the lens. In the real-world order of operations, it happens after the layers of the scene, but before such "effects" as film grain and color correction.

Since our color corrections arsenal simulates real-world events (such as relighting an object), there is a right and a wrong sequence in which to perform them. Below is the correct order of operations for your color correction layers. There are detailed descriptions of most of them in the next section, "Tools of the Trade." And don't worry, you don't necessarily have to do all of these things!

1. Remove DV artifacts.

2. Add any visual effects elements.

3. Optimize the shot (see "Rebel CC" below).

4. Relight and change object colors.

5. Add gradients, diffusion, and other on-lens filter effects.

6. Include vignetting and other in-lens effects.

7. Perform color correction.

8. Simulate a particular film stock.

9. Add dissolves, fades, and other transitions, along with titles.

10. Perform specific color conversions, resizing, and sharpening for specific output formats.

The way to think about this is that you're applying the effects in the order that things happen in real life. You fix things that you wish had been different in front of the lens, then you add lens effects, then you pretend that all your shots look perfectly consistent, and then you simulate having shot all this on some kind of funky film stock that makes everything look super sexy (much more on that in a bit).

It might surprise you to learn that this kind of flexibility, and specifically the capability to do localized color corrections both before and after the primary grade, exceeds the capability of many high-end color correction systems used on feature films. Those systems, some costing hundreds of thousands of dollars, are so fixated on operating in real time that they impose very specific workflows on their operators. Real-time feedback is great, and especially important when working with a client. But since you are your own client, you can sacrifice the expensive luxury of real time and take advantage of the power and flexibility of using a full-blown compositing application as your color correction station. There's nothing magical about a Da Vinci 2k or a Lustre, and there's nothing they do that you can't do in After Effects. In fact, you can do much more than they can—but you will have some rendering time ahead of you.[3]

Tools of the Trade

This section covers the actual hands-on techniques involved in color correcting your film in After Effects.

---

3 *The Last Birthday Card* was made on an Apple G3 and took over two days to render. I chose to take these enforced breaks from working on my film as opportunities to strike up a new hobby, one that I still practice today: staring at my After Effects progress bar.

THE GOODIES

Oh yes, there are goodies.

On the included DVD, in the Goodies folder, are two folders: **copy ToPresets** and **copyToScripts**. Copy the contents of copyToPresets to the Presets folder in the Adobe After Effects 7.0 application folder. Copy the contents of the copyToScripts folder into the Scripts folder while you're there. Relaunch After Effects.

If you've done this all correctly, there should be a new script in your File > Scripts menu, enticingly called rd_DVRebelTools.jsx. Select it.

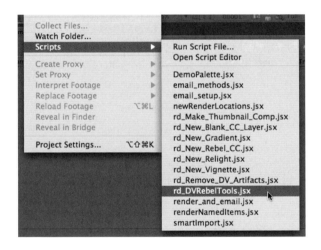

A palette will appear. Do not be alarmed if rays of light shoot out of your screen and angels descend from heaven with trays full of breakfast sandwiches—such is the power of the DV Rebel Tools palette.

Damn.

Jeff Almasol

The DV Rebel Tools palette and the scripts it launches were crafted for this book by Jeff Almasol. Jeff helped develop scripting products for After Effects called Useful Things and Useful Assistants. These plug-ins brought scripting power to After Effects before it was built into the application. Now Jeff has gone straight to the source and works directly for Adobe as a quality engineer on the After Effects team.

Jeff has a Web site, redefinery.com, where he maintains a growing list of utility scripts that automate complex tasks in After Effects. A couple of my favorites are rd: Scooter and rd: Statesman. Check 'em out!

THE BASICS

I realize that you are probably excited to play with the new goodies you just installed. But before I get into that I need to go over the basics. Ninety-nine percent of the color correction you'll ever need to do in life can be accomplished with two basic effects, and you should master them before trying Rebel CC. The two effects are Levels and Hue/Saturation, and at The Orphanage, we've actually color corrected entire feature films using only these effects.

The reason Levels is important is that it provides a means of controlling the shadows, highlights, and midtones of an image separately. The reason you often need Hue/Saturation as well is that Levels cannot change one color to another, nor can it control the saturation of a color. Levels provides surgical control over the three channels of the image— red, green, and blue—whereas Hue/Saturation allows you to mix and match colors among those three channels. With these two capabilities, you can do almost every kind of color correction possible, including anything you can do in a million-dollar DI suite.

I couldn't possibly do a better job of explaining these effects than Mark Christiansen has done in his book *Adobe After Effects 7.0 Studio Techniques* (Adobe Press). Read up on these two fundamentals (and while you're at it, revel in his explanation of Curves as well).

REMOVE ARTIFACTS

While there are commercial plug-ins out there that do a terrific job of removing the specific color glitches that plague consumer digital video formats, Magic Bullet chief among them, I refuse to let this book be an ad for Magic Bullet, so here's a nifty trick for getting a pretty darn good "de-artifacting" effect. Not as good as Magic Bullet's, but good, and really cheap.

Use the Remove DV Artifacts button in the DV Rebel Tools palette to clean up the nasty color edges that make DV sad. Before is on the left, after on the right. In this example, the difference is most profound in the blue channel (bottom two images).

In After Effects, select your clip in the Timeline and click the Remove DV Artifacts button in the DV Rebel Tools palette. A new adjustment layer will appear with only one effect on it—Median. Many people know the trick of blurring only the color channels of an image to smooth out DV artifacts, but Median works a lot better than blur. Blurs can ruin good edges while smoothing chunky ones, whereas Median has a magical way of attacking only the nasty bits of blocky color.[4]

---

4 The default value is 3, but you can try 2 or 4 as well. Use the smallest value that satisfactorily reduces the blockiness.

This effect works because the adjustment layer uses the Color transfer mode. With only one quick layer, you've drastically reduced the blockiness of your DV's color.

REBEL CC

OK, it's finally time to try out the Rebel CC in the DV Rebel Tools palette, a powerful three-way color corrector built out of common household items!

What's this fascination with "three-way" color correctors? Would a four-way not be 25 percent better? Maybe, but it seems that we simple film people like to think about images in terms of three ranges of values: "shadows," or that which is, you know, kinda dark; "highlights," i.e., bright stuff; and "midtones," presumably whatever's left in between. We can look at an image that's funky and assess it with a statement like, "The highlights are OK but the shadows are all brown and the midtones are a gnarly puce." Beyond that, we find it hard to say what might be off about an image.

Glibness aside, it is no accident that most color correction is designed around this shadows-midtones-highlights model. It works equally well for correcting images as it does for artistically designing a look.

Not all three-way correctors are created equal. The one in Final Cut Pro HD behaves differently than the one in Premiere Pro, which bears no resemblance to the one in Sony's Vegas. The truth is, I don't care for any of those three-way correctors. As you read earlier, I like Levels (you did read the exciting section called "The Rules," right?). Levels is actually a three-way color corrector that works almost, but not quite, like the ones inside those million-dollar DI suites I keep insisting you should not envy.

But let's face it, Levels is hard to drive. If you want to make the midtones less magenta, you need to know that means either to raise green gamma (well, actually lower it) or to nudge blue and red gammas in the opposite direction. If you wanted to do some combination of the three, you'd have to click as many as six different UI elements to do so. Levels is precise, but unwieldy.

Enter Rebel CC. Rebel CC is an animation preset that allows you to drive Levels with color swatches. Want to make midtones less magenta? Just pick a slightly greener color for the Midtone CC swatch.

Rebel CC also splits apart two common tasks that you've already read quite a bit about. It provides two sets of three swatches, the first for correcting or *optimizing* the image's color, and the second for designing it.

You can apply Rebel CC in many ways. You can select a layer and then click on the New Rebel CC button in the DV Rebel Tools palette, which will automatically create an adjustment layer over the selected layer. Or you can find Rebel CC in your Effects and Presets panel by typing "rebel" into the search field, and from there drag it onto the layer you wish to color-correct.

The first swatch is called Step 1: Set Black. The "Step 1" part is a little reminder to use these three swatches in order, otherwise they won't work. So the first order of business is to tell Rebel CC what color in your image is "black." Do this by clicking the eyedropper that's next to the swatch, and sampling the darkest color in your image.

Use the eyedropper to sample the blackest pixels in the image. Tip: If you hold down Cmd (Mac) or Ctrl (Windows), you sample a larger area, which can help you work around the inevitable noise in your image.

Your image should then change to reflect the new setting. If you picked a good color, the shadow tones of your image should look more neutral now. If that's not the case, undo and try again. If no amount of sampling yields a more neutral look to the shadows, that's fine—just reset the picker to pure black and skip this step. Don't worry if your image gets darker than you thought it might.

Next up is Step 2: Set Highlights. Here you are looking for the whitest white in the shot. If the brightest color in the shot isn't white, you may want to skip this step. The image at the top shows what my image looks like

after sampling the white collar on Mike's shirt.

The last step in optimizing the image is to set the gray value. The second image on this page shows the fully optimized image after sampling Mike's jacket.

Looks to me like I picked a black value that wasn't quite the blackest thing in the shot. The shadows are a bit *blocked up,* or crushed. I'm clipping off some pixel values, which I should not do when optimizing. No problem though—just grab the Shadow Brightness slider and gently nudge it up. To better see what you're doing when fine-tuning the blacks, you can crank up Highlight Brightness to a very large value. This way you can clearly see when you stop clipping blacks. You want the smallest Shadow Brightness value that still shows no clipping, or flat, detail-free black areas. When you're done, set Highlight Brightness back to 1.

Left: Cranking up Highlight Brightness reveals that I've crushed my blacks a bit. Center: The result of lifting Shadow Brightness until the blocked-up areas are cured. Right: Resetting Highlight Brightness to 1.0 results in perfectly optimized shadow tones.

From here on, you can use the rest of the Rebel CC preset as you please, but there are some common practices to observe. For example, most colorists work in exactly the sequence I just ran through—shadows first, highlights second, midtones last—both when optimizing an image and when designing a creative look. You will get the best results by following this sequence.

The mechanism by which you color correct with Rebel CC is the set of three color pickers that begin with "CC." You pick colors for these swatches to nudge the relevant value range in that direction. A little color goes a long way, and if you ever want to get back to a "zeroed out" setting, simply enter a value of pure white.

When you click on any of the CC swatches, the After Effects color picker pops up. Although it won't be very interactive (in the sense that your image won't update while you adjust the colors using the picker), this color picker can be made to behave almost like the color wheel in a more traditional three-way corrector. The key is to click on the radio button labeled "B."

Left: Using the Adobe color picker in Brightness mode results in an unfolded color wheel, ideal for use with Rebel CC. Right: Slightly more intuitive, but also less informative, the Apple color picker's color wheel tab is another good choice for use with Rebel CC—if you're on a Mac.

In Brightness mode the After Effects color picker is at least a little more friendly to color correcting. It's still not a color wheel, but it's as close as I can get ya.

Unless you're on a Mac! Mac OS X has its own color picker that features a color wheel mode. After Effects doesn't use this picker by default, but if you'd like to use it instead of the Adobe picker, just install the free Redefinery script called rd: PickerSwitcher (redefinery.com). This will allow you to switch back and forth between the Adobe and system color pickers.

For a detailed tutorial on using Rebel CC to create a creative look, see "Push and Pull" later in this chapter.

MASTER WITH A CARD

Rather that scrounge around for decent black, white, and gray tones for your optimizing process, why not roll out the red carpet for yourself and shoot a gray card? Just tape the thing to your slate and you'll always have one at the head of each shot. Of course, to be useful, it should be in the key light of the scene and free from glare. If you use the fancy Kodak one shown here, you get black and white patches as well. The black patch will probably not be the blackest value in your shot, so you'll need to lift Shadow Brightness after sampling.

This gray card from Kodak runs about $80, but I'll tell you a secret—if you print your own on nice white card stock, you'll probably get totally decent results from it. Consistency is more important than accuracy.

MASKS

One of the biggest reasons for grading in layers is the ability to confine your corrections via layer masks. Masked corrections are sometimes called *localized corrections,* and they are very powerful tools. While many high-end real-time systems restrict localized corrections to "power windows" that are either rectangular or oval, in After Effects you are free to use any mask shape, or combinations of several shapes.

Any mask applied to an adjustment layer serves to restrict the effect of that adjustment. It's like matting between the affected and unaffected image. This is perfect for us—all you need to do to define your color correction region is to add a mask to your adjustment layer.

Usually you will want to feather these masks to create a soft boundary to your corrections. Don't be afraid of very large feather values—they help hide the transition and keep you from having to set a ton of keyframes to track your mask into a moving shot. If you'd like to see what your mask actually looks like, including the feathering, double-click on the adjustment layer to view it and hit Opt + 4 (Mac) or Alt + 4 (Windows) to view the alpha channel.

Using masks to confine color corrections to a particular region of the frame is a powerful capability made easy by the use of adjustment layers. In the center is the mask used to brighten up Billy Brooks in the "Not So Secondary Corrections" example.

RELIGHTING

While you can't truly "relight" a scene in post, you just saw an example of a localized color correction that appeared to change the lighting of a scene. What you cannot generally change about the lighting in a shot is the quality of the light. But you most certainly can change the quantity. When a colorist talks about relighting a shot, she's usually talking about adding or subtracting light. You can add light to focus attention on a particular area, such as a face, or you can subtract light to add shadow and mood to a scene, or take focus away from a distracting element.

This is best viewed as a method for enhancing lighting that is already pretty good, rather than a way of "fixing" bad lighting—although I would be lying if I said I'd never done the latter in cases where I was my own DP!

A relighting correction is simply a masked adjustment layer with a specific kind of effect on it. In most cases, the effect of choice is Exposure, found in the Color Correction submenu in After Effects.

Scott's arrival at Baxter's studio in *The Last Birthday Card* was shot with only natural light. Somehow in my excitement over shooting at magic hour for the dusk coloration in the sky, I neglected to notice that

Scott wasn't centered properly in the pool of light cast by the bare bulb above the door. The following figures detail the process of hammering this shot into submission in After Effects.

The untreated footage (left) looks almost passable, but once I applied an overall look (right), the added contrast made it clear that this was a shot about Scott's shoulder.

My first task was to add an adjustment layer to color correct the face. I added this below the look adjustment layer, since relighting needs to occur before creative grading.

 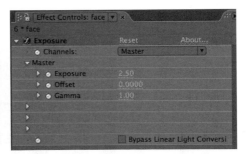

I then created a mask on this new layer. The mask is not all that precise, and is feathered considerably (about 45 pixels at NTSC resolution). I applied the Exposure effect and boosted the light on Scott's face by 2.5 stops.

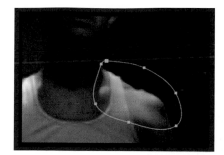 

Next, I created a second adjustment layer for the shoulder. Same deal here as the face, except here I exposed down by a stop and a half. Note how in both cases the mask is rough and extends beyond Scott's silhouette. Since both masks are feathered, a little sloppiness means that I might not have to animate the masks if Scott moves around a little.

The results (left) look much better, but Scott still looks like he's in the dark. My last step was to add a third adjustment layer with a super-soft (350 pixels!) oval mask, and expose up a "spotlight" area around Scott. Note that the brightening effect happens everywhere within the soft matte, not just on Scott. You can totally get away with big, broad localized corrections like this. Try it—you'll be surprised how much you can get away with.

The final image (right) with the original for comparison. What was my point about not using these tricks to fix bad lighting?

GRADIENTS

In "The Camera" chapter on the DVD I extolled the virtues of the ND Grad filter as an exposure control device. I recommended that you stick with neutral gradients because you could always color them however you like in post. Here's how you do that.

The DV Rebel Tools palette has a button called New Gradient. Select any single shot in your Timeline and click this button. A new layer will appear above yours, and a Ramp effect will appear in the Effect Controls pane.

There's nothing that special about this new layer—it's simply a solid set to Overlay mode with the good old Ramp effect on it. You can reorient the ramp by moving the Start of Ramp and End of Ramp point controls, and you can adjust Start Color to change the color of your virtual grad filter.

Don't touch the End Color picker—that puppy's set to 50% gray because that's the transparent color for the Overlay Blend Mode.

Feel free to experiment with other blend modes, including Multiply—but I've found that Overlay deals well with footage containing problem highlights. If you do switch to Multiply, ignore what I said about End Color—you'll need to change it to pure white, the transparent color for Multiply.

VIGNETTES

As with gradients, a vignette is only a button-push away. Select your layer and then click New Vignette in the DV Rebel Tools palette.

This will result in two new layers hovering over your shot, labeled Vignette Matte, Controls and Vignette CC. You don't need to touch Vignette CC—all its functionality is driven by expressions in the Controls layer above it.[5]

The UI is simple. Ignore the effects with parentheses around their names—these are driven by expressions and require no loving caresses from your mouse pointer. You drive these beasts with three simple controls: Vignette Center, Falloff, and Strength.

---

5 Speaking of "above it," make sure to always maintain the layer order of these two vignette layers. The bottom one has expressions that will break if they can't find the Controls layer.

The user interface for the Vignette effect.

Vignette Center is a point control that places the "hotspot" of the vignette on your image. Drag it to the area you want the viewer to focus on.

Strength controls the intensity of the effect, and Falloff controls how gradual the darkening makes its way from the center to the edges.

TRANSITIONS

On the included DVD, there's a supplemental section for this chapter (**Chapter6/Transitions.pdf**) *all about creating multilayer transitions in your After Effects online project. You'll definitely want to read this to see how to fit these important effects into your project correctly.*

BLEACH BYPASS

I've mentioned *Saving Private Ryan* enough that I'd better talk about everyone's favorite color treatment, the *bleach bypass* look. While many people have heard this term, few know what it refers to. In 35mm color negative film processing, there's a stage during which the silver, which holds blacks of the image (sort of like the K in CMYK), is bleached off the negative. If you skip this step and then continue to process the negative, you wind up with a desaturated and contrasty image.

A decent approximation of the popular bleach bypass look can be achieved with two simple effects in After Effects.

There are a number of ways to emulate this look, but here's one you can do without any third-party effects. As you might guess, the way to make your image look desaturated and contrasty is to reduce the saturation and add contrast. But the latter part of that equation can be implemented much more elegantly than the Brightness & Contrast effect would ever allow if you bust out the oft-overlooked Curves effect.

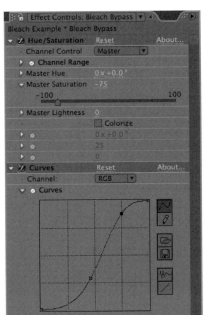

It's that S-shaped curve that's the key. It adds contrast without crushing detail, making for a much more film-like look. In fact, you can use a curve like this without the Hue/Saturation effect as a look adjustment for your project and you'll instantly lend it a more cinematic appearance.

You can dial in that S-curve however you like—there's no one correct setting. But do beware of slamming the curve flat against the top or the bottom of the box— when you do that you're clipping off detail in a harsh way. Some-times clipping might be a part of

One possible configuration for a bleach bypass effect—dial it in to your own taste, as there's no one right way to create this look. Note that the only value changed from its default in Hue/Saturation is Master Saturation, which has been reduced to -75 percent.

the look you want, but you should add another control point to the curve to ramp into your clip more gently.

Clipping off values in the shadows and highlights may be a part of the look you're going for (*Sin City*, anyone?), but there's a good and a bad way of doing it. On the left, the clipping (the flat area of the curve) is accidental and has an abrupt transition. On the right, I've smoothed the transition, preserving the aggressive contrast but maintaining detail in the shadows.

THE FILM LOOK

After Effects 7.0 introduced the beginnings of a CMS, or Color Management System. Using the Color Profile Converter effect, you can convert your images from one ICC color profile to another. Using this same mechanism, After Effects 7.0 also provided a means for film compositors to preview their work as it will appear projected on 35mm print film in a theater.

What this means to the DV Rebel is that there's actually a definitive recipe for that most sought-after of Holy Grails—making your video "look like film." You can actually apply a carefully measured simulation of a popular Kodak film stock to your DV footage!

1. In After Effects, import a clip and add it to a comp. Add the Color Profile Converter effect (Effect > Utility > Color Profile Converter) and set the Input Profile to one that matches your footage. If your footage is DV, you should use SMPTE-C; if it's HD, you should use HDTV (Rec 709).

2. Set the Output Profile to DPX Scene—Standard Camera Film.

3. This next step is very important. Set the Intent to Absolute Colorimetric. If you forget this part (which is easy to do, because what

the hell does that mean anyway?) the conversion won't work correctly.

4. Now add another Color Profile Converter effect after the first. Set the Input Profile to DPX Theater Preview—Standard Print Film. Set the Output Profile to the correct profile for your output medium. If HD, use HDTV (Rec 709); if NTSC, use SMPTE-C. Leave Intent alone.

5. You will probably find that your shot looks dark. Apply the Brightness & Contrast effect to the layer and place it between the two Color Profile Converter effects. Increase Brightness to taste.

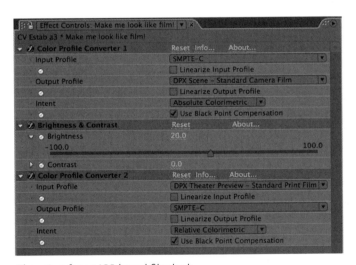

The setup for an ICC-based film look.

What just happened? The first Color Profile Converter effect converted your video image into a Cineon log color space—the color space of scanned film images used in visual effects and high-end DI suites. This was a somewhat accurate process because you knew the color space of the source (video) and of the destination (Kodak's 5218 color negative film stock). Then, you previewed this image using the lookup for Kodak's 2383 print film stock, also known as "Vision."

Left: An untreated DV shot. Right: The same image as if it had been shot on Kodak 5218 and printed on Kodak Vision stock.

Do you like the way it makes your image look? It's OK to say no. Mapping video to a film gamut should not necessarily look "good" without any intervention, and this whole process is only as accurate as the match-up between your camera's unique characteristics and a generic color ICC profile (the first Input Profile). As fun as this trick may be, I'd advise you against getting too excited about it. The truth is, most current action films are color corrected digitally. Their look is determined much more by the colorist's hand than by any particular film stock. Use the tools you like to make your film look the way you like.

But if you do like the way it looks, and still want to imbue your film with a custom look, you can actually apply the Rebel CC effect in between the two Color Profile Converter effects (after the Brightness & Contrast effect, if you used one). You'll then be color grading in what is known as "log color space," which is exactly how 35mm movies are digitally graded. The first three color pickers (Step 1 through Step 3) won't be of any use, but the Shadow, Midtone, and Highlight CC pickers will work just fine—although the controls will be a little more sensitive than you might be used to.

If you want to grade your whole film this way, I recommend applying the first Color Profile Converter, the one that goes from your video's color space to Standard Camera Film, to the individual clips in your Timeline. Then add an adjustment layer over the whole Timeline with the second Color Profile effect (Standard Print Film to video). Now you can work just as you ordinarily would, using the DV Rebel Tools palette to add color correction layers to each shot. Everything you do will be under the film look adjustment layer, so you'll always be obeying the same restrictions that the pros have when grading under a film LUT.

Jargon Watch

LUT means Look Up Table, which is just a fancy name for a color correction stored in a single file that can be read into some software and applied to an image. When you save an .acv file out of the Photoshop Curves window, that's a LUT. One common use of LUTs is to provide an accurate preview of what an image will look like on film.

Color Theory

It's a funny thing how forgiving and clever our eyes are. If you go into a room lit with only red light, you can still tell the difference between a red object and white one. In the lighting section of Chapter 3 you read a bit about how our eyes correct for light sources of different color temperatures. You can watch an entire movie from a crummy seat way off to the side of the theater and after a minute forget completely about the distortion. You can become engrossed in a TV show playing on a tiny iPod screen.

Think about the extreme color treatment in *Saving Private Ryan*. The contrast is so high in this film that details in shadows and highlights are obliterated completely. One could say that the audio equivalent of this would be to play the movie's soundtrack through a bad telephone connection—something the audience would never put up with. But not only do they effortlessly look past the harsh color-drained bleach bypass look of the film, they are actually *more* transported and *more* immersed in the film as a result of the look.

The ultimate proof of this is the audience's acceptance of black and white. If you've done much digital photography you've probably experienced the transformation that can occur when you take a mediocre photo and convert it to grayscale.

In short, you can get away with just about anything when color correcting your film. The audience will buy it. But this discovery is not a license to douse your film in some arbitrary, extreme look, "just because." It's an opportunity to enhance the storytelling power of your film in a way that the audience will inhale without even realizing how profoundly they are being affected.

PERFECT REALITY, MAGICAL FILM

Grade first for consistency, then for look. You've read that enough by now, but it's worth a quick philosophical look at why we do things this way.

The not-so-exciting tasks of evening out shots, correcting for inconsistencies in natural light, removing unwanted colors, and enhancing your already brilliant lighting are more than just necessary polishing steps in getting your film out the door. It's where you visually reinforce that the events of your film are larger-than-life. Honing a verisimilar cohesiveness across shots staged in a variety of conditions is how you make your movie feel not just real, but realer-than-real. Only in a movie can a beautiful blonde woman carry a golden rimlight with her wherever she goes, or can a vampire lurking in the shadows always have a cool blue glow in his ashen face. Only in a movie can it always be sunset in Miami, or perpetually overcast in Detroit. Grading for consistency is about creating an impossibly perfect reality.

But as you read only a couple of paragraphs ago, reality is for suckers. So what do you do after you craft this more-perfect-than-could-ever-be reality, where all shots match precisely and all mistakes of nature have been quelled? Why, you rephotograph your reality onto a magical film stock of your own design.

This is what's happening when you lay that "look" adjustment layer over all the shots in a sequence and give them that *Private Ryan* look, or that *Matrix* green twinge, or that dusty pallor of *O Brother, Where Art Thou?* You're inventing a film stock with just the characteristics that you like, and you're reshooting your movie with it.

This is why it's so important to maintain the correct order of operations. For example, if your magical film stock for a particular scene desaturates blue to the point where almost no blue can get through, then it would be a mistake to add a secondary correction after the look that pumped up blue for just one shot. The audience would read the inconstancy and feel somehow that something was wrong. But if you pump up blue underneath the look, you know that there will be a consistent maximum blue saturation to the entire scene, as if you'd shot on some kind of magical film stock that really didn't like blue. Another way of thinking about this is in the context of the greenish look that demarks the electronic reality of *The Matrix*. No matter how purple (the opposite of green) something might be inside the Matrix, it will never be as purple as it would be in the cold blue decks of the Nebuchadnezzar.

Upper left: An uncorrected image of a pinkish-purple house. Upper right: If you put that house in the greenish world of *The Matrix*, it still reads as purple, even though its actual color is a green-gray. Lower right: To insist that the house remain purple in the Matrix world blows the gag and makes the viewer aware that the tint is an arbitrary affectation rather than organic reality. Lower left: In a cool blue color scheme, the house becomes even more purple, without any help from a secondary color correction.

PUSH AND PULL

As you discovered, the shadow, midtone, and highlight corrections in Rebel CC are closely intertwined. It's hard to adjust one without affecting the other two. If this seems like a limitation, I'd like to encourage you to look at it another way.

Color correction systems that allow a more distinct isolation between the value ranges may seem to offer more precise control, but instead they encourage unpleasant results. Nevertheless, it can be a bit frustrating to carefully set a Shadow CC color, only to seemingly have it countermanded by subsequent midtone and highlight settings. How do you get the three value ranges to get along?

The answer is that you must play them off one another. Like a NASA flight engineer plotting a course by slingshoting off of planetary orbits, you must push and pull the three color swatches against each other until the correct values appear in between.

This is why colorists in real-time suites always have their hands on those three knobs. Any real color correction system has that same mysterious trio of knobs, and you almost never see a seasoned colorist adjust them one at a time. Instead, you find them massaging them in concert, like a race car driver in a tight corner guiding his car with both the steering wheel and the throttle. Until you upgrade to a Da Vinci, though, the three CC swatches in Rebel CC are your knobs. And while you can't tweak them simultaneously, you can play them off each other to produce your desired results.

Let's look at an example. You can follow along with the **scottBrushes Crop.tif** image located in the Examples/Rebel CC folder on your DVD. Say you have in mind that the shadows in this shot should be blue (are you detecting a pattern yet?). Not cyan-blue, not magenta-blue, but pure blue. So you apply Rebel CC and set Shadow CC to a neutral blue tone:

Pushing shadows towards a neutral blue produces intuitive results.

Success! The paintbrushes and other dark regions of the frame have been tinted to exactly the hue you specified. Now you want to push the highlights to a warm, golden color. You pick an appropriate value for Highlight CC as shown:

After pushing highlights warm, those blue shadows have gone a cyan-green.

When you exit the color picker the highlights have indeed gone warm, but look what happened to the shadows. Gone is that neutral blue cast you specified, and in its place is a cooler, more greenish tone. In fact, the whole shot has gone green—which looks kinda cool, but it's a flat, even green. You can do better.

Start by recovering what you liked about the shadow color. You made it blue, but then by pushing the highlights towards yellow you nudged the shadows that way as well, creating green. Now it's time to pretend you have your hands on the knobs and can push shadows away from green (or toward magenta) while you simultaneously nudge highlights towards a redder yellow color than what you actually want.

Things get even a bit more dynamic if you push the midtones slightly toward green. Suddenly your shadows and highlights, which you just pushed away from green, now both look green again! So you have to revisit shadows and highlights a second time, pushing them even father away from green. By the time you have an image with blue shadows, green midtones, and warm highlights, your CC swatches may well be pink, green, and peach-colored, respectively!

In order to maintain the appearance of blue shadows, you must counteract the green tint introduced by the highlight color. You do this by pushing your blue color more towards magenta, the opposite of green.

Yes, this would be much, much easier with a dedicated color correction plug-in (if you have one, please feel free to use it!). Easier still with a hardware control surface sporting that trio of trackballs. But Rebel CC will get you there with a little patience. At least it's easier than Levels!

PICK A PALETTE

By now you've probably noticed that a few consistent color correction schemes have come up several times: an overall green look like that in *The Matrix*, the green-to-warm push thing you just did with Scott above, the classic bleach bypass treatment, and many variations on the bluish shadows look.

I'm Being Followed by a Blue Shadow

Why do so many looks seem to push shadows cool and highlights warm? This color scheme seems to emulate the natural beauty we find in those *magic hour* moments you read about in Chapter 3. When the sun is low, it casts a warm light, and shadows appear to turn blue. The color contrast makes skin look golden and makes all colors seem to pop. I guess it shouldn't surprise us, then, that a color correction that invokes this scheme triggers a positive response in the viewer—it's as if you've bottled a sunset.

It's true that there are some go-to looks that colorists draw on again and again. But there's a popular misconception that a look can be applied to any old piece of footage and produce good results. This is not the case. The look that a seasoned colorist selects for a shot or sequence will be based on an analysis of the colors in the scene, and will follow certain rules that you might remember from grade school art class.

Here's an interesting exercise: Take a shot from any movie the look of which you admire. Freeze-frame the shot on your DVD player and count how many colors you see. Chances are, there will not be more than three. That's right, only three! Try it if you don't believe me. You might find a scene with up to four dominant tones, and you will certainly find some with only one or two, but three is the average. Art directors, cinematographers, wardrobe artists, and directors conspire to restrict the palette of a movie, a concept that I touched on in Chapter 3 ("Show Less").

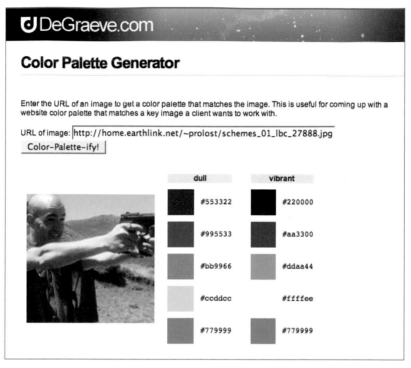

Designed for Web developers, DeGraeve.com's Color Palette Generator is an excellent tool for extracting the salient colors from your image. It's an important first step in deciding how your color correction can enhance, rather than overpower, your scene's inherent palette.

If you're finding it hard to count colors in an image, there's a cool online tool to help you at degraeve.com/color-palette. This tool allows you to specify any image on the Web, and it will show you a simplified color palette derived from that image. If you do some online image searches for frame grabs from *The Matrix*, you can then pass those image URLs to the Color Palette Generator and see how their color schemes can be boiled down to a few primary hues that feel related to one another. Give the Color Palette Generator a random snapshot from the Web and you'll see that most images don't have this kind of restricted, harmonious palette.

The idea that certain colors balance each other harmoniously and others clash is something that I learned the hard way from some giggly girls in junior high after wearing brown shoes with black pants. I guess I didn't pay enough attention in art class when they showed us this:

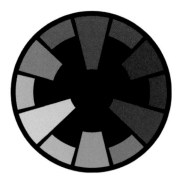

The subtractive color wheel. Clockwise from top center: red, red-violet, violet, blue-violet, blue, blue-green, green, yellow-green, yellow, yellow-orange, orange, red-orange.

That's the color wheel, with the three primary colors represented by the longest pie slices. Why are the primary colors red, *yellow,* and blue, rather than red, *green,* and blue? This is the subtractive color wheel—in other words, it represents the relationship of color pigments, not illumination. If you had only three light sources and you wanted to create any imaginable color, you'd need a red, green, and blue light. That's how your computer monitor works. But if you were going to paint a painting and could only afford three tubes of paint, you'd want red, blue, and yellow, since you can create green by mixing yellow and blue paints together.

Because our computer graphics tools emphasize the RGB color model so strongly, it's very important to remember that color harmonies, or pleasing combinations of colors, are best extrapolated from the RYB color wheel. There are a number of ways to drive color schemes using the color wheel, but they all start with the idea that you have one *base color* for which you want to derive a complementary color. The following figures show three common methods of deriving color complements. For these examples I started with red as my base color, but the concepts apply to any hue.

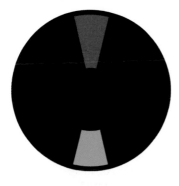

The simplest rule of color theory is that the hue that is opposite your base color is its complement. For any color on the wheel, the color facing it will always balance it equally. A film that uses this two-tone complement scheme well is *The Exorcism of Emily Rose,* where entire scenes seemed composed of no colors other than red-orange and its direct complement, blue-green.

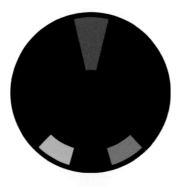

The most common method of deriving complementary hues is the *split complementary* rule. For any base color, take the two hues surrounding the opposite position on the wheel. An example of this can be found in *The Matrix* when Neo first meets Morpheus. Morpheus sits on a red chair in a yellow-green room, wearing a blue-green leather trench coat.

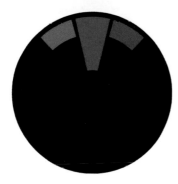

Another common rule in color theory is that of *analogous* colors. The analogous colors are the ones to either side of the base color. You can optionally use the base color's complement as well when using its analogous pair. The dusty debris that surrounds the asteroid in *Armageddon* consists of pure blue and its analogous hues. A splash of orange shows up from time to time, introducing blue's complement into the palette.

Remember that these rules are for finding complementary hues. The lightness and/or saturation of the colors does not matter. That's why you see a lot of color wheels like the one on the next page.

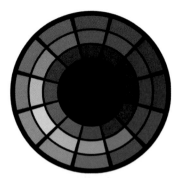

Many color wheels display alternate color *tones*, or degrees of saturation and/or lightness. When selecting complementary colors, you may choose any tone you like from within the appropriate hue.

There's a great online tool you can use to help select color schemes using the above rules. Another filmmaking tool masquerading as a Web tool, you can find it at wellstyled.com/tools/colorscheme.

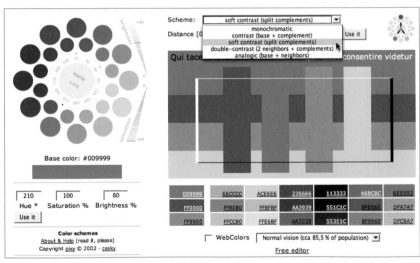

Color Scheme (wellstyled.com/tools/colorscheme) is a Web design tool created by Petr Stanicek, but it's a handy online reference for anyone who needs to quickly find a color palette based on a known color.

It's easy to see how working within a palette of harmonious hues can be an important concept to keep in mind when designing a set or a wardrobe, but how does it affect the colorist? The fact is, many of the scenes I used as examples above derive their palettes as much from their color grading as to their physical designs. Take the *Matrix* example—sure, that room may have been painted a greenish tone, but the palette wouldn't have nearly the punch it does if the color correction didn't make green a major player in the scene.

And that is the ultimate point of this section: The look that you choose for a sequence should be an integral part of the color scheme you've designed. And hey, I'm realistic—I know that sometimes the DV Rebel cannot fully design a world with as much meticulous control as a film-maker with an army of set builders and art department PAs. But whatever lack of control you had on your guerrilla shoot, you can still refine and enhance the palette of your scene in the grade, rather than slather a look across it like peanut butter.

As an example, take *The Green Project* on the DVD (the one that you're about to become quite familiar with). As you know, I shot this in a com-pletely uncontrolled environment: a festival in San Francisco's Chinatown. The only thing dictating my palette was luck and the pre-art-directed quality of Chinatown itself. The one choice I could make to help myself out was to select a bright orange color for the fugitive's wardrobe.

Here's a raw, untreated frame from that footage run through DeGraeve.com's Color Palette Generator:

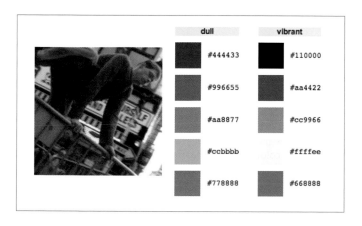

dull		vibrant	
	#444433		#110000
	#996655		#aa4422
	#aa8877		#cc9966
	#ccbbbb		#ffffee
	#778888		#668888

Although the colors are not inharmonious, they could be better. Check out the same frame after some color tweaking using Rebel CC:

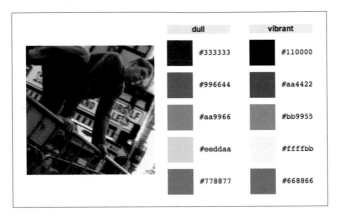

The result seems more harmonious, but is it? Let's go back to the Color Scheme site and check.

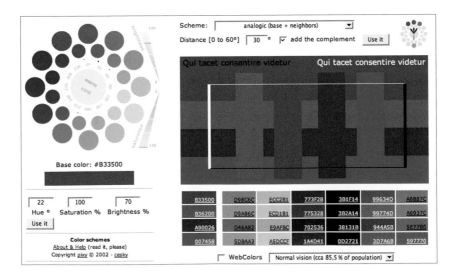

The colors aren't identical, but the hues are in the right places. The color correction has brought the color ranges of the image into harmonious accord, both according to the rules, and to the eye. This is the look you'll use for *The Green Project* when you follow step-by-step instructions to online it yourself in a few pages.

Now, am I suggesting that you must vet your every color decision through a complex series of Web tools? Not at all. Consider these tools to be training wheels in your journey to understanding color. I still like to keep these links in my toolbar even after years of coloring my own projects, but after time you will develop an intuitive sense of how colors relate, which combinations are pleasing, and how you can enhance this in your grading. As a handy cheat sheet, and in the spirit of this book being a true guide, this page features a wheel of color wheels showing the split comple-ments for all 12 positions on the color wheel.

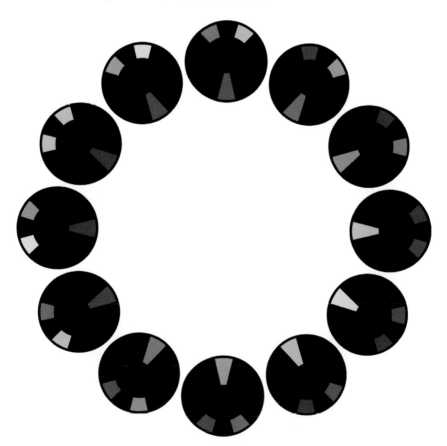

Three "color plots" from the movies *Pearl Harbor,
Crimson Tide,* and *Top Gun.* Can you guess which strip
belongs to which film? Hint: They're not in the order I
listed them, of course!

TELL A COLOR STORY

It's not enough to create a cool look for your scenes. I hate to keep going back to *The Matrix,* but it's a film that uses color schemes to excellent story effect. When you first saw the film, you probably didn't even real-ize how green Neo's world was until the first moment you saw him in the real world. The green tint of the artificial reality of *The Matrix* was working along with many other cues in the film to give you the subtle impression that something wasn't right, but it wasn't tipping the filmmaker's hand.

Color association can be a powerful filmmaking tool, and it's as old an idea as color in films. Watch Hitchcock's *The Birds* and pay close attention to the use of red. You will find that bits of red scenery appear in other-wise cool color schemes just before an attack by the birds. Next time you watch *American Beauty,* see if you notice a distinctly American flag color scheme to almost every major shot in the film, especially in a poignant moment near the end.

The larger your filmmaking endeavors the more people will be asking you questions. Nine out of ten of these questions are along the lines of "What color should this be?" or "Which of these five vintage cars do you like best?" If you've plotted out a color association for the major events of your film, you'll always know the answer to these questions.

In *The Last Birthday Card,* I designed the following color associations: Scott's "happy place" of painting and artistic expression would be a pale pink color. Red would of course be the color of killing and death. Nak's signature color would be bright yellow. These decisions were sometimes practically motivated—turns out the actor playing Nak really did own that awesome yellow Land Rover. But assigning red to be the color of death led to some fun explorations, including a citywide search for a hotel room in San Francisco with red walls. A minor setback occurred when I found out that the red envelopes I wanted Scott's birthday card hit assignments to arrive in were discontinued because they confuse the Post Office's optical sorting robots. But when Scott and I were looking through his closet for a shirt that he should wear for the final scene, I instantly knew I wanted the orange-red button-down you see him in.

Even after finding a hotel with a red interior, I didn't stop there. The scene where Scott goes to assassinate Jacob Billups (David Beyers Brown) is color corrected to be almost entirely red. I wanted each scene to have a distinctive color scheme and each major idea to have a color, and when a scene arrived that fully expressed that idea, that scene would be in the color of the major idea.

Have you figured out which movie goes with which color plot? The answer is, from left to right, *Top Gun, Pearl Harbor,* and *Crimson Tide.*

SINS OF THE FLESH

There's one last bit of wisdom that I've gleaned from my time spent with some of the world's most respected colorists. These guys are often asked to create extreme looks, looks that are pushed strongly in contrast and tint. This is something that anyone can do—but what sets the big boys apart is their ability to create crazy looks without damaging skin tones.

Even *Underworld,* which is nearly a black-and-white film for how cold and icy blue it's been tinted, allows the pale flesh hues of its nocturnal denizens to rise above the blue-black depths. In *Spy Game,* Brad Pitt somehow manages to maintain a healthy complexion even as he's escorted into a monochromatic blue-green Chinese prison.

How is it possible to push a scene so completely blue and not destroy flesh tones? The answer lies in the push-pull technique you just learned about. The fact is, with Rebel CC, you can push shadows one direction and highlights another, and if you're very careful, you teeter-totter the tonal scale around that magical flesh-tone value without affecting it.

If this sounds challenging, it should. There's a reason those colorists I was talking about all drive such nice cars. But I've got a trick you can use to help develop skin-tone-friendly looks.

It starts with a chart. Go to babelcolor.com/main_level/ColorChecker. htm and download one of their digital versions of the GretagMacbeth colorchecker chart. You'll have to scroll past a ton of really useful and utterly unimportant information to get there, but two-thirds of the way down the page you'll find some download links. The one you want is the sRGB 16-bit TIFF from the left column. The direct link is:

www.babelcolor.com/download/ColorChecker_sRGB_from_Lab_16bit.tif

If you haven't seen this chart before, here's what it looks like (right):

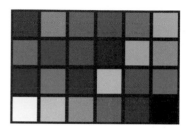

The purpose of the chart is the same as that gray card I showed you in the Rebel CC section: It provides a known set of color values that can be used in post to ensure that you've correctly characterized an image. But for our purposes you won't need a physical version of this card—what you're going to do is experiment with some color correction on this image you've just downloaded, paying special attention to one of the 24 color patches.

See, each of these patches is supposed to represent some real-world color, and the one second in from the left on the top is supposed to be an average white dude. Er, I mean, a representative Caucasian flesh tone.

Load this chart image into After Effects and apply Rebel CC to it. Your goal is now to experiment with the most extreme looks you can imagine, while trying to keep that white guy square as close to the original as possible. Snapshot the uncorrected image (Shift + F5) and then use the F5 key to compare it against your corrected image.

Here's an example of that tried-and-true blue shadows, warm highlights, green midtones look. I've placed the original colors in small squares superimposed over the corrected image. The gray squares show just how "pushed" this look is, adding contrast and radically adjusting

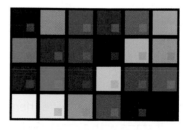

the tonal range. And yet the pink square is almost unchanged. If anything, it's gone a bit warm, which is usually a good thing for skin tones.

Once you think you have a pretty cool look brewing, move it from the squares to an actual image. Start with a shot that has decent skin tones, like the one on the left, and then apply the Rebel CC settings.

I've managed to give the image a highly aggressive look (image on right) without making the butcher's looks inhuman. And in the process I've decided maybe I'll just have a salad for dinner tonight.

There's only so far you can take this concept, so another handy thing to remember is it's OK to warm up the flesh tones as a part of the shot-by-shot correction, knowing that the look will cool them back off. A handy tool for doing isolated, secondary-style color corrections in After Effects is the Change Color effect, found under Color Correction.

These are the Rebel CC settings I used on my chart.

LIGHTING FOR THE GRADE

Lighting and color correction have a symbiotic relationship. It probably won't surprise you to learn that good lighting can be color corrected to look bad, or that even the best color correction cannot save a poorly lit shot. But what few DV shooters realize is that there are some specific things you can do with lighting that will greatly improve your color correction process, as long as you light with a specific color correction scheme in mind.

For example, let's say that you have a scene that you know you will be tinting a cool, desaturated blue. This is an overall look you're going for—you want the whole scene to appear cold, dark, and metallic.

If you shoot your scene normally, making it look nice and balanced in the viewfinder and watching your shadow and highlight detail, you will most certainly be able to color correct the scene cool and blue later. However, there will be only so far you can go with that look, because if you push it too far, even if you observe the push-pull technique, the flesh tones may prevent you from going too far with your look.

There's a technique common on music videos and commercials that can help with this. What you do is light your talent with a warmer tone than the rest of the scene. It's like building a spot-correction into the shot—you're essentially pre-counteracting your cool look on the actor's skin. This is definitely something you want to test before you commit to it. It's especially important that you watch your clipping—it's quite easy to light skin so warm that it clips in the red channel, rendering it unrecoverable in post. Clipping in red alone is sometimes not enough to trigger your camera's zebra effect, making this all the more risky a move.

Left: The lovely Michelle on a brisk morning in Minneapolis. The warm light is natural, and this is the raw image as it appeared in my viewfinder. Right: I was able to apply a very aggressive look to this image, cooling down the entire scene and yet still leaving a pleasant warm tone in Michelle's face.

A Sample Sequence

OK, it's time to take all that you've learned so far and apply it to a sample sequence included on the DVD.

1. In the Examples/Green/Project folder on the DVD, find **green.aep** and copy it to your local hard drive. Open it from there.

   When you first open the project, it may have trouble finding the footage. If so, you can double-click on the missing footage icons and locate the files found in Examples/Green/Footage, /Effects, and /Audio. Alternately, you can copy these files to your local disk as well for faster performance (recommended). If you do that you must reference them in that location (see the After Effects help manual on replacing footage).

2. With the project open and all footage located, choose File > Scripts > rd_DVRebelTools.jsx. Place the DV Rebel Tools palette somewhere convenient.

The Green Project as it appears when you first load it in.

3. Open the Color Correct comp in the Onlining Comps folder. Your setup should look something like the above figure.

    What you're looking at is what you might get straight from Automatic Duck or from importing a Premiere Pro project into After Effects. It's your movie raw, unrecompressed, and ready to be color corrected.

4. The first order of business is to swap in the effects shots. You may notice as you examine the footage that the hit man is carrying a green plastic gun. Luckily, the visual effects elves have been up all night baking fresh de-greened gun shots for you. Import these five effects files from the DVD, or copy them locally, from **Examples/Green/Effects** and then import the copies. Place them in the Source Footage/Effects folder in your project.

    It might seem a little anal retentive to be placing these few shots in their own folder, but when you have hundreds of shots and dozens of effects, it will all make sense. Remember, onlining is the least rebellious part of the process.

5. Now begin carefully laying in the effects shots over their corresponding shots. As you do this, you should see nothing about the shot change except the gun, which will go from green to steely gray. Toggle the effects shot on and off to check your lineup, i.e., ensure that you have placed the effects shots to their proper frames.

6. Once all the effects are placed, I like to use the label colors to help differentiate things. Go ahead and assign the effects shots a unique color (I chose pink) and switch the old shots they replaced to another color (like blue). Turn off the visibility of the old shots but do not delete them—they're good reference in case you have a question about sync.

Replacing the effects plates with the rendered shots. Your next step will be to switch off visibility for the old plates so that After Effects doesn't try to render them.

You're almost ready for the fun part. You're going to use the Make Thumbnail Comp button on your DV Rebel Tools palette to create a helpful master view of your entire Timeline, so you can see all your shots at once and compare them for color consistency and look. But first you need to fix a few details and set your poster frames for each shot.

7. A few of these shots, being hand-held and uncontrolled, could use a little reframing. Select Shot 2 and press Cmd + Opt + B (Mac) or Ctrl + Alt + B (Windows) to set the comp work area to just this shot. RAM preview and notice that Eric's head keeps bobbing out of the top of the frame. This shot would look better if you used the headroom provided by the letterbox—in other words, repo it down. Grab the layer and slide it down as shown.

8. Scan through the other shots and see if any of them could use repoing. For my taste, Shots 2 and 3 look better repoed all the way

Some shots in *Green* look better with a slight vertical repo—one of the benefits of shooting standard def for a widescreen master.

down, and Shots 4 and 7 work well repoed up as far as they'll go. Remember to RAM preview each shot to ensure that your repo works well over the entire length.

Now it's time to set each shot's poster frame. The poster frame is the frame that best encapsulates the look and intent of the shot. Sometimes a shot may require two or more poster frames, especially if it is a long shot or contains many story beats.

9. Go to Shot 1 and scrub through it. Select a frame that you like and, making sure that Shot 1 is selected, press the * key on your numeric keypad to create a marker. I chose Frame 17.

10. Continue this for each shot. For the shots with effects, be sure to place the marker on the effects layer.

    When you're done, your Timeline should look about like this:

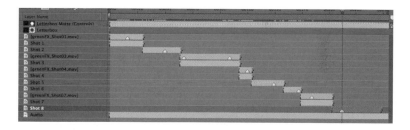

    Note that I selected two poster frames for Shot 6. While not strictly necessary, I just wanted to show that it's possible.

11. It's time to push the button! Select each layer that has markers on it. This should be every shot, and only the effects layer, not the plate that you turned off, as shown in the next figure. When you have all the layers selected, press the Make Thumbnail Comp button on the DV Rebel Tools palette.

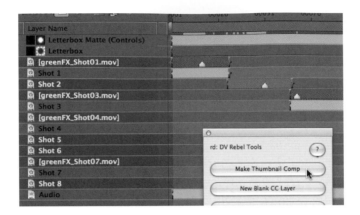

12. When the script is done running, a dialog will appear asking you to open the selected composition. Select OK and open the new comp that you just created, called Color Correct Thumbnails.

You should see something much like the previous figure. In case it's not obvious, let me try to explain just how cool this is. Each layer in this comp is a freeze-frame of the poster frame you selected. It doesn't matter where you are in time, this comp will always show you the same image.

The markers you see on the layers are live. If you ever want to change your poster frame, just move the marker to the new frame and the thumbnail will update.

The sort order is live, too. You can reorder the layers in the comp and the thumbnails will resort automatically.

The sorting of the thumbnails reflects the visibility of the layers. Try selecting three of the thumbnails (you can shift-click directly on them in the comp view) and then solo those three. The three layers shift to the top. In this way you can easily view a set of similar shots together, or break a larger sequence down into bite-size chunks when working on a longer project.

You can change the size of the thumbnails. Select the Controls layer and examine its effects controls. Adjust Tiles Across and watch your thumbnails update. If you have more tiles than will fit on one screen, you can use Scroll to scroll through them. If you're viewing your thumbnails on a video monitor that doesn't have underscan, your tiles may get cut off at the edges of the screen. Drag Scale All down to about 80% to fix that. And if your images are letterboxed like those in *Green*, you can adjust Trim Letterbox (%) to get rid of the blank areas between the rows of tiles.

But the real power of the thumbnails comp comes when you lock its view and place it alongside your Color Correction Comp view, like this:

With this setup you can work in the color correction comp, adjusting your shots and creating your look, and you can always see a live overview of your entire sequence updated in real time.

13. Can I get an amen?

14. It's time to start color correcting. You are going to want a Rebel CC effect on each layer, so select all your layers (again, only the visible ones) in the Color Correction Comp and click New Rebel CC. Rebel CC adjustment layers should appear above each shot, neatly trimmed to match. These new layers should be selected—take advantage of that opportunity to label them all some unique color. I chose violet. Now your setup should look like this:

15. Select the first Rebel CC layer and go to your poster frame for Shot 1. Using what you know of Rebel CC, optimize the shot by first sampling a black color for Set Black, then the whitest color in the shot for Set White. I found that Set Gray was unnecessary on this shot after I set my black and white points. Remember, if Set Black gives you too much crushing in the shadows, increase the Shadow Brightness slider. If Set White causes any clipping in the highlights, back it off with Highlight Brightness.

16. Repeat this process for every shot, checking your work as you go in the thumbnail view. You can easily navigate from one poster frame to the next using the J and K keys. Cool! The truth is, these shots don't require a ton of evening out, but at the end of this process you should have a very neutral and consistent sequence.

17. Now it's time to create a look. Select the Letterbox Matte layer and click on New Rebel CC. No, you're not color correcting the letter-box—this is just an easy way to get a Rebel CC adjustment layer the entire length of the comp. After it appears, name it "Look" and move it below the letterbox as shown.

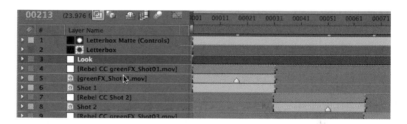

18. You already read how I came up with the look for this scene using the color wheel, but feel free to experiment on your own. You may have noticed that when you were working on the shots one at a time, the thumbnails updated very quickly because only one shot changed. As you tweak the look, all the thumbnails will re-render, so things get a little slower. Feel free to close the thumbnail view if this gets too annoying, although eventually you'll need to check your look across the whole sequence.

Step back and look at the whole sequence. RAM preview it and watch it a few times. It's looking pretty good. What's nice about the scene is that, for a project staged in the ultimate of uncontrolled environments, it feels like it has a nice, consistent palette—like a movie.

Except one shot.

What is the deal with that dude's purple shirt in Shot 4? Does that guy not know we're trying to make a film with a tastefully restrained palette? Did he not get the memo?

19. Select your Rebel CC layer for Shot 4 and scroll down through the effects controls to the Hue/Saturation effect. Select Magenta from the Channel Control pop-up menu and drag Magenta Saturation all the way down.

Whew. I feel much better.

20. Hey, while we're on this shot, I think we could emphasize our killer a bit more here. Select the shot and click New Vignette. Remember, the Vignette goes above the shot's optimization and below any other corrections. Select the Controls layer (if it isn't already selected) and use Vignette Center to position the vignette on the killer's face.

21. For good measure I also put a vignette on Shot 7 to help maintain focus on the fugitive as he ducks away. You kinda can't go wrong with vignettes, but try not to go crazy. I only wish there was a shot in this sequence that could use a gradient.

You could stop here, or you could keep going. There will always be some little bit of color consistency that you could improve, some little tweak you could make to the look. I recommend that you render the sequence and watch it a few times before you make that decision, though.

I just can't stop tweaking his scene. Here I upped the saturation of Eric's orange shirt slightly in Shot 5 to make it match the surrounding shots. Note that I've soloed only the Eric shots in the thumbnails comp and set my Tiles Across to 2, so as to better examine the pressing issue of orange shirt continuity.

Output

There are many destination formats that you might want to render to—DVD, DV, HD, or Webcasting formats such as Flash video, DIVX, or H.264. But there's only one format that you should render to before you think about any of those others—the *digital master. This section continues on the included DVD* (**Chapter6/DigitalMaster.pdf**), *where you'll pick up where the mastering tutorial leaves off and learn how to create an archival-quality digital master of your film from which you can create any output you want, from a Web video to a film print.*

Boom.

Dude, you made a movie!

Or wait, did you just read a book on making a movie?

There seem to be as many books about making a low-budget film as there are screenwriting books. I have about a hundred screenwriting books and no matter how fervently I read them, I never seem to make as much progress by doing so as when I simply sit down and write. That's why I envisioned this book as a field guide—it's not a book about how to fly a plane, it's the emergency instructions in the seatback in front of you. So here's one last step-by step:

Original photo by Andreas Jankowsky.

1. Stuff book in back pocket.

2. Go shoot a movie.

3. Repeat, until the faux tattering on the cover is replaced with the real thing!

Movies Referenced in this Chapter

American Beauty

The Birds

Crimson Tide

The Exorcism of Emily Rose

The Matrix

O Brother, Where Art Thou?

Pearl Harbor

Saving Private Ryan

Spy Game

Sin City

Top Gun

Underworld

Index

Get free online access to this book!

And sign up for a free trial to Safari Books Online to get access to thousands more!

With the purchase of this book you have instant online, searchable access to it on Safari Books Online! And while you're there, be sure to check out the Safari on-demand digital library and its Free Trial Offer (a separate sign-up process)—where you can access thousands of technical and inspirational books, instructional videos, and articles from the world's leading creative professionals with a Safari Books Online subscription.

Simply visit www.peachpit.com/safarienabled and enter code TBIZTYG to try it today.